STAGE
WRITERS
HANDBOOK

STAGE WRITERS HANDBOOK

*A Complete Business Guide
for Playwrights, Composers,
Lyricists and Librettists*

DANA SINGER

THEATRE COMMUNICATIONS GROUP

Stage Writers Handbook is published by Theatre Communications Group, Inc.,
355 Lexington Ave., New York, NY 10017.

Singer, Dana
Stage writers handbook : a complete business guide for
playwrights, composers, lyricists and librettists / Dana Singer.
ISBN 1–55936–116–6 (paper)
1. Theater—Vocational guidance. 2. Theater—Economic aspects.
I. Title.
PN2074.S56 1996
331.7'02—dc20   96–7093
CIP

Book design and composition by Lisa Govan

First Printing, February 1997

*This book is dedicated to my partner Jane Grochowski
and my best friend Karen Abbott.*

Acknowledgements

FIRST, I interviewed many, many people who spoke with me confidentially and off the record. This information was truly invaluable and much of this book could not have been written without their input. I wish I could thank them publicly, but they know who they are.

I would also like to thank the following:

Paul Aiken at the Authors Guild, The Association of American Publishers, Jeffrey Brabec and Todd Brabec for their book *Music, Money and Success*, Stephen DiLauro, Steven d'Onofrio, Bill Downs, Patricia Felch, David Friedlander, Richard Garmise at the Dramatists Guild, Elana Greenfield, Stuart Greenman, David Grossberg, Nikki Harmon, Robert Harris, Sharon Jensen, Susan Lee, Literary Managers and Dramaturgs of America, Susan Lowenberg, Gary Marshall, Lauren Marshall, Phillip Mattera and the National Writers Union, Sarah Montague, Scott J. Parker, Maria Pillante, David Pritchard, Sarah Schlesinger, Roger Hendricks Simon, Helen Sneed, the Society of Stage Directors and Choreographers, David D. Wright, Lou Anne Wright, and Blake Edwards, Terry Nemeth, Steven Samuels and Wendy Weiner at Theatre Communications Group.

Special thank-yous to Peter Stone and everyone on the Council of the Dramatists Guild, Elliot Brown, Jere Couture, Alvin Deutsch, Seth Gelblum and, again, Robert Harris, from whom over the years I have learned an immeasurable amount about the theatre industry.

Last, I used many resources in researching various parts of this book, but two in particular deserve special recognition: *The Rights of Publicity and Privacy* by J. Thomas McCarthy and Melville Nimmer's four-volume treatise on the *Law of Copyright*.

Contents

Contents

Introduction

STAGE WRITERS, like many others, are a vulnerable group, most often left to their own devices to try to navigate the murky waters of the theatre industry. The majority of stage writers don't have agents, and many find the cost of retaining a lawyer prohibitive, particularly when the money the writer might earn is not much, as is often the case in the theatre.

This book can help stage writers learn and understand the basic information and issues they will confront in their careers. The order of the chapters tries to anticipate a reasonable progression and to show how one's career might unfold. There is no single path that all stage writers follow, but the information in this book represents the most commonly asked questions and the most frequently encountered situations and contracts.

One of the primary goals of this book is to demystify the industry, the process of getting your work out into the marketplace and your various relationships. The playing field is not level and you should not count on it being transformed overnight into a "fair" place. But you can become a better, more-educated player, and that will change the tenor and the parameters of negotiations. You can't successfully negotiate what you don't know about or fully understand. For example, you should never sell your copyright to a publisher; but, if you don't learn what is normal in publishing contracts, you might mistakenly sign a document which includes such a damaging clause. If a producer wants you to sign away forty percent of your subsidiary rights income, you need to know whether that is appropriate to that level of production.

A career as a stage writer does not have to take place in a long dark tunnel, nor are you required to wear a blindfold in order to make your way through it successfully. If you choose to conduct your business blindly (whether with collaborators, underlying rights owners, agents, theatres, producers, publishers and so on) that is your prerogative. But you do have a choice, and I've written this book so that every writer can, at a minimum, make certain basic decisions about how to create and structure a career in the theatre.

This book has eight chapters: copyright; collaboration; underlying rights; marketing and self-promotion; production contracts; representation: agents and lawyers; publishers; and developing areas (addressing the director/playwright relationship, the author as creator, electronic rights issues, radio drama and videotaping). In some situations, there are answers to specific questions or there is detailed information that will enable you to understand and negotiate your contracts from a stronger bargaining position. In other situations, clear answers simply don't exist, but I hope to indicate which issues you need to think about and which questions you need to address. Where there are choices to make which depend on your particular circumstances, I try to help you think through the issues to arrive at a personally acceptable resolution, knowing that different people will establish different priorities and make different choices. Where relationships with others are involved, I try to provide practical suggestions concerning both tangible and intangible factors that need consideration.

Information and knowledge are empowering, to use an overused word in its proper context. Most writers are not naturally business people, and yet developing and honing your business skills is an essential part of being a professional writer. Many writers say, "I can't possibly understand business," but I have not found that to be true.

You will notice the absence of form contracts in this book. My primary goal is to get stage writers to think through the issues and situations they will encounter, rather than just reach for a form in the hope that it will solve their problems. I know that reading through this book may conjure up questions it doesn't answer, but as a practical matter one book simply can't answer every possible question. In part, like any book, this one exists to provide a general educational base in a range of different areas and, in part, many questions that arise are specific to a particular set of circumstances.

Certainly, it can be overwhelming to tackle the type of information contained in this book, but I have tried to present it in plain English, and to make it accessible and manageable. For the most part, these are not difficult concepts to grasp, but they are certainly foreign to most writers, and you may want to read through some explanations more than once.

There are a number of recurring themes for stage writers, of which you should be aware. The first is the fact that certain essential elements of your career will cost you money, which you simply must accept. Your career as a professional stage writer is a business for which there are necessary business expenses; each person must decide where she or he can afford to draw the line, but investing a certain amount is unavoidable. For example, don't try to avoid proper copyright registration just because it costs twenty dollars, and don't send out poor quality copies of your script to save ten or even fifty dollars. The amount you might save is paltry compared to the risks of what you might lose in the long run. If you are committed to being a professional writer, you will not want to take these risks.

Second, you must understand that building a career requires a long-term commitment. There are no guarantees of success, and you may experience periods of extreme frustration about how time-consuming and difficult getting produced or published is. A well-written play or musical is obviously an important part of the equation, but it is only the first step to establishing yourself professionally. It requires hard work and perseverance to get your work produced or published, and the competition is fierce; but, it can be done. Don't fall into the trap of thinking, "I wish I had an agent so I could just turn all of this over to him or her and not have to think about it anymore." Not only is it fairly difficult to obtain an agent; but, once you have one, you must continue to foster the contacts you have already made and to try to establish new ones. Besides, agents are not infallible. Whatever their level of experience, you should always strive to be an active participant in your career, understanding the issues to be negotiated and comprehending the documents you sign. It is your work, and your career, at stake.

Third, try to have confidence in yourself and your work. This is one of the hardest lessons to learn. I realize that when someone wants to produce or publish your work, it will be one of the greatest moments of your life, for to have your work acknowledged and appreciated is the highest compliment. Of course you don't want to "blow it" or do anything that will offend the producer or publisher; but, at the same time, you must protect yourself and your work. As discussed at greater length in "The importance of contracts" in the chapter on production contracts, a negotiation is the normal way to conduct business, and if you are an educated negotiator you will be respected by the producer or publisher.

Unfortunately, at some point in your career you will probably be offered contracts that were drafted without your concerns in mind. Depending on the producer or publisher, the document may be sweepingly one-sided or even incomprehensible; but, don't just give up. You may not win all of your points, but through knowledgeable and careful negotiating you will improve the offer that's been made (not necessarily just in financial terms), and you will start down the path of establishing yourself as a professional writer.

Yes, there is an inherent imbalance of negotiating power in these relationships, an inequality which is most prominent when you are at the earlier stages of your career (although you will probably always entertain these feelings). No one likes to turn down offers of production or publication, and rarely will you consider rejection an option. But you must move through these relationships with your eyes open and your integrity intact. Don't assume that at the beginning of your career you must accept degrading or offensive contract terms or relationships in order someday to find someone who will treat you with respect; reject this "boot camp" mentality. Don't think you must sell your soul on your first work in the hopes of being able to obtain a decent offer on your second work. Some terms in contracts are freely negotiable, others are more difficult to change and some you may find are simply impossible. Don't think that because you're not Neil Simon, Wendy Wasserstein or Tony Kushner you have no right to ask for anything to be changed in the offer. Ultimately, you may decide to sign a not-so-great contract because the benefits outweigh the terms with which you aren't happy, but don't hesitate to give it your best shot and know that at least you understand what terms you are agreeing to and why you made that decision. One of the worst feelings is to find out later on, after the deal is over, that you could have easily negotiated terms that everyone else was able to obtain if only you had spoken up, or to discover that you've signed something dreadful without realizing the full import of the language.

Throughout any negotiation, you may feel natural pangs of desperation and fear, but try to quell those feelings and replace them with knowledge and self-esteem. In other words, don't give up before you've tried. Too many writers walk into business relationships with a dangerously self-defeating attitude. If there are any absolutes in discussions with potential producers or publishers, one of them is that if you negotiate from fear it is more likely than not that you will end up with an inferior agreement. Fear is often unfounded and should be replaced with information and understanding.

One must strive to become someone with whom others want to work. You have certain rights, obligations and responsibilities in any situation, but it is equally important that you understand industry customs and practices. For example, when your show is in rehearsal you have the right to attend, but you must also understand the protocols of working with your director. If you are writing in collaboration, think twice before trying to convince a co-author that your contribution is the most important element. If you have submitted your work for consideration by a theatre company, don't make persistent, demanding, angry or petulant calls to the literary department. You shouldn't be anyone's doormat, but it's crucial to understand generally accepted guidelines of behavior. This understanding will enhance and advance your career in an industry where word of mouth and reputation are of paramount importance.

After reading this book, consider becoming involved in the community of stage writers in order to learn from them and to share information. When you write you are usually alone, and it is all too easy to become isolated from your natural community. However, there are both personal and professional benefits that can result from reaching out to other writers. Even though you are technically "competitors" in the marketplace, you are also each other's best allies and often you can help each other shed light on difficult issues or serve to illuminate theoretical concepts by placing them in practical contexts. Furthermore, unsavory business practices shouldn't be kept a naughty secret, mushrooming in the dark. If you have an unsatisfying or unpleasant experience with a publisher, producer or anyone else in the profession, talk with other writers to find out if they have encountered similar situations and discuss ways they can be resolved or avoided in the future. A simple conversation with a peer can go a long way towards improving the stage writer's life.

Last, if you wish to discuss specific questions or issues, or to have access to model agreements, consider joining the Dramatists Guild, the national organization for playwrights, composers, lyricists and librettists. And here, please note that this book is not intended to represent the "official Guild position" on the broad spectrum of issues addressed. I have written *Stage Writers Handbook* to be informative and educational. While there will necessarily be a certain amount of overlap, don't mistake my experience, research and inclinations for the Guild's advocacy, particularly with respect to some of the more volatile issues, such as the director/writer relationship.

STAGE
WRITERS
HANDBOOK

Chapter 1

COPYRIGHT

COPYRIGHT is your ownership in the work you create; for the stage writer, in the plays and musicals you script. Once you have written the work, you automatically own it. It is no longer necessary to register the work with the Library of Congress in order to obtain the copyright (although, as discussed below, registration is strongly recommended).

Think of copyright as a bundle of twigs, each twig representing a possible disposition of the work. You alone have the ability to control the script's reproduction, distribution and performance, and the creation of derivative works in all media. The rights can be disposed of singly, in clumps, or the entire bundle at once, in any variation the copyright owner wishes.

These rights are very powerful and, on a practical level, include such matters as the right to decide if and by whom the work will be revised, produced, filmed and/or published; the right to choose the agent who will represent the work; the right to negotiate all contracts and make decisions about working conditions, etc. In other words, copyright is the right to make *all* decisions about the work itself, subject only to the fair use doctrine addressed below.

Ideas alone are not copyrightable; only the tangible *expression* of those ideas—the written script, music and lyrics—is protected by copyright. There can be an infinite number of works addressing the idea of corruption in government, for instance, but each person's expression of that idea is protected by the copyright law from being copied or otherwise infringed.

There is a fairly widespread misconception that because you can't physically hold or visualize a copyright it is less protected by the law than, say, owning an apartment, but this is simply incorrect. The fact that copyright is intangible may make it somewhat difficult to comprehend, but that has no bearing on whether it is legally protected. People need to distinguish between possessing the physical embodiment of the work (e.g., the playscript, a book, a painting) and the copyright in that work. You could sell a famous script at auction, but the buyer would own only that copy; the purchase of that object would not extend to the underlying copyright in the work itself.

Copyright protection extends only for a finite period of time, as discussed below. It is intended to encourage creativity and artistic endeavors by guaranteeing that disposition of the work and any financial rewards it may engender belong to the copyright holder, but it doesn't last forever. After the copyright term runs its course, the copyright expires and the work enters the public domain, thus belonging to the public rather than to one person or party.

COPYRIGHT OWNERSHIP FOR STAGE WRITERS

Whoever creates a work is the owner of that work. Stage writers always retain ownership of the copyright in their theatrical works, and this is probably the most fundamental tenet of being a stage writer. Consequently, stage writers always work as "independent contractors," not as work-for-hire employees, in their relationships with producers, theatres, publishers and the like. By contrast, "work-for-hire" is an arrangement in which the employer, not the creator, retains ownership of the copyright, such as in the film and television industries, in which the writers sell their copyrights and any ability to control the content of their work, usually in return for substantial sums of money. For stage writers, the upfront money is typically low, but by retaining ownership of the copyright the stage writer retains control over the work. Remuneration is therefore structured differently than in other media, with the stage writer remaining able to make money from the work in all of its manifestations. The concept of work-for-hire is anathema in the theatre.

COMMISSIONS

Even when a stage writer is commissioned by a producer or theatre to create a script, the writer should always retain copyright ownership. It doesn't matter whether the commissioning party came up with the idea for the play or has a specific piece that it wants written or pays the writer well for the work: The writer always retains copyright ownership. Note, too, that since the writer automatically owns the work once it is written, there would have to be a signed agreement between the writer and producer to turn ownership of the copyright over to the commissioning party, if that is what the parties agree. If that contract doesn't exist, the writer retains ownership.

Consequently, all stage writers are warned to be particularly vigilant when writing a commissioned work. The contract should state clearly that the copyright ownership remains with the writer, because there are, unfortunately, producers and theatres that aren't as well-versed in this area as they should be. Some assume that because they pay the writer to create the work, or have obtained the right to have an underlying work adapted, or provide specific ideas or guidelines for the work, somehow they "should" own the copyright. Your answer should be, resoundingly, "no."

Don't think the commissioning producer is left with nothing. As discussed further in the chapter on production contracts, what the commissioning party receives is the right to be the work's first producer without having to compete with other producers, which also affords the producer significant caché for its local and national fundraising efforts. It's also possible, depending on the terms negotiated between the commissioning party and the writer, that the commissioning party may have the right to produce the work more than once, perhaps even entering into a long-term, usually non-exclusive license with the stage writer that spans a number of years. Under some circumstances, the writer may share with the commissioning party a small percentage of her or his subsidiary rights income for a specifically defined period of time, but the negotiated "goodies" must not go so far as to encroach on the stage writer's copyright ownership.

TERM OF COPYRIGHT PROTECTION

In order to obtain a copyright in a work created before January 1, 1978, you had either to have the work published or to file the unpublished work's registration form with the Library of Congress Copyright Office, which would start the clock running on the legislated period of copyright protection. The initial term of protection, in those days, ran for twenty-eight years after that publication or filing; the registration would have to be renewed to obtain a second twenty-eight year period of protection, for a total term of fifty-six years. Subsequently, this renewal period was extended by Congress to forty-seven years, for a total term of seventy-five years. However, as of June 28, 1992, the renewal registration is no longer mandatory, as discussed below. Definite advantages exist to encourage the filing of renewal forms, but if a writer decides not to file (or forgets to do so), he or she no longer loses copyright ownership.

For works created since January 1, 1978, the period of copyright protection has changed significantly; it runs for the rest of the writer's life, plus fifty years. As of this writing, another amendment to the copyright law is being discussed in which the copyright term would be extended to the life of the author plus *seventy* years. This proposed change is due, in large part, to the fact that the European Community changed its copyright laws, effective July 1, 1995. If the U.S. copyright law isn't changed, American writers will lose out on twenty years of royalty payments in the European Community, because the works here will enter the public domain that much earlier. This new proposition is not without detractors, however, who assert that copyright law already prevents or seriously restricts access to certain information and works, and that extending copyright protection will only exacerbate the situation.

REGISTRATION

There is only one proper way to register one's work with the Copyright Office: For plays and musicals, this involves filling out Form PA, which stands for Performing Arts, and sending it to the Copyright Office, in one envelope or package, with a twenty-dollar check, bank draft or money order accompanied by the "deposit copy" of the work that will be retained by the Library of Congress (so be sure you have another copy). Rest assured that the deposit copy is safe; there are strict procedures that prevent someone from just walking into the Library of Congress, making a copy of someone else's script and walking out.

To order forms or circulars prepared by the Copyright Office on a wide range of topics call 202-707-9100, twenty-four hours a day, seven days a week. If questions arise, the public information number is 202-707-3100, 8:30 AM to 5 PM Eastern Standard Time, Monday through Friday, or you can speak with an information specialist at 202-707-5959.

Form PA is fairly straightforward and is always accompanied by detailed instructions from the Copyright Office. The form asks for or about: 1) the title and nature of the work, such as whether it is music, song lyrics, words and music, drama or musical play; 2) the name(s) of the author(s); 3) the year in which the work was created and, if applicable, first published; 4) the name(s) of the copyright claimant; 5) previous registration of the work or an earlier version of the work, if applicable; 6) whether or not the work is derivative or a compilation; 7) the deposit account and correspondence designation of the copyright claimant, if any; 8) certification by the person submitting the form that the information is accurate; and 9) mailing instructions.

The completed registration form should be sent to: Register of Copyrights, U.S. Copyright Office, Library of Congress, Washington, D.C. 20559. It is recommended that you send it by registered or certified mail, return receipt requested, because the registration begins to run from the date all the required elements are received in acceptable form in the Copyright Office, regardless of how long the Office takes to process the form. The return receipt signed by an employee of the Copyright Office is evidence that it has been received; no other notice of mere receipt will be sent. Once the registration moves through the appropriate channels, you will receive a Certificate of Registration.

Keep in mind that more than 600,000 people file copyright forms each year for their plays, musicals, books, videotapes, movies, works of art and so on. Depending on the number of filings received by the Office at any given time, it can take up to six months to process an individual form; thus, it makes great sense for the writer to have tangible evidence of filing in hand, such as a signed return receipt, while waiting to receive the actual Certificate of Registration. (Also note that an author does not have to wait to receive this Certificate to begin showing the work to others.)

Some people try to cut corners. Instead of registering with the Copyright Office, they mail themselves a copy of the work but don't open the envelope when it arrives, hoping to use the Post Office's cancellation as evidence of the date of original creation. There is disagreement among lawyers about whether this type of evidence will sufficiently protect the creator in court. Another alternative people choose is to file the script with the Writers Guild of America, because they think one filing is just as good as another. This is not true. Filing in the Copyright Office is the best copyright filing you can effect.

This issue can be debated ad nauseum, but for the writer the bottom line is protecting the copyright. There is no risk attendant to filing the proper form with the Copyright Office and, as addressed below, there are significant potential benefits to filing in a timely fashion. Do not risk wasting time and money arguing in court about the validity of the method chosen to protect your copyright; you might lose the gamble. If you need to save twenty dollars, think of another place to cut expenses or take chances. Don't mess with the copyright filing.

What registration means

The Copyright Office is an office of record. Its function is limited to performing the necessary administrative tasks—processing properly submitted registration forms. It does not issue or grant the copyright itself. The law alone assumes that substantive function.

The Copyright Office cannot help:

♦ Compare copies of works by looking for similarities;
♦ Offer advice on possible copyright infringement or prosecution of copyright violations;
♦ Draft or interpret contracts;
♦ Enforce contracts or recover manuscripts;
♦ Recommend publishers, agents, lawyers or the like;
♦ Get a work published, recorded or performed; or
♦ Grant permission to use a copyrighted work.

To give an extreme example: Anyone could copy the script of *Inherit the Wind* word for word and register it on Form PA with the Copyright Office. The person in the Copyright Office receiving the form would sign the receipt for the envelope and process it like any other work. No one in the Office would review the form or the script for substance. No one in the Office would call and ask, "Are you sure you wrote this script?" No one in the Office would make any substantive rulings or determinations.

That the form was accepted and processed by the Copyright Office would not change the fact that only Jerome Lawrence and Robert E. Lee own the copyright to that play. Issues of substance, content and ownership are decided in courts, not in or by the Copyright Office. In the example cited, the true authors could sue the copyright infringer and present as evidence the original copyright filing. The person who filed the later registration would have to explain *and prove* her or his rights to the work.

Timely registration

Registration is not a condition of copyright protection, which vests automatically upon creation, but it is crucial to register the work in order actively and properly to enforce your rights. Certain important benefits are lost if you fail or take too long to make this registration.

All the hassles and ambiguities described below can be avoided by filing the appropriate form as soon as the work is finished (meaning the work is ready to be shown to others, not the minute the first draft pops out of the printer). It is strongly recommended that you establish a habit of timely registration. It's too easy to postpone, to place at the bottom of a list of things to do, and there is always the risk that taking care of the paperwork will fade from memory as more pressing matters demand immediate attention. The consequences may be grave if registration slips out of mind.

Registration required before lawsuit

If copyright is infringed and a lawsuit is necessary to enforce ownership rights, the law mandates that the proper copyright forms must be filed *before* the lawsuit can begin. Some argue that the chances of someone infringing one's copyright are not high, so this situation should be addressed only if it arises, since it would be just as easy to file the registration when a lawsuit seems necessary rather than beforehand. This is not wise.

In any copyright infringement dispute, the issue of which person created the work first will arise, and this must be established through evidence. The act of registration will be very important in proving the order of creation. The copyright law states that if the registration filing is made before or within five years after first publication (not production), the filing will be considered by the federal courts to be the strongest possible evidence; that is, the certificate of copyright will be *assumed* to be valid. For example, if Writer A presents a properly filed registration for Work A, Writer B will then have to present evidence of prior creation of competing Work B. Writer B's evidence must be strong enough to rebut or override Writer A's registration, which can be a very difficult hurdle to overcome.

Without the benefit of advance registration, Writer A will be forced to prove, through external evidence, that he or she was in fact the first writer of the work. Examples of such evidence include testimony from witnesses who can swear they saw Writer A creating the work, that they received a copy of that exact work from Writer A or attended a reading or performance of the work on a specific date. Given the passage of time between the creation of Work A and the alleged infringement (which, in most situations, will be years), and the myriad ways in which individual works are created, Writer A may not be able to produce this type of evidence: She or he might not know how to locate particular witnesses or may find the witnesses' memories faulty or inexact. Even if Writer A is able to produce this external evidence, doing so during the lawsuit will be both burdensome and expensive.

Besides, merely providing the evidence is only half the battle. The next issue is persuasion; that is, presenting evidence substantial and credible enough to persuade the judge or jury. While a lawyer could perhaps estimate the likelihood of success based on an analysis of existing evidence, no lawyer could ever guarantee that the judge or jury would be persuaded by it. Without proper copyright registration, a certain degree of risk inevitably exists.

Risk of losing important copyright benefits

Next, there are two very practical and important "rewards" granted by the copyright law for timely registration—first, the winning party may have its legal fees and expenses paid by the losing party; second, the winner is entitled to statutory damages—but they apply only if the infringement of an unpublished work began *after* the registration, or if the infringement of a published work began *between* first publication (not production) of the work and the effective date of its registration *provided* the registration was made within three months after the first publication. In other words, if the work has never been published, then registration must come before the alleged infringement or you will not be able to avail yourself of these two benefits. In addition, if the work *has* been published, and the infringement occurred *after* the publication but *before* the registration was effected, you are again precluded from these two benefits, with one exception: If you registered the work within three months after first publication. Thus, you can be a little late in filing the post-publication registration and still take advantage of these benefits, but you can't be later than three months. If these conditions aren't met, the two benefits will not be available, and their absence can have a serious, perhaps devastating, effect on a lawsuit.

For instance, assume Writer B has copied Work A and is sending it around under her or his name. Writer A seeks legal representation in a copyright infringement lawsuit which, if it proceeds beyond the initial stages, will likely be so costly that few people could afford to pursue it without financial assistance. One of the basic issues a lawyer would have to resolve, in addition to evaluating the substance of the claims, would be the likelihood she or he would get paid.

If Writer A filed the registration form in a timely fashion, the lawyer would be more inclined to take the case, knowing that the winner's fees and expenses could be paid by the losing party. If Writer A had *not* filed the registration form within the required time and, as a result, could *not* take advantage of the "loser pays" provision, Writer A would be in the possibly difficult position of having to prove she or he could afford to pay before the lawyer would agree to take the lawsuit.

For most people, this is a burden that cannot be met. Even with the best, most damning evidence, Writer A could be left without legal representation.

Statutory damages are no less significant. In a copyright infringement case, Writer A needs to prove not only that the copyright in Work A has been violated, but also that Writer A suffered damage—*financial* damage—as a result of Writer B's infringement. Depending on the circumstances, this may be difficult to prove in court; consequently, the copyright statute provides for statutory damages, meaning that the judge, within her or his discretion, can award Writer A between $200 and $20,000 in damages (up to $100,000 if the court finds the infringement was willful) that Writer B has to pay even if Writer A is unable to provide proof of actual financial damage.

For another example, let's say that Writer B sent Writer A's play to producers under B's name and that it was optioned by Theatre C. Writer B, working with the director, rewrites the play in such a way that the play is torn apart by the critics, and the work's future looks grim. What financial damage can be *proven* by Writer A? It's very difficult to prove that if Writer A had done the rewrites, the play would have been loved by the critics, become a huge success, moved to Broadway, yielded Writer A hundreds of thousands of dollars in royalties and changed the course of Writer A's future. Obviously, it's all too speculative.

So while under certain circumstances, a writer may be able to prove actual damages, often writers need to be able to pursue statutory damages, which can be achieved only by filing for copyright registration within the time stated in the law.

Registering revised works

The question often arises whether to file a second registration encompassing revisions. There is no hard and fast rule. While you want to know a work being shown to potential producers and others is fully protected, it is not necessary to file time and again for every single change made in the text. When you believe the work has changed substantially from the original deposit copy, then it's time to file again. Use discretion and common sense: Don't file for registration of your very first draft; give yourself time to work on the play and make the necessary rounds of revisions. Know your own work habits and establish ground rules: If you know you are likely to work through five drafts, wait to file until you have in hand the product you know will be worthy of professional consideration.

Extremes are always easy to identify: If the writer has changed the name of one character, or has decided that two characters should enter from stage right instead of stage left, a second filing would not be necessary. If the writer has completely rewritten the second act, a second filing would be advisable. However, most situations will fall somewhere in the middle and become a matter of subjective comfort. The issue is protecting the content one has created. If changes are superficial and the true content is essentially unchanged, the work would remain sufficiently protected by the initial filing. A new registration encompasses only the revisions; consequently, if the writer feels the changes are *not* merely superficial—or is simply unsure—then it might be best to file a second form. When in doubt, err on the side of safety rather than risk.

The proper form for registering revisions is also Form PA, but the focus this time would be on lines 5 and 6. The form asks whether this work or an earlier version of the work has already been filed for copyright registration. The answer would be "yes," and then the writer would indicate, by checking the appropriate box, the reason another registration is sought. The form also requires the previous registration number and year of registration for accurate record-keeping and cross-referencing.

Combining multiple registrations

If a writer has written more than one work and would rather not pay twenty dollars apiece to file each work separately, it is possible to file these works as a "collection" (as long as they are all unpublished). However, this type of filing comes with its own set of conditions:

♦ The elements must be assembled in an orderly manner;
♦ The combined elements must bear a single title identifying the collection as a whole;
♦ The person or persons claiming copyright in all the elements individually and in the collection as a whole must be the same; and
♦ All of the elements must be by the same author; or, if they are by different authors, at least one of the authors must have contributed copyrightable material to each element.

The potential disadvantage is that the entire collection will be indexed only under the collection title, not under the individual titles of the works that comprise the collection. This means that if someone were to run a copyright search in the Copyright Office looking for an individual work by its individual title, the search would reveal nothing; only persons knowing the collection title would be able to locate any information about the individual works.

While this is not a recommended method, if you cannot afford the individual registrations but can satisfy the law's requisites and are comfortable with the risk, this may be an avenue to pursue.

Renewal term registration

Over the years, Congress became aware that the renewal term filing requirements were causing the copyrights on many works to lapse inadvertently into the public domain; human nature dictated that some people simply didn't remember twenty-eight years later to effectuate the filings. Consequently, in 1992, President Bush signed an amendment to the 1976 Copyright Act abolishing the mandatory renewal requirements. For works affected by this change—those that were filed for copyright registration between January 1, 1964 and December 31, 1977—the term of copyright is now a flat seventy-five years from the initial filing date.

However, even though the renewal filing is now optional, the 1992 amendment created many benefits that would accrue to the copyright owner if, in fact, the renewal forms were filed. This area of the copyright law is so dense and complex that a simple list cannot possibly explain all the essential points, and a thorough explanation is beyond the scope of this book.

One example: when a writer dies before the twenty-eighth year of the original copyright term and a statutory renewal claimant takes care of registering the renewal within the twenty-eighth year, that claimant can terminate an assignment made by the now-deceased writer authorizing the exploitation of a derivative work. In other words, if a writer had disposed of the film adaptation rights to a play, then died before the twenty-eighth year of the copyright, the writer's spouse (or others allowed by law) could file the renewal within the twenty-eighth year and then terminate that previous agreement, presumably in order to renegotiate more favorable terms. This is an obvious benefit that you would not want to have foreclosed inadvertently.

Unfortunately, many writers decide that because the law's incentives are so difficult to comprehend, it is easier to ignore them and rely on the new safety net of automatic registration. Even though the full range of benefits is not understood by the layperson, it makes no sense to relinquish potentially valuable benefits. To the contrary, the best protection for any affected writer is somehow to schedule the renewal registration early in the twenty-eighth year of copyright. It would therefore be best to keep a comprehensive, readily accessible list of both the original filing dates and the corresponding renewal registration dates.

The necessary Form RE is also fairly straightforward and comes with its own set of instructions. Essentially, it asks for or about: 1) the names of the renewal claimants, 2) information about the work being renewed, such as the title and whether this is a new version of the previously copyrighted work, 3) the author(s), 4) the original registration number, 5) the copyright claimant, and 6) the date of copyright.

Again, the issue of renewal pertains only to works filed for copyright registration between January 1, 1964 and December 31, 1977.

PUBLIC DOMAIN

The term "public domain" is referred to often in copyright law; people will say that a work has "fallen" or "entered" into the public domain at the end of the copyright term, which means that no one any longer owns the copyright on the work in question; instead, the work now belongs to the public. The practical results of a copyright entering the public domain are that permission is not needed to use the work (for example, to produce it or to write an adaptation based upon it) and that royalties no longer have to be paid to that copyright owner for such uses.

As a general rule in the United States, once the copyright in a work falls into the public domain, it stays there forever; the copyright cannot later be returned to its original protected status. (There are now two exceptions to this general rule, one under NAFTA for works created by foreign nationals and another under GATT for works still under copyright in a foreign originating country.)

It may be difficult to conceive of the finality of a work entering the public domain. Writers frequently ask whether public domain status can be reversed simply by changing the title of the work and refiling, but the answer is always unequivocally negative.

DEATH OF THE COPYRIGHT OWNER

Copyright can be passed on to others when the copyright owner dies. Copyright in works can be included in a will (bequeathed to someone) or, if the deceased never created a will, it will be passed on as personal property according to state law concerning intestate succession. (For works originally copyrighted between January 1, 1964 and December 31, 1977, the rules of who can claim renewal copyright may be different; if you fall into this category, read Circular 15 from the Copyright Office.)

The laws that govern the order in which property will be distributed in the absence of a will vary from state to state, but an example will clarify the concept. Typically, the first recipient is a spouse. If the deceased was not married, then next in succession might be the deceased's children. If there are no children, the deceased's parents are often next; but, if there *were* children and *they* are dead, it's possible that *their* children (the deceased's grandchildren) might be next. If the deceased's parents are also deceased, then the deceased's grandparents might receive consideration, and so on. (This scenario should serve notice of the importance of having a will, particularly if you are not married or don't have children. You might want your life partner or your best friends to inherit your possessions, but partners and friends are never given the same legal rights as "family" defined by society, even though they may have been much closer to you in life than your relatives. If you don't want your property passed along in a predetermined way, make a will that explicitly spells out your wishes.)

Copyright succession will often involve more complex issues than disposition of royalties, such as the right to make decisions about the content and future of the work. Furthermore, if you are part of a collaboration, the inheritance of copyright control has significant, long-lasting consequences, as discussed in the chapter on collaboration.

The law surrounding inheritance and other types of transfers of copyright as well as how to file those registrations in the Copyright Office is rather complicated. If this or a related situation applies to you, consult with an attorney knowledgeable in these areas, and read Circular 12 from the Copyright Office.

USING ANOTHER PERSON'S WORK

For writers, the issue of obtaining permission to use another person's work cuts very close to home. An oft-cited but *erroneous* "rule of thumb" states that it's legal to use a certain amount of another's work before being required to request permission. Sometimes this amount is quantified (five lines or eight bars are both popular numbers) and sometimes it's amorphously referred to as "just a small amount."

Neither is true. Technically, it remains a violation of copyright to use any part of a work without permission. The question of whether someone will actually sue for copyright infringement when the taking is insubstantial is a different issue—a risk the infringing writer would have to assume—but in terms of legality, it's definitely *not* encouraged.

Consider, too, the ethics of using any amount of someone else's work without permission. Reverse the situation and think honestly how you would feel sitting in a theatre and hearing your own words as part of someone else's work; perhaps you wouldn't mind the use, but certainly you would like to have had the choice. Or perhaps you won't like the context or nuances that now become attached to your work. If a writer believes that his or her own copyright carries significance, then a healthy respect should exist for everyone else's copyrights, even if it is frustrating at times.

For two very clear reasons, then, writers are always encouraged to request permission to use another's work, even when the amount being used is small: as a matter of law and as a matter of courtesy. How to go about obtaining permission is addressed in the chapter on underlying rights arrangements.

Fair use

An author has exclusive rights under the copyright law to authorize or do any of the following: reproduce copies of the work; sign agreements for dispositions of the work; perform and display the work publicly; and create derivative works based on the original. Anyone who violates these exclusive rights can be held liable for copyright infringement. However, the law explicitly creates a few exceptions to this general rule whereby, in certain limited situations, someone can use material that belongs to someone else *without* their permission. This is known as "fair use," which could be a viable defense against the claim of copyright infringement.

It's important to understand the concept underlying fair use. A defendant is not saying, "I didn't use your copyrighted material." What she or he is saying is, "Yes, I used your copyrighted material, but I am protected in this use for certain public policy reasons. So I don't have to get your permission, and I will not be considered to be infringing your copyright." In other words, Congress believed that the exclusivity of copyright should give way in limited instances for which it would be counterproductive to society as a whole to deny access to the copyrighted material.

(Although a thorough discussion is beyond the scope of this book, the following constitutes a rudimentary outline of fair use. If you are working on a piece in a manner you believe falls within fair use, you should consult with an attorney who can provide you with a legal opinion and advise you of the potential hurdles and pitfalls.)

The law allows as fair use reproduction of passages for purposes such as criticism, comment, news reporting, teaching, scholarship or research; generally, these uses would not be an infringement of copyright. Consequently, if someone uses a portion of a copyrighted work (not the entire work) in a news report, that would ordinarily constitute a fair use of the materials. If someone analyzed a play in their master's thesis, that would constitute a fair use of the material and would not be an infringement of the author's copyright. In other words, another person can use copyrighted material for such purposes without having to obtain permission, and the copyright owner doesn't have the right to deny permission.

This seems pretty clear, but note that fair use is *not* limited to my examples, which are only illustrative. In trying to determine whether a particular use is fair use, the law also considers the following four factors:

(1) the purpose and character of the use, including whether such use is of a commercial nature or is for nonprofit educational purposes;

(2) the nature of the copyrighted work;

(3) the amount and substantiality of the portion used in relation to the copyrighted work as a whole (what is known as the "conjure up test": whether or not you used only what was truly necessary to conjure up the original in the audience's mind); and

(4) the effect of the use upon the potential market for or value of the copyrighted work (considering whether there was an adverse effect on the potential market, since fair use is not intended to supplant or fill the demand for the original work).

Once again, note that this is not an exhaustive list of factors. The law says only that the analysis and determination will *include* these factors. As the courts, including the Supreme Court, have interpreted this language, there may be other factors to consider, and there is no indication of how much weight each factor should be given. What this means as a practical matter is that each set of facts and circumstances will be evaluated on a case-by-case basis (ostensibly grounded in the fundamental purposes of copyright), with each court given a fairly significant degree of latitude in arriving at a decision. (Remember that fair use is a defense against a lawsuit brought for copyright infringement, so you would be in court making these arguments.)

What you might have gleaned from the above is that there are very few hard-and-fast rules. This can be disconcerting when you are trying to figure out how, and if, your work fits in. Any attorney would read the existing case law to provide you with an opinion as to how a court might view your situation.

Parody and satire

Parody and satire are also defenses against a claim of copyright infringement. Again, you are saying, "Yes I used something that you own, but I should be protected in this use and not have to obtain your permission." Historically, it was assumed that parody and satire fell within the parameters of the fair use doctrine because they were considered useful forms of social and literary commentary, but the Supreme Court did not address this question until 1994.

Here, copyright also bumps right up against important First Amendment considerations. The First Amendment right to free speech is not absolute, and certainly would not be interpreted as a license to steal another's work; but, obviously, our society considers social commentary worth protecting fiercely. Consequently, there must be careful analysis of the content of a work at issue, making it nearly impossible to predict neatly the outcome in any such case.

Generally speaking, the core of parody is to mimic a particular original work, and this necessarily entails using some of that original. By contrast, satire stands on its own, exploring general issues in society rather than one particular copyrighted piece.

For stage writers, these issues often arise when one wants to create a revue using well-known songs but changing the lyrics. Here, some distinctions must be made. The courts have indicated that, for parody, it's not enough that someone adds a few funny or silly words to someone else's song; the issue isn't whether or not the new version of the song is "funny"—an impossibly subjective judgment—but rather whether or not the parody provides social commentary about the original. Courts do not look favorably upon someone who uses another's work either to attract attention or to avoid the labor-intensive task of creating something original.

If the new work *is* just about putting funny lyrics to established songs, and not commentary on them, then the writer needs to contact the owner of the original song and obtain permission to use it in that way. (This typically requires contacting the music publisher, but the songwriter often retains approval over any change in the lyrics, which means that permission would have to be granted by both the songwriter *and* the music publisher.) Sometimes it will be possible to obtain permission from the copyright owners for this purpose, but the copyright owner might not want the song used in that fashion.

Where "true" parody is involved, the courts have acknowledged that the copyright owner of a "serious work" may be unlikely to grant a license to the parody writer. In its 1994 case, the Supreme Court did not reach the decision that the song before it—by 2 Live Crew—was a parody of an older Roy Orbison song ("Oh, Pretty Woman"). Instead, it sent the case back to the lower court for another trial to make that determination. However, with that case the Supreme Court established, for the first time, that parody is in fact encompassed by the fair use defense, reiterating the four factors enumerated above. But the Court did not go so far as to decide what would constitute a protected parody, leaving that to be decided by the lower courts on a case-by-case basis.

This was a victory for parody writers, although not a complete victory. If the Supreme Court had decided that only scholarly or educational works could qualify as parody, it would have made the legal battles surrounding such use much more difficult for parodists to win; ultimately, that would probably have had a silencing effect on people who write parodies. And the Supreme Court did go so far as to say that making money *doesn't* eliminate parody protection; in other words, the question as to whether or not parody is "of a commercial nature or is for nonprofit educational purposes" was not believed to be dispositive, and the Court refused to state unequivocally that commercially oriented work deserved no protection under the fair use doctrine, because the Court felt the case before it *could* involve legitimate social commentary as well as "commercialism." Thus, while establishing parody and satire as protectible under the fair use doctrine, the Supreme Court left unresolved many questions as to what works will be held fairly to constitute parody and satire.

TITLES

Titles are not copyrightable; the copyright statute is very clear on this point. Only the content of the work is covered by registration, not the title. Consequently, it is not unusual to find multiple works with the same title, all registered with the Copyright Office, and they would all be valid, for purposes of copyright protection, assuming that they are substantively different (non-infringing) works.

This is not to say that there are no rights that one can hold in a title; it means only that *copyright law* does not protect it, and the Copyright Office has no jurisdiction in this area. A writer could acquire certain proprietary rights in a title, but completely different areas of the law govern that determination. The applicable federal and state laws on unfair competition and trademark address the many factors to be taken into consideration. The following provides a fundamental understanding of how titles may be protected, but an in-depth study of the applicable laws is too vast to undertake here.

A title must acquire what is known as secondary meaning in order to vest the writer with the legal right to prevent others from using that title. In a nutshell, secondary meaning applies when a title becomes so intimately acquainted in the minds of the public with a particular work that it would be misleading to allow others to use the same title for different works.

An example would be writing a musical and calling it *The Sound of Music.* Everyone immediately associates a particular musical with that title, and if a production of a new *The Sound of Music* were advertised and people bought tickets thinking it was the tried-and-true version they have loved for years, the writer of the new version would have benefited unfairly from using that title.

At this point, you might be thinking: How, then, can there be so many shows called *Phantom of the Opera* or *A Christmas Carol?* Remember that the underlying works on which those shows are based are in the public domain; thus, there can be an infinite number of adaptations (or as many as the traffic will bear) all based on the same underlying work. This is substantively different from writing a new, original play and calling it *A Christmas Carol* when it has no relation to that well-known work.

What can become important is making sure the theatre-going public is acutely aware of which version they are buying tickets to see. Using *Phantom of the Opera* as an example, every producer must be sure that the audience does not confuse the Arthur Kopit/Maury Yeston musical version with the Andrew Lloyd Webber musical version, which is not to be confused with the Ken Hill musical version, and so on with all the other musical versions of this public-domain book.

The question inevitably arises as to *when* a title has achieved this special secondary meaning. In some cases, one work is unequivocally associated with a particular title; in others, multiple works may be equally unknown, so no writer can make a claim to exclude the others from using the title. (In the latter situation, it may be easier simply to change the title before trouble arises.)

As always, it is in the middle that disputes occur. One of the hardest sets of circumstances exists when two works with the same title have both been shopped around and produced, but one acquires secondary meaning before the other. It becomes difficult at that point for the writer of the less-famous work to change the title because the work has already appeared in the marketplace under that appellation. But this difficulty *must* be overcome, because at that point the writer whose work *has* acquired secondary meaning is afforded substantive legal rights to which one must defer.

Admittedly, titles can hold a great deal of emotional significance, and once a writer has become attached to a particular title, the idea of changing it can turn into a struggle. One writer might feel inclined to fight the battle while another would change the title and deal with the logistics of the change. Consequently, writers are encouraged to try to create titles that are unique, to think ahead and to try to increase the chances that there won't be two works with the same name.

COLLABORATION

A nuts-and-bolts discussion of collaboration appears in its own chapter, but for copyright purposes, be aware of the most basic—and sometimes stickiest—issues. The author is the actual creator. If a person contributes only ideas, the prevailing view is that that does not constitute co-authorship; actual writing is the requirement for this. Additionally, it is understood that a collaboration agreement should be between the authors of the work, which excludes directors, actors and others who interpret the work, regardless of their input.

If writers who collaborate do not have a written arrangement between them, the copyright law (meaning both the statute and the judicial decisions) establishes certain governing presumptions. For example, the law deems the authors to be "joint authors," which means that each author owns an undivided interest in the *whole* work, not just in that portion written by that author, which can become a problem if the collaboration decides to disband. It also assumes that all monies are to be divided equally between or among the authors without regard for each individual's contribution. Because these presumptions may not represent the manner in which the collaborative relationship would have been structured had the collaborators addressed the issues themselves, writers should be aware that inaction carries important legal ramifications. Collaborators are encouraged to enter into collaboration agreements in order to avoid these presumptions.

INTERNATIONAL COPYRIGHT RELATIONS

It is important to understand there is no such thing as a monolithic "international copyright" that protects the writer's copyright everywhere in the world. Each country decides independently whether, and to what extent, to enact its own laws protecting works created by both domestic and foreign authors. They may, as the United States has done, become parties to certain international treaties that protect against unauthorized uses (primarily the Berne Convention and the Universal Copyright Convention); but, they may not. Thus the existence and extent of copyright protection varies from country to country.

Most countries *are* signatories to the two primary treaties; but, unfortunately, there are still some countries which not only aren't signatories to these treaties but which also have not enacted laws protecting foreign authors. Nationality becomes an important factor in analyzing whether works are protected by copyright throughout the world. Foreign copyright is a specialized area of the law, and one may have to consult an expert to obtain specific information about a particular country. (The Copyright Office does not provide this information.)

Chapter 2

COLLABORATION

C<small>OLLABORATION</small> is a special area full of twists and turns. The primary focus in this chapter will be musicals, since the majority of stage writing collaborations occur in the musical context. However, the important precepts apply equally to dramatic collaboration; there are simply additional concerns particular to music and lyrics.

A collaboration is, on its most basic level, a relationship between two or more people, and thus one will encounter the full range of emotions inherent in any interpersonal relationships. Some writers find it difficult to locate and connect with others who are compatible both creatively and in work style, and this is not surprising; a good match is cause for celebration. The results may be wonderful, yet it may be difficult or impossible to work together, and vice versa. Collaboration, like any working partnership, is a blend of business and personal. While it is a labor of love, ultimately you must attend to business if you want the collaboration to be successful.

It's a good idea for collaborators, in the early stages, to talk to each other honestly about their work styles. This should not be intended to convince anyone that they need to change; to the contrary, it should enable the collaborators to understand each other, to begin working together with reasonable expectations on the day-to-day level and in the long term.

The following are suggestions of some topics you may want to discuss: how you best work (a few hours a day; only on weekends; just before a deadline); whether you are a disciplined writer or a procrastinator; whether the collaborators will write simultaneously or serially (particularly if it's a musical); whether you work best alone, sending drafts back and forth, or would prefer actually to sit down and write together; whether you work well under pressure, and need or want to establish deadlines, or have trouble meeting deadlines; whether you are capable of giving and receiving constructive criticism; how you feel about revising (some writers need reassurance of the simple truth that all work needs revision); and how the parties will resolve differing opinions about the direction the work should take. If you need a rigid set of guidelines, be clear about those expectations. If you are more freewheeling let that be known, too.

Talk openly about each writer's vision and hopes for the work, and allow yourselves to dream in addition to being pragmatic. Collaborators should have an idea of each other's expectations—it will not further the collaborative effort to discover two years in that one collaborator envisioned a big, splashy Broadway affair while another was thinking of an intimate, Off-Broadway production. This is not to say that you must agree on such specifics from the outset—ideas and people change as the work develops, and will continue to change as you meet potential producers, directors, etc. But it's enormously helpful to talk about these issues.

The more you know about each other, the better the collaboration will be. Perhaps it's just human nature, but unmet expectations can sometimes be more devastating and hard to resolve or overcome than the underlying issue had the collaborators hashed it out.

THE "RIGHT" COLLABORATOR

A common question that arises is how to know if you've met the "right" collaborator. There is no clear answer. For some people there will be many different "right" collaborators in a lifetime. If you like each other's work and you've had your crash course in getting to know each other, then you've done your best research—it's time to trust your instincts and get to work.

Not all collaborations work out—risk is part of the arrangement. It's not a scientific equation, so you may one day find yourself trying to figure out how to break up and move on. Whatever you do, don't berate yourself for failed collaborations. No one can control the many tangible and intangible variables.

It's also important to establish who is *not* a collaborator. Collaborators in this context are writers, not directors, designers, actors and so on. There may be exceptions to this, based on individualized circumstances, but those situations or relationships are exceedingly rare. (See the chapter on developing areas for a discussion of such relationships.)

THE ABSENCE OF A COLLABORATION AGREEMENT

Once you decide to work together, it is unequivocally necessary to have a collaboration agreement. Copyright law encourages all collaborators to assume responsibility for their affairs and, consequently, there are substantial risks and consequences to ignoring these responsiblities.

In the absence of an express agreement, copyright law (i.e., a combination of the statute and judges' decisions that have interpreted the statute) governs the collaboration. In most instances, the law decides important issues differently from the way the collaborators would have done if they had had a written agreement.

Another reason it's important to have a collaboration agreement is that producers, publishers and other parties with whom you hope to do business down the road will want to know that the collaborators have resolved their working issues. They won't want to risk involvement with a production or publication that may be held hostage to a collaboration gone sour.

Joint ownership

In the absence of a written agreement, the law provides a presumption that the collaborators intended to create a "joint work," and that each collaborator, as a joint owner, has an undivided ownership interest in the whole product. This means each collaborator retains an ownership interest in *all* the elements, not just those to which he or she contributed. (It's not necessary for individual contributions to be equal, either in quantity or quality. It doesn't matter if one person creates music and another creates the book and lyrics, or if one person conceived the project and therefore has a greater emotional stake in it: The collaborators will be deemed joint owners if there is no collaboration contract.)

If collaborators work together for a while and then one decides to break up for whatever reason, in the absence of a written collaboration agreement she or he cannot simply say, "I'm taking what I contributed and leaving," because the other collaborators can reply, "You can't do that, because we share ownership with you." Under such circumstances, if the collaborators can't come to an agreement about how to break up (which would not be unlikely, since differences might have already created ill will), the work already completed (i.e., their respective contributions) cannot be used again in other ways (such as removing songs to use in a different musical), and the work can't be marketed on an exclusive basis. The project may be dead, and all the work that went into it wasted.

Non-exclusive rights

Joint ownership also means no single collaborator has complete control over the work, and each has equal rights to market the work. Each joint owner could sign non-exclusive licenses for the work without obtaining the other collaborators' signatures (so long as each collaborator would receive their fair share of any resulting monies).

Exclusive licenses are granted to just one person or company (one producer, one publisher and so on) but non-exclusive licenses can be signed with any number of people simultaneously. If one collaborator could sign exclusive agreements without the consent of the others, it would preclude them from marketing the work, which would be patently unfair.

The practical problem is that until a work has gained a reputation enabling multiple productions (e.g., has had a regional, Off-Broadway or Broadway production), most producers will probably not be interested in non-exclusive rights because there's too much risk attached (e.g., the risk of a competing production, which would significantly reduce each production's chances for financial success).

In addition, since producers are not interested in getting involved in disputes, they will ordinarily insist on obtaining every collaborator's signature on a contract. Consequently, the fact that non-exclusive rights are made available by law may, in fact, be only an illusory benefit.

Division of money

If the work is deemed a joint work, all money would be divided equally between the collaborators, regardless of their contributions or intentions. As an example, consider a team of two—one creating the music and lyrics, the other creating the book—and assume that in the beginning they might have liked two-thirds of earnings to go to the composer/lyricist and one-third to the book writer, but they never really talked about it directly and they don't have a written collaboration agreement. In the absence of such an agreement, the book writer could legally claim half of the monies flowing from the musical, and the composer/lyricist would be forced to concede (unless he or she could convince the book writer to agree to a different division).

Defining the existence of a collaboration

The law answers many other questions: For a finding that a collaboration existed, the collaborators don't have to have worked together, either physically or even at the same time. The key is the parties' intention that different elements be put together. For example, a writer could draft a book before even looking for collaborators to write music and lyrics, and even if they ultimately fail to complete the project, the chosen composer and lyricist could be judged joint owners of the work so long as they did, in fact, create material intended to go with the book.

The intention of the parties

As stated above, the crucial issue is the *intention* of the parties at the time the work is done. So long as the writers intend to collaborate, they are subject to the presumptions established by law.

However, intent also encompasses the question, "Who is a collaborator?" Consistent with copyright law's general precepts, the answer is that a collaborator's contribution must be one of actual *authorship* (i.e., expression, not mere ideas), *and* the parties must intend to work together in a *collaboration*. Thus, the context is important too: There are some projects on which people work together that are clearly never intended to result in a collaboration. One obvious example is that of an editor making stylistic changes to a fiction or nonfiction book; yes, the intent is to merge different elements into a whole, but the parties clearly never intended themselves to be collaborators in the sense of joint authors.

The law may seem harsh, but there is a reason, a policy, behind it that sends a loud message to all collaborators: Take care of your business affairs; focus on these issues and resolve them; get your understanding in writing and signed by all collaborators so that nothing is left to be decided by the copyright law. Don't shirk your responsibilities, either because you're intimidated by the issues or because you're afraid to raise the difficult ones with your collaborators. These excuses will not be persuasive later on.

Consequently, writers don't need a collaboration agreement to *create* a joint-author relationship—working together as collaborators creates that relationship automatically. The purpose of a collaboration agreement is to define, explain and memorialize the parameters of the working relationship—each person's rights, responsibilities and obligations—before the law steps in and does it for you.

THE COLLABORATION AGREEMENT

Here, as with other contracts, there is a natural desire to avoid tackling difficult issues for fear that the relationship will be damaged or ruined. The strong suggestion remains the same as in other chapters: Yes, there will probably be some rough moments of discussion, but overall your relationship will be stronger if you address all issues and reach a resolution. Once you've signed a collaboration agreement, you will have laid the hardcore business-related issues to rest; this will enable the collaborators to move forward together and focus their energies where they belong: on the creative elements and on getting the work produced.

The following discussion addresses the core concepts of any collaboration agreement. Because each collaboration is inevitably different, this discussion is not intended to be exhaustive. Thus, the circumstances of each individual situation should always be addressed clearly.

Copyright

First, understand the difference between copyright registration and a collaboration agreement. Registration fulfills certain legal requirements to afford the work the complete protections of the copyright law (as discussed in the chapter on copyright). By contrast, the collaboration agreement defines and explains the substantive relationship between collaborators and the parameters of that relationship; specifics about how to structure the collaboration and how in practical terms to make it work are embedded in the agreement. It is important, however, that *both* the copyright registration and the collaboration agreement exist.

Where there are distinctly separate elements (e.g., the book, music and lyrics of a musical), there is more than one way to file for copyright registration of the complete work. The first is to file a registration for each individual element, and the second is to file one registration form for the whole work. The Copyright Office advises that these are both valid registrations.

Sometimes the creation of the piece will naturally decide this question. Individual elements may be created at different times, so it may make sense to file forms when each element is finished. (This may be particularly compelling if any parts of the work are shown to people outside the collaboration.) For example, if the book is written first, the book writer may have filed the registration form before beginning a search for collaborators. If three collaborators create a musical simultaneously, their inclination might be to file one form for the completed work.

Where timing doesn't compel a particular decision, the collaborators need to think about their personal preferences. Some people would be more comfortable keeping the registrations separate; perhaps it's easier, or the separation of ownership gives them peace of mind. (And the collaboration agreement would explain how the individual elements would be brought together.) Others want the musical to be viewed as a whole, rather than in discrete parts, and perhaps symbolically this becomes important to the collaboration. (And the collaboration agreement would also explain what will happen to the work if the collaboration breaks up.) There may also be financial considerations, because at the time of this writing each registration with the Copyright Office costs twenty dollars plus the costs of the deposit copy (although it is suggested that collaborators try not to make cost the deciding factor).

Regardless of which method of filing the collaborators decide to adopt, it's important that the collaboration agreement be clear in stating how and in whose names the copyright registration has taken or will take place.

Money

Everyone always wants to know how to share the money. It is strongly recommended that this issue be addressed very early in the relationship, because it is easier to arrive at resolutions when only concepts are being discussed. People tend to get a little crazier about percentages when actual dollars are on the table and can be calculated. Start by defining what money may be at stake.

Money attributable to the complete work. All money that flows from the work itself, be it a musical or a play, is shared by the collaborators. This is not limited to stage productions, but also includes such dispositions as translations or adaptations that may be made in all media. (In the musical context, this is to be distinguished from the use of "separate music and lyrics" and from publication, addressed below.)

There are no hard and fast rules about how to divide money,

although there are general concepts that may help collaborators decide for themselves how to handle it. (As an aside, always keep in mind that the manner in which collaborators share money is *not* tied to their voting structure for making decisions; the voting structure is a completely separate issue, addressed in more detail below.)

Don't think in terms of specific percentages of gross. (For example, collaborators on a musical often ask whether money should be divided two percent, two percent and two percent, thinking only of the theatrical industry custom of paying the authors six percent of the gross box office receipts.) Think of the bigger picture: how the collaborators will divide *all* money earned over the life of the work, regardless of where the money comes from and how that particular deal was structured. It's percentage of *dollars*, not percentage of gross box office receipts, that matters. (Using the example above, the collaborators would be dividing the dollars into thirds; where the arrangement was for six percent of gross, that would translate into two percent per collaborator.)

Work contributed/time spent. For a number of reasons, it is impossible to figure out shares based on actual work contributed, in terms of both tangible results and time spent on the project. As a practical matter, collaboration agreements should be signed in the beginning of the relationship. That means you simply won't know what each person's ultimate contribution to the work will be at the time of signing.

Even if the collaborators were inclined to revisit the issue after completion of the work, good collaborations will result in a free flow of ideas back and forth, and not be constrained by artificially constructed formulas. (For example, the book writer may give the lyricist ideas; the lyricist may give the composer ideas; and so on.) It would be absurd to sit down with a calculator once the work is completed and try to tally each person's contribution (who came up with which idea, or which word, phrase, lyric could be attributed to whom). If the collaborators are lucky enough to work well together, they should focus on capitalizing on the output rather than nitpicking about whether one collaborator really deserves thirty-five or thirty-eight percent. Don't lose sight of the real goal: a wonderful work that has a long life.

The calculation *can't* be based on time spent on the project since some writers think about their work for a long time before writing anything down, others write it down right away but spend more time revising, etc. Realistically, it's not quantifiable.

Even if the collaborators wanted to quantify the actual work created and time spent, experience has shown that to be counterproductive; in the end, it may do more harm than good to the collaboration (and ultimately to the work) to assign actual "value" to each contribution. Collaborators would find themselves arguing over minute details, and it naturally would spill over into other parts of the relationship.

Without a doubt, it is important that each collaborator feels that her or his contribution is acknowledged and fairly compensated; but, if you get into a bind, try to step back and think of yourselves as a team pulling together towards a mutual goal. Maximize appreciation of each person's strengths rather than tallying creative output as if it were beans to divvy up.

General guidelines. Sometimes establishing percentages means fairly allocating the risk that contributions may turn out to be a little different than originally envisioned, since no one can predict with precision. The true goal is to arrive at percentages which, given natural fluctuations over the life of the collaboration, might fairly and reasonably reflect total contributions, and with which the collaborators can work comfortably.

The easiest (and fairly common) scenario is one in which three people collaborate, with each person creating one distinct element of the musical (one writes the book, one writes the lyrics, one writes the music). In this situation, there is a natural inclination to divide money earned into thirds. There are no rules that say it must be this way, but this particular situation generally suggests an easy division into thirds, with which the parties are usually satisfied.

Complications crop up with different combinations; for instance, when there are two people collaborating on the three elements. If one person writes the book and the other writes music and lyrics, what guidelines should they use to divide the money? There are several schools of thought on this subject. (The same principles also apply when there are more than three collaborators involved.)

The work as the reference point. The first approach is to use the musical itself as the reference point, not the number of people involved. Thus, the musical could be viewed as three distinct elements—book, music and lyrics—and the money would be divided according to these elements rather than the number of people involved. This arrangement is based on the following idea: If three people were involved, each writing one element, the money would most likely be divided into thirds. Consequently, if one collaborator is talented enough to write two of the elements, he or she should not be penalized, in a sense, for being able to do so; conversely, the person who writes only one element should not receive a windfall just by virtue of working with a collaborator who can write the other two elements. Thus, the collaborator who writes two elements would receive two-thirds of earnings and the collaborator responsible for one element would receive one-third.

The number of collaborators as the reference point. A second approach would be that the money should be divided equally between two collaborators without any reference to the work created by each person, because this arrangement symbolizes an equal partnership. This situation is sometimes emotionally charged, with the collaborator creating one element not wanting to feel like or be treated as a lesser participant. The emotions can ride high on both sides, however, with the collaborator creating two of the three elements feeling that the extent of his or her contribution is not being fairly recognized.

To better appreciate this discussion, try putting yourself in the other collaborator's shoes. (And consider, for example, if there were four collaborators rather than two: You might be less inclined to divide the money equally.) In these situations, no collaborator should ignore the importance of the emotional issues on the other side. Focus, instead, on finding ways to address these to the satisfaction of all parties.

Compromise. A third line of thought defines a middle position. It is possible to structure financial arrangements so that the collaborator who has created two elements receives more than half but less than two-thirds of the proceeds, which means the collaborator who created one element receives more than one-third but not a full half-share. For example, the collaborators might arrive at a sixty/forty division, since that brings the collaborators closer to an equal partnership symbolically, yet still recognizes the fact that there *is* a difference in their contributions. A variation on that theme is to retain the two-thirds/one-third division on earnings from the work, but to look at *other* monies which flow to individual collaborators and which are often not shared by all the collaborators (e.g., publication royalties or money paid for separate use of the music and lyrics, as discussed below). Adjustments in those other areas might satisfy the emotional or symbolic issues.

At all times, try to avoid the trap of asking questions like, "How did Rodgers and Hammerstein divide their money?" The answer to that question is irrelevant to the discussion between other collaborators; there will always be intangible or personal factors that significantly influenced other collaborators' decisions which will never be known and simply cannot be evaluated. (What if Rodgers was motivated to offer Hammerstein an equal split of the money because Hammerstein once helped Rodgers out of a tough spot; how could that information have any bearing on a collaboration now? Even if the specific relationship and discussions between Rodgers and Hammerstein could be researched, would today's collaborators also have to research Rodgers and Hart's relationship, and then compare that to Sondheim and Lapine's relationship, and then compare that to a comprehensive list of other collaborations that have existed in the last seventy-five years in order to arrive at a mathematically sanctioned answer?) The fact is that your collaboration is not that of Rodgers and Hammerstein, or of anyone else. So keep the focus on your particular collaboration and talk about your feelings. The resolution you reach will make for a much healthier and more productive collaboration than if you try to compel your collaborator to accept a particular division of monies just because someone else did it that way.

The negative approach. Don't fall into the trap of trying to decide which element is most important. For example, some composers have been known to say, "It's called a musical. That means people are coming to hear the music, so I should get a bigger share." Composers and lyricists have been known to denigrate the book as "just dialogue," when in fact the book usually creates the foundation and structure from which the songs are created. These arguments can be twisted into any number of configurations from each collaborator's perspective, but the result is the same: It throws the collaboration off-balance and creates bad feelings. And truth be told, a musical is a work in which *all* elements are interdependent and must hold up their respective ends.

Everyone has sat through musicals that had great music but not interesting lyrics, or a wonderful book but boring songs, and so on. No one element is inherently more important than the others, but the success of the whole certainly depends on the success of all the individual elements working together.

Maintain perspective. If collaborators find themselves haggling over the last few percentage points, sit down and think through both best- and worst-case scenarios. If the work is successful, there will be plenty of money to share; if the work is not successful, you may find yourselves at loggerheads over just a few dollars. This is not to say that money isn't important—obviously it is, not only for its intrinsic value (it pays the bills), but because there are often important emotions attached. However, there comes a point when collaborators may be well-served by perspective.

Weigh the last few percentage points in question against the intangible human/personal parts of the collaborative relationship. Try to address the emotions and realities of collaboration as you would any personal relationship; ordinarily, people will try to find reasonable compromises on common ground.

The flip side of this, however, is that collaborators should not agree to a division with which they're truly unhappy or angry. Don't allow yourself to walk away feeling taken advantage of. Any lingering resentment may surface again when other issues or situations arise.

Figure out what you can live with and move on. Don't tally up compromises as chits to be called in later.

Money from separate uses of individual elements of the work

With musicals, there are situations which may arise that do not automatically involve all the collaborators sharing money (plays typically do not confront these issues because they lack distinctly separate elements). The first is the use of "separate music and lyrics." The second is publication.

Separate music and lyrics. Separate music and lyrics means the music and lyrics are used *outside* the context of the complete musical work (i.e., book, music and lyrics). The two most obvious examples are the cast album (although a small amount of dialogue might be used for continuity between songs) and when a performer wants to record a particular song from the musical. Other examples are synchronization rights (when a song is used in a movie) and small performing rights (the royalties collected by BMI, ASCAP and SEESAC for songs played in restaurants, bars, elevators, etc.)

It is assumed that the composer and lyricist will share these earnings. Thus, the core issue is whether the book writer will share in any money that flows from the use of the separate music and lyrics. This is freely negotiable between collaborators, and here there are two schools of thought:

The book writer shares. One position is that the book is more than just the literal text of the story that links the songs: It's foundation and structure, and therefore the book is integrally related to the songs. This theory posits that even though the book isn't technically a part of the songs, the songs grew out of the book. Thus, ignoring the book's influence on the music and lyrics would be unfair. A corollary of this proposition is that the *entire* musical generates interest in the individual songs, and therefore the book writer's contribution is just as important as that of the composer and lyricist, and should be recognized with a share of the earnings.

The book writer does not share. The other line of thought is that only the collaborators whose work is actually used in another context (i.e., the composer and lyricist) should share those earnings. The "reality" is that ordinarily very little tangible material from the book, if anything, appears on a cast album or an independent album or in a movie which uses a song, etc., and it could therefore be unfair to have to share such earnings with the book writer.

Publication monies. It is common for the published version of a musical to contain the book and usually the lyrics, but not the score, so the money received is usually shared only by the book writer and the lyricist. A book writer might have a harder time making the argument for a share of the separate music and lyrics money if he or she is not also willing to share publication earnings. A composer could argue either that it's not unfair to exclude the book writer from separate music and lyrics money, since she or he is excluded from the publishing money, or that there should be equal/bilateral sharing in both areas.

The collaborators need to think: When individual elements are used, will the money be shared only by those collaborators whose work actually appears in the separate use, or will the collaboration treat *all* money as belonging to the team, regardless of its source. This is a question for each collaborative team to answer for itself; there is no one "correct" answer. Either way, out of fairness the solution would probably apply equally to both circumstances addressed above, unless the collaborators decide to the contrary.

Decision-making power

Probably the most important issue to resolve is how to make joint decisions. The collaboration needs to establish a clear voting structure. This concern encompasses a wide range of questions and issues that will need to be addressed over the life of the work. For example, where to submit the work—contests, staged readings, workshops, nonprofit theatre, commercial producers? If two producers are interested in the work at the same time, how will the collaborative team decide which producer to choose? Once a producer is selected, how will the collaborative team negotiate the production contract? Assuming that the authors collectively have the proper artistic approvals in the production contract, how will the collaborative team actually make those decisions? If there is a successful production and Dramatists Play Service, Dramatic Publishing Company and Samuel French are all interested in publishing the acting edition and licensing the work, how will the collaborators decide which company they want to work with? With luck (and hard work), the list of questions will be quite long.

Number of collaborators. If there are two collaborators—whether it's on a play or a musical—each person should have one vote and the decisions should be made unanimously; it would be fundamentally unfair for the structure to be otherwise, since both collaborators should be actively involved in making decisions about the work. Collaborator A may have written two elements and Collaborator B may have written one element, but it would destroy the relationship if Collaborator A could automatically outvote Collaborator B on every issue. In some collaborations it is possible that one collaborator, for personal reasons, would decide to relinquish active participation in the decision-making (or in a particular decision); but, as a general rule, collaborators should *not* try to exclude or ignore each other.

At times there might be a collaborator who thinks that joint decision-making won't work; he or she decides that "someone" must have final authority, and unilaterally appoints him- or herself as that person. This doesn't teach collaborators how to work together. Mutual decision-making will not be really mutual if one person knows, in the back of his or her mind, that if the collaborators can't agree one of them can "pull rank" and simply tell the other what the final decision is. Inevitably, there will be times when collaborators don't agree. The best answer to such situations is, "Learn how to work with others, to share and compromise, and to resolve your differences." Again comparing collaboration to a relationship: The best relationships are those in which the participants have learned to listen to each other and to work together, not those in which one person has established him- or herself as the "master."

If there are three or more collaborators, then the team must decide whether to make decisions by majority vote or to insist on unanimity. Again, there is no "correct" way to go; the collaboration must choose what is most comfortable. Keep in mind the potential advantages and disadvantages of each method.

Majority vote. If the collaboration uses majority vote, there will be times when one collaborator will be outvoted and may not be happy. One might assume, however, that over the life of a work each collaborator will be outvoted at some time and an overall fairness will still be achieved. Depending on the parties involved, having only to achieve a majority vote could alleviate problems and disagreements that would otherwise thwart the work's forward movement and success. However, if one collaborator is concerned that the other collaborators will always join forces, that person might want to consider establishing unanimity as the means of making decisions.

If there are more than three collaborators, it means that there is more than one person writing one of the elements (e.g., there might be two lyricists, one book writer and one composer on a musical). Ordinarily each unit, or element, would have one vote, and then the collaborators on that one element have to figure out how to cast their one shared vote. Overall, this would mean that the voting remains divided into thirds according to the *elements* of the musical, rather than giving each *person* one vote. However, the collaborators can decide to handle this any way they like, and if you prefer to give each person an equal vote, then do it.

Unanimity. If the collaboration chooses unanimity, there will inevitably be times when the parties cannot reach an agreement and must then be prepared to explore other alternatives rather than arguing endlessly over who is right and wrong. Some collaborative teams may decide it's easier in the long run to opt for majority vote than to negotiate around deadlocked votes. Others believe that "true" fairness occurs only when all the collaborators are in agreement.

Whenever there is a situation requiring unanimity, regardless of the number of collaborators involved, the collaborators will need to know how to work creatively around disagreement. As mentioned, there will inevitably be issues that result in conflict. The first rounds of discussion usually involve each person stating his or her preference and then explaining why he or she believes it is the best choice to make. It's possible that the other collaborator(s) will decide to change their mind(s). If not, then the second rounds often consist of discussion and debate, with each person trying to convince the other(s) to adopt his or her position. Again, sometimes this will be "successful" and can result in changed positions and agreement.

If, however, the collaborators cannot reach agreement even after moving through these two stages, it is incumbent on the collaborators to try to find a compromise. This can often be done by putting aside all the previously stated positions and working together to find some other resolution that wasn't already on the table. For example, when it comes time to exercise artistic approvals, the collaborators might not agree on their first choice of director. If Collaborator 1 wants Director A and Collaborator 2 wants Director B, and they cannot reach agreement through the first two stages of negotiation, then in the third stage they might try to think of *other* directors' names in the hope of being able to agree on Director C. While not the first choice of either Collaborator 1 or 2, there is usually more than one "good" director, and a third choice might represent a compromise that enables the collaborators to arrive at a joint decision. (Someone once defined a compromise as a resolution in which all parties walk away a little unhappy because no one person gets everything he or she wanted. This is not necessarily bad.)

Arbitration/mediation. Even though all collaboration agreements should contain a provision for arbitration or formal mediation of disputes, stay away from these as the means to resolve issues if you possibly can. Distinguish between the inevitable *issues* that arise within collaborations and the substantive hardcore *disputes* that more often than not damage collaborations. While more expedient and less expensive than litigation, arbitration and mediation still signal a substantial breakdown in both communication and the overall relationship. In practice, resorting to arbitration or formal mediation to resolve the most ordinary collaborative issues could indicate to potential producers and others who would be interested in the work that serious problems exist which could either encumber or destroy the work.

There are so many works on the market that collaborators should do everything possible to avoid attaching this stigma to theirs. (Given a choice between a work that is fraught with intra-collaborator problems and one that is not, the latter would probably be more appealing to a producer.) Consequently, such formal means of resolving disputes should remain drastic measures; that is, the very last resort.

(As an aside, there may come a time in a collaboration when you simply can't get over a hurdle, and the parties may decide that an informal yet facilitated discussion would help them to communicate better. Often collaborators in these situations will choose an objective third party to help facilitate their conversation. The purpose is to diffuse the problem or anger, so that the parties can find a resolution. This is more like going into therapy than asking someone to cast a deciding vote.)

Arriving at a structure. Each collaborator needs to be an active participant in decision-making, and the structure needs to be fair. It is rare to find a collaborator who will invest time, energy and money in creating a work but who will not want a voice in decisions. It would probably be detrimental to the collaboration to try to reduce or eliminate their participation.

The collaboration agreement should actually state clearly that every collaborator will be given the opportunity to be involved in all discussions, issues, questions, negotiations and the like. In addition, each collaborator should agree to participate in a reasonable and cooperative manner to further the possibilities of exploiting the work as much as possible; collaborators can't just vote against proffered deals because they're still angry about an unrelated issue. And again, while an individual collaborator may decide at any time to relinquish participation, even on a situation-by-situation basis, the collaboration agreement should plainly state that the person is entitled to be involved.

Exceptions. Having established the general rule for group decision-making, there are a couple of limited exceptions to point out.

The first is in the area of script approvals. If the work in question is a play, collaborators will usually retain equal decision-making power over alterations in and/or omissions from the work. However, if the collaborators are working on a musical, it is more common for each collaborator to have final approval over the element he or she wrote; thus, the book writer would have final approval over the book, the composer would have final approval over the music and the lyricist would have final approval over the lyrics. This is not to say that the collaborative team shouldn't address these issues as a team—they definitely should—but no collaborator should have his or her work summarily changed by the other collaborators.

Second, it is common for the composer and lyricist to have approval over the musical elements of a production. Choice of conductor, orchestrator and the arrangements should be their prerogative.

If one person creates two elements of a musical, that person needs to think of her- or himself as wearing two separate and distinct hats when addressing these issues. For example, if a person is both the lyricist and the book writer, it is better to focus on the lyric issues wearing only the lyricist hat and the book issues wearing only the book writer hat, as odd as it may feel to divide your personality in this way.

It bears repeating that the issue of decision-making power should always be addressed separately from the issue of how to divide money; the two are not really related. For example, there might be two collaborators sharing money on a two-thirds/one-third basis, yet the collaboration simply could not work effectively if one person had a two-thirds vote on all matters that needed to be decided. So think about these areas individually and arrive at appropriate conclusions by isolating the relevant concerns.

Division of labor

The division of labor (as regards marketing, promotion and related areas) is not typically addressed in a collaboration agreement, although how to handle expenses incurred on behalf of the work should be. This seems an appropriate place, however, to address both.

There are contributions to any collaboration that will not be exclusively creative. There are necessary (and not always thrilling) administrative tasks, such as researching submission possibilities, writing cover letters, making copies of scripts and tapes, and organizing, making and tracking submissions. Then there are also the "hustling" and "schmoozing" factors which, as discussed in the chapter on marketing, are not to be taken lightly. It's very important to be visible in the industry, to be comfortable meeting people and making connections, and to take advantage of opportunities when they arise. Without a doubt, these tasks, individually and collectively, are time-consuming and carry significant responsibility.

Some collaborators work together in all aspects of marketing the work. However, in other collaborations, different tasks or responsibilities may be assumed by different collaborators, according to such factors as who is comfortable being the "out front" person (people who either have a lot of business contacts or who enjoy the marketing and business side) and who enjoys the organizational aspects (or is better at them). Again, every collaboration is different and the individuals involved should work out how these tasks, responsibilities and obligations are going to be handled. This does not have to be established up front, but it's a good idea at least to begin talking about these matters.

The collaborative team should evaluate all the work that needs to be done and try to allocate it in a fair and reasonable fashion, which should mean *not* dumping all the least desirable work on one person. No one wants to feel taken advantage of, in terms of either time or dollars spent. This is not to suggest that the person whose contribution is, for example, organizing mailings and doing follow-up should somehow be compensated for the time spent; no collaborator should expect to be paid by the other collaborators for any of their work on the project.

Expenses incurred

In a related vein, then, the collaboration agreement must also address the fact that marketing the work will involve outlays of money and how those expenditures will be handled. Don't incur expenses without obtaining advance permission from the other collaborators or, at least, have some structure in place to deal with expenses, such as requiring approval for any expenses in excess of fifty dollars. Generally, collaborators share responsibility for money spent to further the work in the same manner that they share the money coming in, although some collaborators make the composer and lyricist responsible for making the demo tapes and the book writer responsible for script copying, based on the idea that the earnings flowing from the use of the separate music and lyrics and from publication would not be shared, as addressed above.

Billing credit

Everyone has an ego, and the importance of billing credit is one area in which people can surprise even themselves. There are two primary decisions to make: the order of the billing (i.e., whose name comes first, second, third, etc.) and whether the billing will be horizontal or vertical. Try to do some soul searching about what emotions may be attached to your billing. Often writers say they don't care about billing . . . until the day they first see the poster. (As an aside, if one collaborator decides that the billing credit really is not important, but there are other issues that have become sticking points with that person, perhaps this could be an area that opens exchange.)

There are certain details pertaining to billing that should be written into every collaboration agreement and which ordinarily should not be negotiable, such as making sure that no one collaborator ever receives billing credit without the other collaborators also receiving credit, or that the type size and style be the same for all collaborators. (The more specific terms, such as the exact type size and placement, will be addressed in a production contract, not in a collaboration agreement, since they involve third parties' concerns.)

The point here is that a collaboration agreement should always strive for fair and equitable billing treatment for all collaborators. This relates back to the question of whether any one collaborator's work is more important than that of another. It is again suggested that collaborators strive to avoid such statements, and if one collaborator feels strongly that his or her contribution should be acknowledged differently, the other collaborators should explore their own feelings carefully before moving ahead together.

Merger

Merger is a very important yet somewhat elusive concept as regards collaboration. Understanding merger requires distinguishing the individual elements that make up the work from the completed work. Merger brings together the individual elements and glues them together into a whole, with the work itself then becoming a separate, tangible entity. Once merger occurs, the individual elements cannot later be broken apart and separated. It is akin to marriage without the possibility of divorce.

Merger is sometimes difficult to conceptualize—because, in a sense, we are creating a legal fiction. Put bluntly, for a successful work to have its own life, there must come a point when its fundamental existence is no longer subject to the whims and moods of its creators. Decisions must always be made about how best to exploit the work, but after merger no collaborator can thwart or destroy the work itself.

Using a musical as an example, before merger takes place what exists is the three distinct elements that make up the work: book, music and lyrics. The elements can still be pulled apart; for example, the collaboration agreement often provides that the collaborators can decide one element isn't working, extract it from the other two and replace it with new material. Another possible scenario is that the collaboration will break up, with each person owning what they contributed and taking that contribution with them for some future use in another work.

Once merger takes place, however, the situation is entirely different. The musical is no longer three distinct elements, but rather one single work with a life of its own. If, after merger, the collaborators can't get along, the active collaborative relationship may grind to a halt but the work will still live on as a complete entity unto itself.

The same principles apply to writers collaborating on a play, except that they won't likely have discrete elements that could be used in other works. Merger remains important in this context for the same reasons enumerated above, but the ability to divide the piece easily doesn't exist.

Protection from risk. The following scenarios may illuminate this idea:

Producer X produces the work and it's been running for six months. Suddenly, the collaborators have a fight and are no longer speaking to each other. Collaborator A announces, "I don't want to work with you any longer. I'm taking my music and going home." It would be nothing short of chaos if Producer X could be left completely vulnerable to a situation in which the work could be used as leverage or for revenge.

Consider the stock and amateur licensing arenas. Imagine there already are twenty-five productions scheduled for next season and requests are still pouring in. Collaborator B decides that Collaborators A and C aren't responding appropriately to his or her opinions about where to market the work outside of the United States, so B states, "If you don't do things my way, I'm not going to let you use my lyrics," holding the work hostage until his or her demands are addressed.

These examples are not as absurd as one might hope, and it isn't hard to see how miserable such situations could become. The work itself, together with future producers, publishers and others, requires protection from the relationship between the collaborators.

And it isn't only third parties who need protection: The collaborators themselves need to know that they will not be exposed to the types of "hostage" situations described above. Think about how long the life of a work can be; consider the classic musicals that have now been around for years and years. Those works need to remain unfettered and untouched in order to garner more and more productions around the world. Imagine, for purposes of this discussion, that three years after *Oklahoma* was produced on Broadway, the collaborators had a tremendous falling out and spoke to each other only through their agents. The musical, having already merged, would still have had its successful life; it would not have "died" when the relationship hit the rocks.

To accomplish this goal, the collaborators' ability to manipulate the *elements* of the work must be eliminated at some point. The collaborators will always maintain ownership and control over *the work* as a whole, but the degree of this control must change as far as individual elements are concerned.

Establishing merger in the collaboration agreement. The collaboration agreement must establish that merger will in fact take place; it will not happen automatically. In addition, the collaborators have to write into the agreement *when* they want merger to occur. Since merger carries important consequences, the collaborators have to consider and evaluate a number of possible triggering events which will occur in the course of the work's life.

The triggering event. Historically, merger has ordinarily been tied to production performances, in terms of both level of production and minimum number of performances. The full range of production possibilities would encompass first-class or comparable (e.g., Broadway or West End), Off-Broadway or comparable, regional theatre, Off-Off Broadway, or any other that the collaborators choose. However, most often merger would not take place until at least the first "significant" production; that is, a level of production that garners a substantial amount of attention. Traditionally, this has meant Broadway or Off-Broadway performances (or the British equivalent), although with the rise in visibility of regional theatre over the last thirty years, many collaborators have also included that level of production as a triggering event for merger. (Agreement language often states that merger occurs when the earliest of these productions takes place.) It is much less common for the work to merge from smaller productions, which are seen as occurring too early in the life of the work to warrant merger. Limiting merger to the higher levels of production is not meant to denigrate smaller productions, but rather to evaluate them honestly in terms of the serious consequences of merger.

Once the collaborators decide on the level of production that will trigger merger, they need to address the required number of performances. In the past, many works merged upon the twenty-first performance, while some required as few as one performance in the designated venue. It is somewhat unusual to see merger postponed beyond the twenty-first performance, but the precise number is entirely within the domain of the collaborators.

Once merger takes place, the collaboration agreement then lasts as long as the copyright in the work. As of this writing the copyright lasts for the writer's life plus fifty years; when there are multiple writers, the fifty years begins running from the death of the last surviving collaborator.

Termination of the relationship or of the agreement

Termination typically can arise in two ways: The parties aren't collaborating well together and they decide to terminate the relationship; or, after a certain amount of time has passed without merger occurring (i.e., without the success desired by the collaborators), any one person on the collaborative team can decide to terminate the collaboration agreement for whatever reason. These situations are especially difficult to codify in an agreement since there are so many variables, not to mention personalities, that can come into play in an amazingly wide range of situations.

Termination of the relationship. The most difficult issue arises when one of the collaborators isn't working out. (Obviously if *all* the collaborators don't want to work together anymore, they just end the relationship.)

How can this happen? One collaborator may be disorganized and unfocused, unable to finish anything on schedule. Perhaps the work was supposed to have been done months ago and one collaborator is holding up all progress. It's possible that one collaborator's personality is so difficult that no matter how wonderful the work is, the other collaborators just can't bear to collaborate any longer. It's also possible that two of the collaborators are disappointed with the quality of one collaborator's work and feel that their ideas simply don't mesh with that collaborator's vision. Any number of situations may ruin a collaboration.

No matter what, don't become stuck trying to figure out how to "force" someone to be a good collaborator. You cannot compel someone else to change her or his habits, and you cannot force people to work together—it's a form of personal servitude. Certainly you must have an honest talk with that person and give him or her another chance, perhaps being clearer about the collaborative team's expectations of each person, maybe establishing a specific timeline with clearly enumerated deadlines for each segment of the work. To some extent people *can* change their work habits if they want to, and if the issues and resolutions are talked through openly. If the signals are clear that the collaboration is not moving ahead smoothly, it may be time to think about whether a different person might be better for the collaboration.

This is not to suggest that any time a collaborator misses a deadline or cancels a meeting he or she should be confronted with the possibility of being kicked out of the collaboration. Voting someone out of a collaboration is a drastic last resort, not a first step. But if a continuing pattern is apparent and the collaborators have done all they can to work together, the problems and issues must be addressed.

Termination structure. If there are three collaborators, it's not unusual to establish a structure in which two collaborators can decide to terminate the relationship with the third. However, if there are more than three collaborators, then the collaborative team needs to decide what number of votes would be required to terminate the relationship with one of the collaborators; often a majority will suffice, but it depends in part on the total number of collaborators in the team. If only a majority is needed, the collaborative team will need to be careful not to subject such important decisions to emotional manipulation and political infighting. If a group of writers decides it must be unanimous on the issue of asking one collaborator to leave, the potential risk is that it will become impossible to reach such a decision, which might stall the work midstream.

If there are only two collaborators, obviously it is a different situation. If one person doesn't want to work with the other person and they can't resolve their differences, the collaboration would seem necessarily to have to end.

Material created by departing collaborator. If it is decided that one collaborator will no longer be a part of the collaboration, the question shifts to what to do with the material that has already been created by that person. There are a couple of possible scenarios and the choice should be made by the departing collaborator after the remaining collaborators have made their preference known.

Depending on the circumstances that led to the departure of the collaborator, the material already created could continue to be a part of the work. For example, the departing person might not be interested in being an active part of the collaboration any longer, but might want her or his work to remain; perhaps she or he has been offered a different project and isn't all that interested in the material already created. In this instance, the departing collaborator would still maintain some stake in the work (both the right to receive money and billing credit), but would relinquish active participation, such as voting power.

The departing collaborator might want to take the material already created and use it in a different work. There are two possibilities in this scenario: limiting that person's ability to use the work already created, or enabling that person to have free use of it. If the remaining collaborators want to limit the departing collaborator's use of his or her materials (out of concern that such other use will compete or interfere with the musical they all worked on), the collaborators will have to work out some reasonable financial arrangement to compensate the departing collaborator. If the departing collaborator refuses to be limited in any future use of the materials already created, he or she should be free to use his or her own materials without restriction, but also without any compensation.

Making room for a new collaborator. If the work isn't finished, the remaining collaborators will have to think about bringing in a new collaborator to start from scratch or pick up the pieces and complete the project. Room needs to be made for that new collaborator in terms of decision-making, financial participation, billing credit, etc. The choices depend in large part on the circumstances: How much of a particular element has already been created and how much more work remains? How far along is the entire work, not just the particular element in question? Will the departing collaborator leave any material behind, or will the new collaborator start with a clean slate? Do the remaining collaborators know who they would want as the new collaborator and has that person expressed interest in and/or decided to work on this project? Is a theatre or producer already interested? Has the work enjoyed any readings or workshops? Will the collaborator's departure drag down the work with emotional issues that surface as a result of the change? If the departing collaborator is taking his or her materials and plans to find new collaborators with whom to work on the same or a similar project, will this create a situation in which two separate collaborative teams are racing to the finish line with similar projects? (Depending on the circumstances, the existing collaboration may be ahead of the person who has to go back to the first step of finding collaborators to work with. But any writer involved with any project should understand there's rarely a guarantee that similar projects aren't being developed simultaneously; unless, for example, the work is an adaptation for which exclusive rights have been obtained.)

There are so many factors to evaluate which can exist in innumerable combinations that, unfortunately, it would be difficult to provide any specific guidelines about how to navigate these waters. Should such a situation arise, the parties involved will have to assess the circumstances and practice triage. It's frustrating not to have an external source to turn to for answers, but this is one of those situations in which there aren't any industry customs or norms that will have any substantive bearing.

Emotionally, this is one of the more difficult situations to move through, and the remaining collaborators must feel free to acknowledge this. It is a divorce, and it inevitably will have an effect on the work and the collaboration. Sometimes it all works out, but collaborators trying to make the best of a not-so-good situation and faced with unsatisfactory options may need to perform a serious cost/benefit analysis before deciding whether or not—and how—to proceed.

Terminating the contract. Ordinarily, any collaborator should have the unilateral right to terminate the collaboration agreement if merger does not take place within a designated period of time. When collaborators begin a relationship, everyone has high hopes and expectations, but for a myriad of reasons the goals of the collaboration may not materialize. As difficult as it may be to hear, at a certain point it could be fair and reasonable for any collaborator to decide that she or he wants to move on.

The collaborative team may *not* be having problems working together, in either the creative or marketing aspects, but the desired result (say, a production that triggers merger) simply doesn't materialize. This is very different from the circumstances addressed above, in which the collaborative team does not work well together. Consequently, there should be two separate provisions in the collaboration agreement, both addressing termination issues but involving disparate circumstances.

Establishing a time frame. The collaboration agreement needs to contain time limits. It's not a good idea for the collaboration to leave this issue completely unaddressed or unresolved. If the collaborators don't establish a minimum period of time that must pass before any individual collaborator can terminate the relationship unilaterally, it could result in a dark cloud hanging over the collaboration. On the other hand, providing a basic period of time to allow for merger to occur is also wise.

Let's be clear about some specifics. First, this type of clause does *not* provide for automatic termination. It simply allows each collaborator to evaluate the situation at a designated time. If each collaborator is still excited and motivated about the work, and feels the work is moving forward even if it hasn't "hit" yet, they won't want to terminate the agreement.

Second, the period of time established needs to be reasonable. The last thing collaborators need is to create unnecessary pressure on themselves to have the work succeed quickly. Think carefully about how long it reasonably takes for a work to be written, marketed and produced.

This will necessarily depend to some degree on the level of production chosen as the triggering event for merger. If a collaborative team decides that what they really want is to have their musical produced on Broadway, and therefore a Broadway production and *only* a Broadway production will trigger merger, then the agreed period of time before "reevaluation" has to be consistent with contemporary Broadway realities. In other words, don't establish a two-year period; some successful musicals have taken six to eight years and even longer to make it to Broadway. Similarly, if the trigger for merger is a production Off-Broadway or at a regional theatre, find out how long that might take. For example, regional theatres tend to plan entire seasons at once, often six months to one year ahead of actual presentation. For commercial productions, the option period for which the right to produce is secured will be at least one year, most likely longer.

Give yourselves a little "cushion" in case things don't work out exactly as hoped. It's impossible to predict all the twists and turns in the road to production, but the one thing you should assume is delay. Remember that if a producer takes an option on your work, it is not a guarantee of production, only a promise that the producer will *try* to present a production.

At the same time, collaborators probably shouldn't commit to too long a time frame. As an extreme example, it could be frustrating for collaborators to be tied to each other for twenty years before having the right to evaluate and terminate.

Although it's difficult to establish absolute boundaries, one could probably say that the pre-merger reevaluation specified in a collaboration agreement should not arise before at least three years have passed, and typically would not exceed eight to ten years, absent extenuating circumstances.

Death or disability of a collaborator

No one likes to plan for death or disability, but it's very important to do so in a collaboration agreement. The discussion here will focus on death, but most of the same considerations can be applied to a collaborator becoming disabled. However, divergence occurs at a most difficult point, which cannot be addressed in-depth: Considering the different degrees of disability, someone will have to determine when a collaborator can no longer work effectively.

Sometimes people never get around to designating who will handle their affairs after death. Even when they do, they may overlook collaborative or other creative work. But copyrights are considered property included in a person's estate. A collaboration agreement must address these issues, because a designee technically assumes the decision-making power of a deceased collaborator.

The absence of a designee. If a writer does not designate someone to handle his or her estate matters, then the laws of the state where she or he lived (or the copyright law, depending on the circumstances) establish a carefully ordered succession for control, as discussed in the chapter on copyright. This is only one of the powerful incentives for collaborators to discuss unpleasant possibilities when creating a collaboration agreement.

Designations that affect literary property. It's fairly common for people to designate spouses or significant others, relatives, close friends

Collaboration

or business advisors to handle their estates. However, even if an heir or a legal representative was chosen to handle the estate, there is no guarantee that that person was chosen with the specific concerns of a collaboration in mind. As a result, the collaborative team could end up collaborating with someone who does not necessarily understand anything about creativity in general or the theatre in particular.

For example, if the work has not been completed at the time of one collaborator's death, then the new collaborative team (including the designee) has to make decisions about a replacement. If the work has been completed, but has not been optioned for production, then the marketing decisions will be made by the new collaborative team. If the work has already been optioned for production, then the new collaborative team will exercise the normal artistic and script approvals, including revising the piece during the rehearsal process. If the new member of the collaborative team is not a writer or lacks experience in the theatre, this could become a very difficult if not disastrous situation.

Surviving collaborators retaining control. To avoid these and similar situations, the best scenario is for the collaboration agreement to state clearly that the surviving collaborators will control the work. This control should include the right to negotiate and sign contracts, the right to make changes in the work, and the right to choose other writers to make changes. It's also a good idea to make sure all surviving parties have to sign every contract, but *not* to require the deceased representative's signature.

Keep in mind that the deceased's legatee or designee remains entitled to collect the money that would have been owed to the deceased, and to receive copies of all signed documents, and that the deceased collaborator will still receive billing credit—nothing stated above vitiates these basic obligations codified in the executed collaboration agreement. But at least the work won't be thwarted or ruined by the collaborator's death.

Bringing in a replacement collaborator. As mentioned, depending on how much of the work had been completed by the collaborator before his or her death, it is possible that the surviving collaborators will have to bring in a new collaborator to finish the deceased collaborator's work. This will necessarily entail a whole new negotiation for financial participation, billing credit, decision-making power and the like for the new collaborator. It's also likely that the person who now controls the deceased collaborator's share may have to be brought into the discussion.

Agency representation

There is no hard and fast rule about whether one agent should represent the entire collaborative work, be it drama or a musical, or whether each collaborator should have her or his own representation.

One agent for the work. One approach is to view the collaborators' interests as being primarily or wholly aligned by focusing on the work itself, not the individuals. According to this position, it is believed that it makes sense to have one person coordinating all representation efforts, and ultimately what is good for the work will also be good for each collaborator. While there is some validity to this position, no collaborator should be pressured into accepting it.

Individual representation for each collaborator. Equally valid is the idea that each collaborator should have individual representation— an agent or agency looking out for his or her best interests as one of multiple writers—and that all the collaborators' agents collectively represent the work.

It is not at all uncommon for writers to be involved in a number of different projects, either serially or concurrently, so it makes sense that a writer would not want to switch agents for each project. Further, some writers may already have representation that encompasses all their work, and it would not be in the writer's or agent's best interest to suspend that relationship on a project-by-project basis.

If a writer is not represented before a particular collaboration comes along and the collaborative team is able to interest an agent in that project, each writer should consider whether she or he wants that agent to represent just that one project or to take on other projects in which she or he is or may be involved in the future. (Of course, the agent may also have strong opinions about the scope of representation, as discussed in the chapter on agents and lawyers.)

Collaborators' respective interests. Another consideration is that the collaborators' interests are not always aligned. If one agent represents the entire work, this could place the agent in a difficult position.

Using the collaboration agreement itself as a simple example, there are issues the collaborators will have to negotiate, such as sharing the monies that result from the use of separate music and lyrics and from publication. In the first instance, the composer or lyricist may not want to share that money with the book writer and similarly, in the second instance, the book writer or lyricist may not want to share that money with the composer. Another illustrative issue is billing credit: The interests of the individual collaborators may conflict if they all want to claim the first billing position. Please note that this is not to suggest that writers need agents to negotiate collaboration agreements—they certainly do *not*—but this example shows complications which could arise for a single agent or agency representing different collaborators in a single work.

In addition, agents are obligated to represent their clients to the best of their ability. It may not be humanly possible for the agent representing the whole work to avoid conflicts of interest between collaborators.

If collaborators decide to have one agent represent the work, everyone involved must be very clear as to how to handle the difficult issues. Perhaps they would agree that the agent for the work wouldn't get involved in issues that present a conflict, or perhaps the collaborators would agree that any individual collaborator's interest would come second to the overall best interests of the work.

As usual, there isn't one particular way to handle these situations. Being aware of them might help resolve them before they can become problematic.

Multiple agents on a work. Do not worry that producers will be driven away by the thought of negotiating production contracts with multiple agents representing different artists. While potentially more time-consuming than negotiating with a single agent, it's a very common situation; producers know to expect this (as do publishers). Remember, too, that the fundamental terms of the collaboration should already have been resolved and codified in the signed collaboration agreement well before such negotiations can begin, so that the agents can focus their attention on the terms of a production or publication contract.

For instance, the collaborative team will have already decided how to divide any money they make from the work. The issue at stake in negotiating the production contract might be the percentage of gross weekly box office receipts allocated to the writers. The agents will undoubtedly agree that a higher percentage is better than a lower one, and between themselves they will figure out how high a percentage to push for and how hard to push. While the potential for differing levels of experience and negotiation strategies still exists (one agent might be comfortable demanding absolute top dollar while another might tend to be more middle-of-the-road), in most instances these differences will ultimately be resolved because all parties want the production to happen.

Most of the discussion about representation for a collaboration will turn on whether or not the individual writers are already represented at the time they decide to collaborate. If they are not, they often won't resist the idea of one agent for the work, but collaborators should not try to manipulate each other into using one agent. If the individual collaborators *are* already represented, they will stay with their own agents (unless other reasons already exist for terminating those relationships).

Negotiation without an agent. When there is no agency representation (which often is the case), one collaborator eventually may assume the role of lead negotiator, whether by explicit assignment or by implicit acquiescence, and will be charged with the responsibility of conveying the collaborators' positions to the producer, publisher or other third party. This should always be done with the entire collaborative team being involved every step of the way, unless collaborators have clearly (and voluntarily) relinquished this role.

All collaborators must be provided copies of each draft of negotiated documents, and each collaborator is responsible for reading all the materials, asking questions that may arise and communicating her or his concerns in a timely fashion. (The collaborators should decide for themselves how much time each person will have to respond.) It is frustrating for the lead negotiator to spend hours negotiating only to discover down the road that there are problems which require backtracking. Ultimately, it will create ill will among the collaborators if the lead negotiator is made to feel foolish with a third party or, conversely, if one collaborator runs with the negotiation and then presents the other collaborators with a "done deal."

Try to avoid obvious manipulations, such as "I assumed you would want this too." Don't make assumptions about what others will consider best for the collaborative team. If you become the lead negotiator, invite and welcome active participation from all collaborators.

Be mindful, too, about how the person with whom you are negotiating (the third party) perceives the collaboration. You don't want to leave the impression that this collaborative team has serious problems arriving at and sticking to decisions. Visible infighting could scare off potential producers, publishers, etc. The lead negotiator should not be put in the position of having agreed to certain terms and then being forced to renege at the behest of the collaborative team. Make sure you are all agreed in advance as to what decisions the lead negotiator can and cannot make in the course of negotiations.

Chapter 3

UNDERLYING RIGHTS

THIS CHAPTER will address the most prominent issues that arise when a stage writer wants to create a theatrical piece based on material that already exists. The preexisting material is known as the "underlying work" and, if the work has not entered the public domain, there is usually an "underlying rights owner." The new work made from the underlying material, whether musical or drama, will be referred to here as the "adaptation." The stage writer will often be referred to as the "adaptor."

Under copyright law, an adaptation is categorized as a derivative work; that is, it is known as a new version which is *derived from* the underlying work, and thus the copyright in the derivative work is dependent on the copyright in the underlying work. Keep in mind that underlying rights owners have their own "bundle of rights" in the copyright to the underlying work, and granting the right to dramatize or musicalize the underlying work is but one of their ownership "twigs." Yes, there will be a separate copyright for the derivative work, but it does not stand wholly independently; again, it remains dependent on the rights granted by the underlying rights owner. Consequently, if the underlying work is still under copyright, the adaptor must obtain permission from the underlying rights owner for use in the derivative work.

If the adaptor does not obtain permission, he or she will not possess *any* rights to the work created; under those circumstances, the unauthorized adaptation will be essentially worthless, as discussed below.

COPYRIGHT OF THE UNDERLYING WORK

When a writer decides to base an adaptation on existing material, the threshold question must be whether the underlying work is still under copyright protection. It's possible that the underlying work has entered the public domain, which would mean that the underlying work is no longer owned by anyone, so permission no longer needs to be obtained. (For a discussion of ownership and the copyright laws, see the chapter on copyright.)

As to those works created before January 1, 1978, when actual registration was a condition of copyright protection, would-be adaptors are encouraged to run a copyright search of the U.S. Copyright Office to find out whether or not the underlying work is still protected by copyright. It is possible that the person responsible for filing the appropriate forms (particularly the renewal form) neglected to do so within the proper time period.

A copyright search can be effectuated in several ways. The writer can go to the Copyright Office and do the research him- or herself, looking through those files that are open to the public, such as the extensive card catalog. (If you are going to search the files, it is suggested that you read Circulars 22 and 23 from the Copyright Office, "How to Investigate the Copyright Status of a Work" and "The Copyright Card Catalog and the Online Files of the Copyright Office.") Since most writers don't live in or near Washington, D.C., it is often not cost-effective to make the trip just for this reason.

A second possibility is to pay the Copyright Office to conduct the search for you. A request to conduct a copyright search must be made in writing, either by personal letter or by using the search request form attached to Circular 22; requests made over the phone simply will not be accepted. Write to: Reference and Bibliography Section, LM-451, Copyright Office, Library of Congress, Washington, D.C. 20559-6000.

Provide as much information in your letter as you have: author, copyright owner (if different from the author), title, type of work involved and approximate year of publication or registration. The more information you can provide, the less time-consuming the search, which will translate into less expense. If you are missing information, don't fret—the search can still be conducted. But do provide the researcher with all the information you can.

A copyright search costs twenty dollars per hour or any fraction of an hour. You can obtain an estimate of how much your search will cost by calling 202-707-6850, and then you must enclose a check for the estimated amount with your written request. Generally, a search for such basic information as whether a work is still protected by copyright will cost twenty dollars, and information regarding who owns the copyright and how to get in touch with that person can cost closer to forty dollars. The search report will be factual and non-interpretive, meaning the Copyright Office will not render any opinions about the information provided.

The response time to a search request is roughly eight to twelve weeks from the receipt of the written request, but it can vary depending on the nature of the request and the volume of requests received by the Reference and Bibliography Section around the same time. There is no shortcut to obtaining this information, since there are no lists maintained of works that have entered the public domain.

Assume for purposes of the following discussion that the existing material *is* protected by copyright. Otherwise, any writer is free to adapt the material.

AVAILABILITY OF THE ADAPTATION RIGHTS

Once you know whether the underlying work is protected by copyright, you need to find out whether the rights to adapt the underlying work as a play or a musical are available. As mentioned earlier, the underlying rights owner controls the right of adaptation, but it is possible that someone else has seen the adaptation possibilities in that work and previously obtained the adaptation rights. If this has happened, you then confront the issue of exclusivity.

In all likelihood, adaptation rights would have been granted on an exclusive basis. Non-exclusive rights are significantly less valuable to the writer creating an adaptation and thus are rarely ever sought, because they put the adaptor at risk that someone else will simultaneously write a competing work based on the same underlying material, with a race to see which adaptation will become successful first. If yours is the second work to appear on the market, producers may not be interested, or it may be harder to pique an audience's interest. It is true that multiple versions of an underlying work have been produced successfully although those usually involved public domain material or works of strong name recognition (i.e., bargaining power). So, if the underlying rights owner has granted non-exclusive rights to another writer and offers you the same, think long and hard before moving ahead with the project.

If the exclusive adaptation rights have already been granted to someone else, then the underlying rights owner won't be able to grant a second set of rights to you simultaneously, and your project must be tabled. As indicated in the discussion below, which addresses the substance of underlying rights agreements, usually there are both option and production stages built into a contract to protect the underlying rights owner's interests, so that if the authorized adaptation does not find a production within a certain period of time, the rights will automatically revert to the underlying rights owner and he or she may again be in the market for an adaptor. Consequently, if another adaptor has already obtained the rights but is not successful in obtaining a production of his or her adaptation, the rights could revert to the underlying rights owner and interest in your proposal may be revived.

There may be other reasons the rights to the underlying work might not be available to you: The underlying rights owner might simply not be interested in having a musical or dramatic adaptation made of the underlying work; the underlying rights owner may decide that you are not his or her first choice as the adaptor; or, the underlying rights owner's terms for granting adaptation rights may be so onerous that the adaptor cannot (either in good conscience or for financial reasons) agree to the terms. None of these responses will be easy to hear.

CONTACTING THE UNDERLYING RIGHTS OWNER

The would-be adaptor obviously needs to find out how to contact the underlying rights owner. It's best to address a letter to the proper person, since writing a blind "To Whom It May Concern" letter may suggest lack of industriousness or seriousness of interest. If the underlying work is published, the best place to start (unless you have obtained information from the Copyright Office) is with the publisher, which must at least know where royalties are sent. A call to the publisher's copyright and permissions, business affairs or legal department might work, but it's easiest and most efficient just to ask the receptionist who is responsible for fielding such requests rather than to guess blindly. The publisher might have the authority to grant adaptation rights but, if not, it should be able to point the writer to an agent or other appointed representative, the underlying rights owner him- or herself, or possibly an estate or executor if the original author is dead.

If the underlying work is unpublished, the Copyright Office will be the best place to look for contact information. If the underlying work is a film or television project, you will have to contact the film or television company since it, not the writer, owns the property. The following considerations apply regardless of whether the underlying rights owner is a person or a corporation (e.g., a publishing, film or television company).

Obtaining permission before adapting

If you write an adaptation before obtaining permission, you are taking a huge risk that all the work will have been done in vain and will have to be discarded if permission is ultimately denied. You may think that the underlying rights owner will be persuaded to grant the adaptation rights once he or she is able to see how beautifully the adaptation has been done and/or is overwhelmed by the adaptor's commitment to and love for the underlying work. This is not an unreasonable possibility, and it may have worked occasionally, but this approach could easily backfire.

The underlying rights owner simply may choose not to grant the rights; that is his or her prerogative, and she or he does not have to have a "good" reason for rejecting your request for adaptation rights. It's equally possible that the underlying rights owner might not appreciate an entire work being created before he or she was even approached, particularly since he or she would then have to worry about the possibility that the unauthorized work will be marketed illegally. Acknowledging up front that you knew you didn't have the right to adapt but went ahead anyway because you wanted the underlying rights owner to be able to *see* the quality of your work might ease the situation, but be prepared to provide written assurances that the work will not be marketed if permission is denied, or the underlying rights owner may not even read your adaptation.

An argument can be made that you're doing the underlying rights owner a good turn by enabling him or her to read the entire adaptation before granting permission, because that enables him or her to make a decision based on the adaptation itself rather than on the concept of the adaptation and/or the reputation of the adaptor. In essence, this also grants the underlying rights owner some degree of approval over the content of the adaptation, which approval might not have been included in an arrangement made in advance of the actual adapting.

This line of reasoning is most often advanced by adaptors worried that their credentials, or lack thereof, won't entice the underlying rights owner to grant permission. This is not an irrational fear, but a better approach would be to adapt one or two scenes to show the underlying rights owner, rather than to do an entire adaptation. This would allow the underlying rights owner to sample your adaptation concept and your ability to realize it, yet it significantly reduces the amount of time you would have invested on spec, thereby reducing the level of disappointment if the project is not accepted. Also, you will not feel as vulnerable about revealing all of your ideas.

If you are convinced it is in your best interest to create the complete adaptation without seeking permission, and if the underlying work is approaching the end of its copyright protection term (after which time it enters the public domain), you may decide to wait to write the adaptation until the copyright has expired, thereby avoiding negotiations with the underlying rights owner. In the absence of that possibility, however, there is no circumventing the underlying rights owner, even if you believe he or she may make the wrong decision. If the underlying rights owner does not grant permission, that is the end of your adaptation, at least until the underlying work enters the public domain. There is no gray area here.

Having taken the risk and been rejected, do not get caught up in thinking, "But I worked so hard to create this adaptation and it's great! I should have a right to do *something* with it." This is a dead end. Any writer who spends time and energy on an adaptation without having first obtained permission from the underlying rights owner may have to live without recompense, reward or recognition.

The choices are clear: Know this risk going into the project and assume responsibility for it, or else obtain the requisite permission before doing all the work. Without that permission, the adaptation cannot be marketed or used in any manner.

All in all, it's probably best to try to obtain permission before adapting, and there's no reason to assume in advance that you'll fail. Even if the underlying rights owner is interested but somewhat doubtful of your ability to accomplish the adaptation successfully, you can always provide reassurance by drafting a scene or two after the subject has been broached.

Letter of inquiry

The primary purposes of the letter of inquiry are to find out whether stage adaptation rights are available and whether the underlying rights owner is interested in pursuing this possibility. In addition, you want to begin to persuade the underlying rights owner that you are the best person to whom to grant these valuable rights. For a would-be adaptor, it's particularly important that the letter of inquiry be well written. This letter is *not* the place to talk specific terms such as dollars or percentages; that will come once you have a better sense of availability and of the underlying rights owner's mindset.

It is suggested that you write briefly about your professional credentials, including information about any productions your other works may have enjoyed and any other adaptations you may have written. Also talk about why this particular work speaks to you and why you believe it will work well on the stage. Provide the underlying rights owner with a general sense of the direction your adaptation would take. Try to convey the sense that you are someone the underlying rights owner can trust to create a satisfying adaptation, someone who understands the underlying writer's vision of the piece. Remember that the person who wrote the underlying work probably feels just as protective of her or his art as stage writers do of their plays and musicals.

If you have not yet amassed an impressive list of credentials, don't throw up your hands and assume no one will be interested in granting you adaptation rights. For example, if the underlying work is older, out of print, has not enjoyed significant success on its own or has not been pursued by others, your interest may be the best shot the underlying work has to reach the stage. If your ideas are fresh and exciting, the underlying rights owner may be intrigued by your creativity and enthusiasm. Don't give up until the underlying rights owner has actually declined to pursue the project you propose.

If the underlying work really interests you, it's worth the time it will take to write at least the first letter. If the underlying rights owner says, "No thanks," you're in no worse position than you would have been if you'd never written the letter. Even if the underlying rights owner is reluctant to grant the adaptation rights to an unknown writer, that feeling may change if your other work *is* produced; that is, when your writing credentials grow. Later, if you make a second contact, the underlying rights owner may respond more positively, particularly if you had expressed interest in the underlying work before becoming better known yourself.

Response

After sending the initial letter of inquiry, be patient. Be very patient. Don't contact the underlying rights owner or agent to find out whether they received your letter. Wait to send a follow-up letter until at least a couple of months have passed.

Most likely, you have been thinking about this project for some time, so give the underlying rights owner a reasonable amount of time to think it over and to assess whether and how he or she wishes to proceed. Don't expect an immediate response. You will not be privy to that person's thoughts or any behind-the-scenes information (such as whether someone else has already shown interest) unless you or someone you know is particularly close to the underlying rights owner.

The response you ultimately receive will fall into one of two general categories: rejection, or interest in pursuing the project. Rejection can take many different forms, from a flat-out "no" to "not at this time," and the specific response will necessarily dictate your next step. For example, if the response is "not at this time," consider sending a gracious letter which makes clear that if the underlying rights owner ever decides to pursue adaptation of the underlying work, you hope the possibility will be pursued with you. If the response is "the rights have already been granted to someone else," your follow-up letter should then state that if the rights become available in the future, you will still be interested and would hope to be informed. If the response is a flat-out "no," lick your wounds, take mental note of the date the underlying work enters the public domain, and move on to another project.

The more complex situation, of course, is when the underlying rights owner's response is, "The rights are available and I find the idea intriguing, so please make me a proposal."

PROPOSAL

As addressed below in detail, there are six or seven elements for a writer to consider including in an adaptation proposal. You will also need to evaluate relative bargaining positions, reduced in this discussion to an analysis of four factors. Financial arrangements are one part of such a proposal, but don't mistakenly think that that's all you need to discuss. The underlying rights owner needs the writer to provide sufficient information to make basic decisions and to open formal negotiations.

There are no absolute rules about what terms to propose, but there are definite guidelines. Underlying rights agreements, historically, are more open to fluctuation during negotiations than production or publishing agreements.

ESTABLISHING RELATIVE BARGAINING POSITIONS
Reputation and credentials of the underlying rights owner

Is the underlying rights owner a known or unknown writer? Is she or he known primarily in a specific field (i.e., literature, theatre, film or television), or is he or she more popularly or generally known? Is he or she known for the particular work you wish to adapt or is this a lesser-known work, a sideline or an experiment?

If the underlying rights owner is well-known, that will improve her or his bargaining position; if not, the adaptor may be in a better position. If the underlying work is a movie or television property, that might indicate a widespread reputation, although this also depends on its age.

Success of the underlying work

Is the underlying work a book that has been on the *Times* best-seller list for fifty weeks; was it published ten years ago by a small but reputable press with a modest promotional budget; or was it published thirty years ago with little success? Is it a popular television sitcom or one that didn't quite get off the ground? Is it a movie, successful when it was first released and remade since, or a cult classic, or an interesting bomb? The questions could go on, but the point should be clear: The more public name recognition and established success attached to the underlying work, the better the underlying rights owner's bargaining position. And vice-versa.

Adaptor's reputation and credentials

What other works has the adaptor written, theatrical and otherwise? Does the adaptor have a production history? Have the adaptor's past works been adaptations or original? If the adaptor has done other adaptations, were they works in a similar genre? What other information should the underlying rights owner know about the adaptor that might have an impact on the decision? Do you teach playwriting? Does your profession combine intriguingly with playwriting or with this particular underlying work? Whatever may be unique about you and your career will improve your bargaining position.

Parties' motivations

How badly do the parties want the adaptation to be made? When people want to make a situation work—any situation—they will usually find a way to make it happen.

If the underlying rights owner loves the adaptor's ideas, he or she may be more inclined to negotiate and compromise. If the underlying rights owner is intrigued, but there is competing interest in the underlying work, the adaptor may have to bend over backwards to make the most attractive offer.

Depending on the terms and how difficult the negotiation is, the adaptor's enthusiasm may eventually wane; at some point, she or he might think, "It's just not worth what I'm being asked to give up." Evaluating these feelings and deciding where to draw the line is very personal and your feelings may shift throughout the negotiations.

Evaluating the four factors

The goal of evaluating these four factors, besides establishing bargaining positions, is to try to divine an answer to the following elusive question: When this play or musical begins performances, will the audience buy tickets because they are intrigued by or attracted to the underlying writer, the underlying work, the adaptor, none of the above or some combination of the above? Figuring out what compels someone to buy a ticket is far too conjectural to be called even an inexact science, but an honest appraisal may help contextualize an adaptation proposal and subsequent negotiations.

Extremes are easy to evaluate; for example, if the adaptor is unknown and the underlying writer is Anita Hill or, conversely, if the adaptor is Marsha Norman and the underlying work, discovered in an out-of-the-way used bookstore in Santa Fe, enjoyed critical success in the 1950s but never achieved name recognition or financial success. Sometimes the situation is clear and the balance, or imbalance, of bargaining power will be apparent. Often, however, the situation is far from clear.

TERMS OF THE BASIC PROPOSAL

The proposal should be written concisely and organized well. It should be informative, perhaps even a bit chatty, yet still business-like. Don't try to draft legalese. This is not a contract, but a document that should allow the underlying rights owner to evaluate the proposed project and decide whether or not he or she wants to proceed to contract negotiations.

Six or seven basic issues need to be addressed in the proposal: 1) the option period; 2) the grant of rights; 3) the financial arrangements, both short term (the option payment) and long term (sharing the money earned over the life of the work); 4) ownership of the adaptation; 5) the attendant approvals (perhaps including the long-term decision-making power); 6) billing credit; and, perhaps, 7) the concept of merger.

You will want to write one to two paragraphs about each issue. Don't write a thesis; organize your thoughts and present them succinctly. If the underlying rights owner wants you to expand on certain ideas, that can easily be done in the next round of talks or correspondence. Start with the fundamental terms and think in broad strokes; don't try to pin down all precise details at this stage. Keep in mind that this is a *proposal*. A fuller contract—the underlying rights agreement—will necessarily come later, and the details will be fleshed out then.

Ownership of the adaptation

Ownership of the adaptation is the most fundamental issue. It is imperative that the adaptor be certain there is a meeting of the minds with the underlying rights owner on this issue early on. Although based on the underlying work, the adaptation is a work created by the stage writer, and thus the well-established general rule is that the adaptor retains copyright ownership in the adaptation. There is *no* correlation between this issue and the amount of the underlying work that will ultimately appear in the adaptation; by its very nature, the adaptation will often contain a significant amount of the underlying work.

The legal relationship here between the adaptor and the underlying rights owner should *never* be structured as work-for-hire, even if the underlying rights owner commissions a writer to create the adaptation (see the chapters on copyright and production contracts, addressing commissions). This issue need not be labored over or handled acrimoniously. Usually it will suffice simply to mention that, consistent with theatrical practices historically, the adaptor assumes that he or she will own the copyright of the adaptation. The underlying rights owner will either agree or disagree with this statement, and that will open that point's negotiation.

Adaptors may encounter underlying rights owners of *very* valuable works which enjoy such significant and widespread name recognition (e.g., *The Grapes of Wrath*) that they may insist on *joint* ownership (50/50) of the adaptation, and they might not allow an adaptation to be created in any other manner. Given the extraordinary reputation of works that fall into this category, this may seem reasonable, but those situations are definitely the rare exception to the general rule. The majority of underlying works do not rest on such a foundation, and thus the adaptations are owned completely by the adaptor.

If an underlying rights owner insists on complete ownership of the adaptation, it is suggested that you rethink the project. Joint ownership, in practical terms, means that neither side can move ahead without the other side's permission, and in some situations this might seem feasible to the adaptor. However, it is very dangerous to work with an underlying rights owner who wants to own and control the entire work (i.e., a work-for-hire relationship with the stage writer). In such situations, the underlying rights owner might say to the adaptor, "In joint ownership, you can't move ahead without my approval anyway, so I might as well own the entire work." This argument is deceptively simple, yet specious. There are ideological and emotional differences between the underlying rights owner owning the copyright, and exercising all control, and his or her entering into a bona fide partnership with the adaptor; that is, sharing control with the actively participating adaptor. If the underlying rights owner understands that fifty percent control remains significant within the relationship, both substantively and symbolically, then the adaptor could just as easily ask the underlying rights owner why she or he should be so *opposed* to joint ownership. (Establishing joint ownership is also important in enabling the adaptor to take the lead in marketing the adaptation, rather than simply leaving that in the hands of the underlying rights owner.)

Some projects may have such phenomenal name recognition or career-advancement potential that you may be tempted to put yourself in a work-for-hire position, and perhaps the rewards will be great enough to offset the rights you signed away, but that should be a very carefully considered decision. Once you sign the documents relinquishing the copyright in your work, the law will probably not be sympathetic if later you say, "But I didn't really want to," or "The underlying rights owner 'forced' me to do it this way." Do not enter into such arrangements blithely. What may be attractive at that moment in your career may come to be one of your greatest regrets.

Option period

The option period should be considered in conjunction with the grant of rights because there is an inevitable overlap between what you want to do with the adaptation and how long you have to do it. Different levels of production will necessarily require different periods of time to accomplish. Thus, the option period must be negotiated with the grant of rights in mind, and vice versa.

The option period defines how long the adaptor will retain the exclusive right both to write the adaptation and to obtain a staged reading or production. Often the parties involved set up an incremental schedule, whereby the work must be completed by a certain date, with a staged reading to follow within a certain time frame, followed by a production to take place within a subsequent time period. For example, the adaptor might have nine months to write the work, then twelve months to present the staged reading, and an additional eighteen months in which to achieve a full production. It is up to the negotiating parties to decide what events will constitute appropriate "triggering events."

The adaptor needs to be honest with him- or herself about how long it will actually take to write the piece and get it heard before a live audience. Don't forget that if there is research involved, you will need to build in time for that, too.

What the adaptor wants to avoid is agreeing to too little time. The worst situation would be if, after writing the piece and beginning to market it, the adaptor's rights to the underlying work lapse. Unless you can go back to the underlying rights owner and obtain an extension, you could be left holding an empty bag, because the terms of the signed agreement govern the relationship, and you cannot assume that the option period will be extended, even if you've done a good job. The underlying rights owner might not be interested in extending the arrangement, or might seize upon this as the perfect opportunity to renegotiate certain terms more favorably. The adaptor could find him- or herself compelled to renegotiate important terms just to keep the project alive. Given the investment of time, energy and probably money, the adaptor's bargaining position may have shifted, possibly not to his or her advantage.

On the other hand, the adaptation may have garnered substantial interest in the marketplace, and both the adaptor and the underlying rights owner might try to use this new information to negotiate a more advantageous financial arrangement. This situation is obviously very different from writing an original work on which there are no time limitations or pressures other than those that are self-imposed (except, perhaps, in the case of collaboration or commissions).

During the original negotiations, the would-be adaptor should be sensitive to the fact that the underlying rights owner is taking a chance on the adaptation and might hesitate to tie up the underlying work for a very long time before seeing a production. Like it or not, underlying rights owners' fears are typically at their strongest when they are approached by lesser-known writers. The length of the option period can be tricky to negotiate, considering the equally valid, competing concerns of each party. The would-be adaptor might have to be more flexible in the beginning than he or she might like.

For example, a powerful underlying rights owner might want to grant only limited first production rights to the adaptor, holding back on committing to a longer-term relationship until she or he has a chance to see that first production and evaluate its reviews. While this is not typical, it's not unheard of, either. This approach can't last too long, though, because producers won't want to take risks if future rights are held too tightly.

In this case, the adaptor would have to decide whether he or she feels passionately enough about the work to throw him- or herself into it knowing he or she could possibly end up with no future rights. Again, the decision comes down to each person's comfort level with risks. Some writers will take the plunge; others might try to find an underlying work that is not so seriously encumbered.

A good middle ground, in terms of the option period, might be to establish the multi-tiered structure mentioned above, concerning dates for completion of the adaptation, for a staged reading and for a full production. Thus, the underlying rights owner might agree to grant *three* successive option periods, with the adaptor needing to jump through certain hoops to earn each period. If the adaptor can't satisfy each successive condition specified in the contract, the option would expire. In other words, the underlying rights owner might be comfortable with, for example, three one-year option periods rather than one three-year option period.

This type of structure may particularly help an underlying rights owner overcome concerns about a lesser-known writer. Just as with the option period between an author and a producer (discussed in the chapter on production contracts), there is comfort in knowing there are natural expiration points built into the contract. Remember, though, that if the work *is* progressing along the time line in the general way the parties had anticipated, and the adaptor *can* therefore fulfill the interim conditions, the adaptor's option periods would continue to be extended. The underlying rights owner could not unilaterally decide to take these agreed-upon rights away.

Grant of rights

The grant of rights provision provides the foundation for the substance of the long-term relationship between the underlying rights owner and the adaptor. It says, in essence, "Until the adaptation proves itself, here is what I, the underlying rights owner, am giving you, the adaptor, permission to do with my original work." At a subsequent point determined by the parties (the point of "merger," discussed below), the adaptor's rights solidify. There will be a shift of focus away from the underlying rights owner to the adaptor, when the work becomes "vested" entirely in the adaptor, allowing the adaptor to move ahead with the adaptation without fear of having rights to the underlying work removed.

The scope of the rights granted is freely negotiable, depending on circumstances. For example, if the underlying rights owner grants the adaptor the right to write a play based on a novel, the adaptor does not have the right to decide later that he or she would rather write a musical based on the novel without returning to the underlying rights owner to negotiate those other rights (the musicalization rights).

In determining the grant of rights, it must first be made clear, contractually, what the adaptor is allowed to do *in creating* the adaptation. As an example, consider this sample of what language from a musical adaptation contract might look like:

> The Owner [the underlying rights owner] grants to the Adaptor the right to write a musical adaptation (the "Play") to be based upon and utilizing the Work [the underlying work] and in furtherance thereof, the sole and unrestricted right to use, adapt, change, interpolate in, transpose, translate, add to and subtract from the Work, its situations, incidents, plot, theme, characters, dialogue and ideas including, without limitation, the right to interpolate and include lyrics and music as the writers of the book, music and lyrics may determine.

Next, the contract must establish what the adaptor is allowed to do *with* the adaptation once it is finished; that is, what levels of production can be sought by the adaptor. (With respect to the post-merger period, the parties will also negotiate the adaptor's rights to the stage work's subsidiary rights dispositions; e.g., the film adaptation.) This part of the grant of rights can be general or specific depending on the needs and requirements of the parties involved. For example, the adaptor might have the right to have the adaptation's first production at any level in the United States within the agreed-upon period of time. It is also not unusual for the grant to be specific at first to particular levels of production or geographic areas, and broader after that level of production is achieved. For example, an underlying rights owner might grant the rights to an initial full production only on Broadway, Off-Broadway, or in a regional theatre; what the underlying rights owner thus says is that having the work adapted is appealing, but that appeal is tied to a certain minimum level of production.

Generally, the grant of rights would not be so specific as to name a particular theatre as producer, unless the adaptor had already secured a commitment from that theatre. For example, it's possible that what attracts the underlying rights owner of a well-known children's book is the fact that a prominent children's theatre has already committed to producing the adaptation. In such a situation, the underlying rights owner might have the grant of rights begin with the production at that particular theatre. In the absence of such a pre-agreement, it would not be fair to the adaptor to place such stringent constraints on the work.

In the proposal, then, the adaptor needs to think carefully about what rights he or she would like to obtain. And here, too, think about both the best- and worst-case scenarios, to give yourself some breathing room. You might believe with all your heart that your adaptation is going straight to Broadway, but that is probably not realistic given the current economics of producing and the many paths that works travel to become successful. You don't want to appear foolish or unbusiness-like to the underlying rights owner, so suggesting a different strategy might actually serve you better. Do your homework, and strive to impress the underlying rights owner with a well-thought-out plan of action.

Explain to the underlying rights owner the general parameters of where you want to present the work and how you believe that can be achieved. For example, suppose a writer wants to adapt the children's book *Charlotte's Web* for the stage. The proposal could state that the writer needs one year to write the adaptation and believes that he or she then needs two more years, broken down into two one-year periods, in which to obtain a commitment to production from one of the theatres in the United States that presents works for young audiences. The writer might provide a list of the theatres she or he believes would be well-suited for this work and perhaps explain why the particular theatres were chosen. This would be a good indication to the underlying rights owner that the writer has performed the necessary preliminary research and has a good sense of the potential market.

The underlying rights owner will also want to enumerate reserved rights. For example, if an adaptor wanted to write a play based on a novel, the underlying rights owner would want to make it clear that it still controlled other rights in the novel not granted to the adaptor, and this might include whether the novel and/or the play can be made into a movie. Thus the contract would have to contain language addressing any potentially overlapping or competitive circumstances. The particulars will change depending on the situation, but do know that the underlying rights owner will be focusing on establishing not only what is being granted to the adaptor, but also on clarifying that which is not being included in the grant of rights.

Financial arrangements

The option payment. Financial arrangements are always an important question on both sides of the negotiation. The broad issues are the option payment (upfront money) and a structure for sharing the monies that flow from the adaptation over its life (which can take many forms). In this discussion we will start with the broadest parameters and then focus on how to strategize and find flexibility in the numbers.

The option payment is money paid by the adaptor to the underlying rights owner in order to retain the exclusive rights to the adaptation for the duration of the option period(s). It is typically a nonrefundable, recoupable advance against first royalties earned from the production of the adaptation. If production never takes place, the underlying rights owner simply keeps the advance; it is not paid back to the adaptor. Each option period ordinarily has a payment attached; so, for example, if there were three one-year option periods, some amount of an option payment would be due for each option period.

Just as stage writers should expect to be paid something for an option on production of a work—and not grant such rights for free—so, too, should adaptors anticipate paying for an option on underlying rights, however difficult that may be. They should certainly not expect to receive the adaptation rights for free. This is not to say that the dollar amount must be high or in excess of what you are reasonably able to pay, but some option payment is always in order if exclusive rights are being sought.

The amounts of option payments are freely negotiable, and the range is rather broad. The amount generally depends on: 1) the length of the option period, 2) the breadth of the grant of rights, 3) how much the adaptor can afford to pay, 4) how much the underlying rights owner needs or wants to receive, 5) how valuable the underlying work is on the market, 6) how much competing demand there is for the work in question and, again, 7) how badly each party wants the adaptation to go forward.

To some people, money is the least of it; to others, it's everything. Some options on underlying works have been granted for fifty dollars per year, most are granted for hundreds of dollars per year, and adaptation rights on heavyweight works can cost thousands of dollars per year.

Just as with a stage writer's option payments, there is a valid argument to be made that different levels of production warrant a different level of option money. An option for dinner theatre should be different from that for young audience productions, versus regional theatre, versus Off-Broadway, versus Broadway, and so on.

Writers should think honestly about what they can afford to pay, since they are assuming the risk that the option will expire without the adaptation having achieved a production. Keep in mind that writers will also still be responsible for the normal business expenses of writing and marketing a play (copying, postage, long-distance telephone, resource books, computer upkeep, etc.) If an offer feels low, but it's the most you can afford, explain this to the underlying rights owner. An explanation of how you arrived at your offer enables the underlying rights owner to consider the project in a different light than in the absence of this information. Be especially mindful of how this information is presented. Don't say, "Since this is all I can afford, you should grant me the rights for this amount." A more gracious statement might be something such as, "I decided two years ago that I wasn't going to be a word processor anymore, that I believed in my writing enough to try to support myself as a professional writer. Consequently, my budget is tight, but I also believe strongly that you should receive a fair option payment which adequately respects the underlying work. Thus, I hope you will accept my offer, though I wish it could be more."

In deciding on your strategy, you need to anticipate the underlying rights owner's response, since he or she will naturally want to negotiate any offer made. There are generally two different negotiating strategies: one is the "cushioned" offer; the other is the "real" offer.

Sometimes people purposely reduce an offer to create a "cushion" for the negotiation, so that they can increase the offer in response to a counterproposal from the underlying rights owner. For example, if you know that you cannot afford to pay a penny over $200 for the option, you might make an initial offer of $150, anticipating a request to increase the offer to, perhaps, $250, in which case you could offer a compromise of the $200 you could actually afford. (Of course, there's always the possibility that the underlying rights owner will simply accept the initial offer, in which case you would have saved yourself fifty dollars.)

On the other hand, some people take a different approach, hoping to eliminate the game-playing of proposals and counterproposals. Making an offer, they are quite honest in stating that this amount is truly what they can afford to pay and that they thought carefully about what would constitute a fair and reasonable offer. There is no cushion with this approach. So, for example, if the adaptor decides that $200 is a fair, reasonable and affordable option, the offer of $200 is made clearly. It is not presented as an ultimatum, but rather as an attempt to eliminate haggling.

Choose your personal negotiating style and, most important, be clear in relaying this information to the underlying rights owner. Don't expect anyone to understand your entire thought process just by looking at the dollar amount stated in a proposal.

Before deciding on a particular amount to offer as the option payment, read through the following, related discussion.

Royalties. The general rule, and one which is eminently fair, is that since the underlying work is, and always will be, an integral part of the play or musical adaptation, the underlying rights owner should share in whatever money the adaptor makes from any and all sources for the life of the copyright. The two parties must decide what percentage each will receive of the whole pot of money, regardless of the specific terms struck between the adaptor and any third-party producer, publisher, etc. Don't try to figure out in advance how those future royalty arrangements are going to be structured (e.g., percentage of the box office, flat fees, lump sum payment). It really doesn't matter whether the adaptor eventually contracts to receive five percent of the gross box office, or $100 per performance, or $1 million for the film sale. What matters is that the adaptor will receive checks for defined amounts of money and needs to know how to divide the number of dollars. All the parties to the contract for underlying rights have to focus on is what percentage of the money earned by the adaptor from the adaptation will be allocated to the underlying rights owner.

So, for example, if a work has been licensed by Dramatists Play Service for the past year, the only thing that matters is that the adaptor receives a check for $20,000. It doesn't matter that some of the productions paid eight percent of the gross, others paid ten percent of the gross, others paid sixty dollars per performance, and so on. The bottom line is that the resulting $20,000 needs to be divided.

Also keep in mind that the underlying rights owner's percentage should be calculated on the money the adaptor holds onto. So any percentage that is owed to an agent or a premiere producing theatre or commercial producer comes off-the-top; that is, *before* the money is divided between the adaptor and the underlying rights owner. This obviously reduces the dollar amounts to the underlying rights owner, but it is fair for both the adaptor and the underlying rights owner to share responsibility for all percentages owed to third parties because of the work done on behalf of, and for the benefit of, the adaptation itself.

The commonly accepted range for the underlying rights owner's share, historically, is between ten percent and twenty-five percent of the money received by the adaptor from all sources, with the twenty-five percent figure reserved for works with a significant tangible reputation. There have admittedly been a few deals made where the underlying rights owner received as little as five percent, and some underlying rights owners with works that enjoy *extraordinary* name recognition have been known to demand one-third to one-half of the adaptor's income; but, the norm for almost all adaptation negotiations remains between ten percent and twenty-five percent. (The most extreme numbers at the bottom and top of the scale are given here in order to provide the most complete picture of possible financial arrangements, but they are widely acknowledged to be just that: "extreme." The point must be reiterated that the overwhelming majority of adaptors and underlying rights owners should not enter into negotiations with these lowest and highest figures in mind. They are completely unrealistic for most relationships.)

Given this range, the parties must again take into account the four factors enumerated above for evaluating the relative bargaining positions of the parties. As with any negotiation involving money, the adaptor would like to give up as little potential income as possible and the underlying rights owner would like to receive as much as possible. Individual circumstances will dictate where the parties end up.

Tangentially, it's important to note that the money to be shared between the adaptor and the underlying rights owner must be earned from the adaption itself, *not* from additional services that the adaptor may render. For example, if the adaptor sells the rights for the stage adaptation to be made into a movie, and then the adaptor is also hired as the screenwriter, the underlying rights owner shares only in the first pot of money (sale of adaptation rights), not the second (additional screenwriter services). The underlying rights owner's only concern is to be sure that the allocation of money between those two deals is consistent with general market value. (Addressing the allocation of money also does not mean that the monies must be divided equally, only that there must be some general regard for the sales price of similar works at the same time, for the payments to other screenwriters with similar experience, and the amounts you may have negotiated for writing other screenplays. Those numbers may be impossible to pinpoint precisely, but experienced film agents will normally know this market information.)

For example, if the total package of both film adaptation rights and screenwriter services equals $1 million, it would not necessarily be fair for the adaptor to try to allocate $950,000 for screenwriter services and only $50,000 for movie rights in order to avoid having to pay the underlying rights owner his or her fair share, not unless the adaptor could present persuasive evidence of extenuating circumstances that would reasonably support such an allocation. (One possibility might be if a very well-known screenwriter has written his or her first play adaptation, which wasn't well-received on the stage. If, because of that person's long-standing Hollywood screenwriting credentials and contacts, she or he was able to negotiate a phenomenal screenwriting deal, then such an allocation might be legitimate. Such situations are quite unusual, and a fairer allocation is typically warranted.)

One exception. The general rule that the underlying rights owner receives a percentage of the monies earned by the adaptor is subject to one exception in certain very limited circumstances. When there is a *commercial* theatre production (i.e., first-class—Broadway or comparable—or second-class—Off-Broadway or comparable), the underlying rights owner may want to be paid the same way as the adaptor: a percentage of the gross weekly box office receipts (subject, of course, to any royalty adjustments the adaptor may agree to), rather than receiving a percentage of the adaptor's money. This percentage of gross box office receipts is paid in lieu of the percentage of the money earned by the adaptor, never in addition to it. There is no double payment.

This percentage of the box office will not be high; certainly, it will not be anywhere near what the adaptor receives. Depending, again, on the relative bargaining powers of the parties, the underlying rights owner's percentage is typically in the ballpark of one-quarter to one percent of the gross weekly box office receipts pre-recoupment, increasing by one half to one percent post-recoupment. So, for example, if you start at one-quarter percent, you could increase the underlying rights owner's percentage to three-quarters or one percent of the gross post-recoupment. If you start at one percent, you could increase the percentage to one and a half or two percent post-recoupment. (The underlying rights owner's percentage should never exceed two percent.) Depending on the figures, there might be a significant benefit to the underlying rights owner from receiving a percentage of the gross rather than a percentage of the adaptor's earnings, as illustrated by the following example.

Assume an Off-Broadway production that can gross $150,000 per week, and an author's pre-recoupment royalty of five percent of the gross, which translates into $7,500 at capacity. If the underlying rights owner has negotiated to receive fifteen percent of the adaptor's monies, the underlying rights owner's share of the adaptor's $7,500 royalty would be $1,125. However, if the underlying rights owner negotiated a royalty of one percent of the box office receipts for commercial productions, that would translate into a $1,500 royalty. Depending, of course, on the level of production and the specific figures, most offers of a percentage of gross would be better deals than receiving a percentage of the adaptor's earnings. (Since underlying rights agreements are negotiated well in advance of ever knowing specific earnings, underlying rights owners are usually given the benefit of the doubt and all commercial productions are thus lumped together under this narrow exception.)

This type of percentage-of-gross arrangement between adaptors and underlying rights owners will ultimately affect the producer, since a percentage of the gross weekly box office receipts increases the weekly operating expenses of the production. Some producers pay the adaptor's royalty in addition to the underlying rights owner's royalty; other producers might try to negotiate for the underlying rights owner's percentage to be blended in as part of the adaptor's royalty. For example, *producers* would prefer to pay a total author's royalty of five percent (for plays), leaving the adaptor and the underlying rights owner to divide that five percent between themselves, say, four percent for the adaptor and one percent for the underlying rights owner (depending on their negotiations). However, the *adaptor* would prefer to negotiate a deal with the producer that leaves fully intact her or his five percent royalty and which pays the underlying rights owner's percentage of gross on top of that. (This will be a point to be negotiated between the adaptor and the producer when it comes time to negotiate the production contract; since the underlying rights owner will not be a party to that negotiation, he or she will simply want to establish his or her royalty in the underlying rights agreement, and leave the rest to the adaptor to work out.)

Strategy. Now, let's jump back to the option payment issue and examine how it relates to the underlying rights owner's percentage of the adaptor's monies. Stage writers seeking to obtain underlying rights often are concerned that they can't afford to pay much upfront money (the option payment). One valuable strategy to keep in mind is that an underlying rights owner might be willing to consider a lower front-end payment if the back-end percentage is increased.

For example, there could be an underlying rights owner who wants a $500 option payment and a ten percent share of the adaptor's money. The adaptor might respond with a counteroffer of a $250 option payment but a fifteen percent share of the adaptor's money. (This strategy can also be employed by the writer making the first offer, rather than responding to an offer made by an underlying rights owner.) If the underlying rights owner is comfortable with the risk inherent in waiting to see how much money is generated by the work, then that person could potentially make a significantly greater amount of money over the life of the work than the $250 difference in the option payment. This could make your offer very attractive, although there is no guarantee; it is, of course, possible that the underlying rights owner needs to see more money up front, or perhaps isn't comfortable taking such a risk on the back-end.

The adaptor should feel free to play with the numbers to arrive at an attractive and comfortable offer. Most important, however, is making sure that the underlying rights owner *knows* that the dollar amount offered as an option payment is lower *because of* the higher ongoing percentage participation. The only way the underlying rights owner will know this is if the writer spells it out, so don't be shy. If the writer fails to explain the basis for the offer, the underlying rights owner may assume (not unreasonably) that the numbers offered constitute the starting point for negotiations. The adaptor could be backed farther into a corner than if a lower offer had been made in the first place.

Specifically, address the situation along these lines in the proposal or cover letter: "Even though I'm confident of my ability to turn your work into a wonderful play, I am not able to offer you a large option payment. However, I'm not asking for any favors or gifts, and I want to uphold my end of this business relationship. So if you are willing to join me in this venture, I would be happy to offer you a higher share of the money I will make over the life of this work. Originally, I was going to offer you a ten percent participation in any money I make from this adaptation in the future. If you could accept this lower option payment, I would comfortably offer you a fifteen percent share of the future monies. To me, this additional five percent seems eminently fair: If the adaptation is a success, we will both have assumed the initial risks and received significant benefits."

Approvals

How much control will the underlying rights owner retain over the adaptation, in terms of the adaptation itself and decisions about its life? This involves script approvals, artistic approvals, rehearsal attendance and decision-making power on a broader scale.

From the adaptor's perspective, the short answer about the underlying rights owner's control should, in most instances, be "none" or "not much." The underlying rights owner will understandably be a bit nervous about turning the project over to the adaptor and, admittedly, the underlying rights owner is taking on some risks; but these concerns should not be used to tie the adaptor's hands, neither creatively nor in terms of future decision-making. The underlying rights owner ordinarily will ask the adaptor to see samples of the adaptation before signing an agreement; but, once the decision has been made to trust the adaptor with the work, the underlying rights owner is generally expected to fade into the background and let the adaptor take control.

Of course, some underlying rights owners will be uncomfortable with such arrangements; in those situations, adaptors must take an honest look at the working relationship. For some people, it may be possible to share control; for others, having the adaptor's work subject to the underlying rights owner's direction might motivate her or him to look for a different work to adapt, one that doesn't come with quite so many strings attached.

Script approvals and the right to attend rehearsals. Script approval is the ability to make final decisions about the script before sending it to third parties for consideration, during the revision process and throughout rehearsals of all productions for which revisions again will be made. Maintaining control over the work is a fundamental issue for adaptors, so the basic question is whether the underlying rights owner has final approval of the script before the adaptor markets it to theatres, producers, contests, etc., and when the adaptor makes changes to the script once it has been optioned for production.

There is a very strong argument to be made that the stage writer knows how to write the dramatic or musical version of an underlying work and that the underlying rights owner needs to trust that person with the necessary creative decisions. This is particularly true if the underlying work exists in a different format or medium, such as a novel or a movie; the underlying rights owner might simply not be well-versed in the ways of theatre, neither in writing nor in production. If the adaptor has to obtain the underlying rights owner's approval of every line written or revised, it could seriously impede the creative process. The underlying rights owner may have an emotional attachment to the work, but at some point the underlying rights owner needs to step back to allow the adaptor to pursue his or her own vision of the work unfettered.

This issue affects the production phase, too. The adaptor has the right to attend all rehearsals, possesses the sole right to make changes in the work, and discusses his or her notes with the director after each rehearsal; the underlying rights owner does not. The producer, too, now has an interest in shaping the work for production and might not be happy to discover that the adaptor doesn't have the exclusive right to make substantive script decisions (which could cause such problems as slowing down the rehearsal process).

Another wrinkle is possible: that the person who wrote the underlying work might not be alive, and the underlying rights owner, who stepped into the shoes of the deceased writer, could be a spouse or partner, a relative, a lawyer, a literary executor, the publisher and so on. In other words, the adaptor might be dealing with someone who is not a creator at all but rather has been charged with responsibility for watching over the work. Sometimes non-writer owners may be more inclined to take a hands-off approach, readily acknowledging that the

creative process is completely outside their realm of experience. Sometimes, however, they take an even more aggressive position because
they feel doubly responsible for the success of the work, even though
they may not truly understand the artistic issues, as a kind of personal
debt to the memory of the deceased. If such a situation presents itself,
the adaptor must be sensitive and try to fashion an arrangement that
retains his or her necessary controls over the work while accommo-
dating the underlying rights owner's needs.

While it's clearly best from the adaptor's point of view not to relinquish or share control, one possible compromise, should adaptors find
themselves with underlying rights owners who refuse to let go (regardless of whether it's the original author or someone who has taken over
responsibility), is to grant that person approval rights over the basic
script, but to retain complete control over the creative process once that
script has been approved. The adaptor might rationalize this middle
position by acknowledging the underlying rights owner's initial concerns—which should be allayed by the completed pre-production
draft—and accepting this level of personal inconvenience so long as
interference terminates when third parties enter the picture.

Artistic approvals. Artistic approvals are the adaptor's active participation with the producer in choosing the director, the actors, the
designers and all replacements thereof; and, of course, these approvals
carry over into the rehearsal and production phase. From the adaptor's
point of view, even if the underlying rights owner negotiates some
level of *script* approvals, shared participation (or final approval) in *artistic* approvals is generally not desirable. Choosing the artistic personnel
and working with them should remain completely within the adaptor's
domain. Again, however, if an adaptor is negotiating with a particularly powerful underlying rights owner, he or she needs to evaluate the
situation and decide whether and how to accomodate the underlying
rights owner's demands or to work on a different adaptation altogether.

Decision-making power. A wide range of longer-term questions and
issues, large and small, will necessarily arise during the life of the adaptation: where to submit the work, what marketing strategies to adopt,

what publicity packet to put together, what agent to choose, what producer to work with, which publisher to sign with, whether and with whom to seek a film adaptation agreement, etc., for as long as the adaptation remains protected by copyright. When the focus shifts from the creation of the adaptation to ensuring its success and longevity, the adaptor must have free rein. Yes, the underlying work is affected by the life of the adaptation, but the primary focus must be on the future of the newly created work and its ability to stand on its own. In the absence of extraordinary circumstances (such as a phenomenally powerful underlying rights owner), the adaptor alone should make these decisions.

Billing credit

Billing credit to the underlying rights owner is essential and should never be overlooked or undermined. The adaptor is not creating a wholly original work—although much originality will go into the new piece, it will always remain rooted in the underlying work, which must be acknowledged. To do otherwise would be deceptive to the public and would violate the spirit of the relationship with the underlying rights owner.

The underlying work and the underlying rights owner should receive billing credit wherever and whenever the adaptor receives credit; the adaptor's name should never appear without that of the underlying rights owner. The size and prominence of the billing for the underlying work and the underlying rights owner must be negotiated with the adaptor, but it's usual for it to be half the size of the adaptor's credit (keeping in mind that the normal size for the adaptor's credit is at least half the size of the title). It is understood that if the adaptor relinquishes certain billing provisions in his or her production contract, the underlying rights owner will follow suit, but whenever the adaptor receives credit the underlying rights owner must receive credit, too. For example, only very prominent stage writers receive billing credit on the marquee of a theatre, and if the adaptor agrees to relinquish this term, the underlying rights owner will automatically relinquish it, too. But if the adaptor's name appears, so must the underlying rights owner's.

There must also be an understanding as to who is responsible if the underlying rights owner's billing credit is mistakenly omitted. Since the underlying rights agreement is between the adaptor and the underlying rights owner, and the underlying rights owner will not be a party to future agreements offered to and signed by the adaptor, the underlying rights owner must be able to look to the adaptor for recourse if this situation arises. The underlying rights agreement should provide that the adaptor will be responsible for remedying any mistakes made in billing; in turn, the adaptor's contract with the producer or the publisher must state clearly that the producer or publisher assumes responsibility for those matters within his or her control.

It is a good idea to establish visually how the billing credit will look. The adaptor's proposal should enumerate the location of the billing credit (e.g., immediately underneath the adaptor's name, on either one or two lines), and then a sample should be included in the agreement. This helps to focus both parties' attention on any details that might be overlooked in the description alone, and it will help to avoid misunderstandings that could arise later. For example, the document might include the following:

The Country Life
by Dana Singer
Based on the book *The Montanan*
by Jeannette Rankin

Never try to limit the underlying rights owner's billing credit. There are certainly areas of reasonable negotiation between the adaptor and the underlying rights owner, but this is not one of them.

Merger

When merger occurs, those portions of the underlying work that are included in the adaptation become part of it irrevocably. After merger, the adaptation has a life of its own, no longer subject to any change of heart the underlying rights owner might have.

It would not be unusual for merger to be addressed in full only when the underlying rights agreement is drafted, but the proposal should contain some mention of it so that the underlying rights owner understands merger is an issue to be resolved. (An underlying rights owner unfamiliar with the concept of merger will need to find out more about it, at least to understand that the adaptor is not asking for extraordinary or quirky terms.)

All adaptations must at some point merge with the underlying work. No adaptor can go out into the marketplace thinking that the underlying rights could be revoked at any point in the adaptation's life. Merger does not mean that the two works become one—that would impinge on those rights the underlying rights owner reserved for his or her own use, as discussed above—only that material from the underlying work can no longer be removed from the adaptation. No producer would invest time, money and energy in a production only to learn that the underlying rights had been revoked, especially considering the potential loss of earnings from stock and amateur licensing around the world, not to mention other professional opportunities, such as film.

Merger doesn't just happen. The two parties to the underlying rights agreement must decide between themselves when it will occur: In the absence of such a designation, it won't happen. Most often, merger occurs after a specific number of performances in a particular venue, such as the first or twenty-first regional theatre, Off-Broadway or Broadway performance of the work.

Merger shouldn't take place at the very beginning of the adaptation's creation. Productions anticipated may never happen, in which case the underlying rights owner would want the rights granted to expire naturally, so that he or she could work with another adaptor eventually.

If every grant of rights immediately turned into an ironclad marriage, underlying rights owners would be so cautious about granting adaptation rights that the number of stage writers with whom they would work would be severely limited. Few emerging writers would be given the opportunity to work with underlying materials, and even better-established writers would have a much harder time convincing underlying rights owners to loosen their grips on the underlying works.

A middle ground must be reached. The parties involved must ultimately agree to a "triggering event" for merger that provides the underlying rights owner with the necessary assurances that the work achieve a level of production which "earns" the right of merger, and which protects the adaptor from an unpredictable, damaging roller coaster ride. They must agree merger will happen, and establish when.

After merger, the adaptor will have the sole right to exercise the full range of normal rights and privileges inherent in copyright ownership of the adaptation, subject to any specific terms agreed to in the underlying rights agreement, and third parties with whom the adaptor signs contracts will know that the work, and they, are not at risk. The adaptor alone will have the power to sign all contracts disposing of rights in the adaptation.

RESPONSIBILITY FOR OBTAINING RIGHTS

Responsibility for obtaining rights to an underlying work depends in part on how the project came about. If a stage writer wants to write an adaptation and then look for a producer, the stage writer will obtain the rights. If there is to be a collaboration, such as a musical adaptation, then typically the collaborative team collectively will obtain the rights. If the collaborative team hasn't yet been put together, there are two possibilities: Either the writer who originates the idea assembles the writing team before approaching the underlying rights owner, or she or he obtains the rights first. If the reputation of some of the collaborators will likely have a positive impact on the underlying rights owner, then the team should be put together first. If the originator has already obtained the rights, then an additional document must be created, linking the writer granted the adaptation rights and all the writers who are actually going to be working on the project.

When a theatre wants to commission a writer or writers to create an adaptation, it is not unusual for the theatre to contact the underlying rights owner and obtain the rights to have the adaptation made and produced first at that theatre. The adaptor(s), however, have a much bigger concern: to retain the underlying rights for the life of the work, rather than just for the first production at the commissioning theatre. Ultimately, the theatre must transfer to the adaptors the rights *it* obtained, so that the adaptors can actually create the work. The theatre also needs to enable the adaptors to work directly with the underlying rights owner to secure the longer-term rights necessary to market the work beyond the first production. Since the adaptors, not the theatre, will own the work (see the chapter on copyright, particularly the section on commissions), the theatre will not be involved in future deals and decision-making after its production rights lapse, but it *might* be able to negotiate a percentage of the adaptor's subsidiary rights income (see the chapter on production contracts).

NONFICTION

Not all adaptations are based on works of fiction. An adaptation could be based on historical or biographical works, interviews with people, unearthed factual information and so on. Rights considerations for these categories of information differ from those of pure fiction, and in some respects the adaptor may be frustrated by the lack of clarity regarding what is and is not usable, and under what circumstances.

Facts do not enjoy copyright protection, which means nonfiction works find less protection in the copyright law than does fiction. Facts are in the public domain and cannot be owned by any one person. The category of "facts" includes historical events or information, facts contained in biographies, news of the day and scientific treatises. Imagine what it would be like in practical terms if any one person could claim a monopoly (which is in essence what copyright is) on pure facts: someone could "own" the subject of the Civil War and control how that event is written about, even deciding that only one account of the War should exist.

Experience has shown that there isn't just one historical "truth," and all writers should be free to present their version of the facts. A copyright on facts would impede the spread of knowledge and eliminate differing interpretations of factual events, thus raising serious First Amendment issues. (Remember with respect to different interpretations of facts that *ideas* are not protected by copyright; only the *expression* of ideas is protected.)

Regardless of how much time, money and effort may go into one person's research, the copyright law does not allow anyone to own factual information. Some courts have stated that such research is, without a doubt, socially important, but it lacks the originality required to claim copyright ownership.

Expression in works of nonfiction has been determined to include actual words (verbatim copying and close paraphrasing are not allowed) as well as organization, structure, style and even punctuation. As an example, an adaptor can use the factual material contained in another's biography, but is *not* free to use that biographer's expression of those facts. (Admittedly, the distinction between facts and the expression of them may not always be readily made, so the adaptor must go to great lengths to avoid appropriating more than just the factual material.)

If you are in doubt about what can and cannot be used from someone else's nonfiction work, or simply want to be sure that there will be no risk of copyright infringement, the safest route is to go back to the source material, do your own research and arrive at your own conclusions. Note that there is nothing wrong with using the existing nonfiction works to figure out where to find the original source materials or to locate relevant people. Doing this type of research is much more time-consuming (not to mention expensive) than taking advantage of someone else's research but, especially in fuzzy, sensitive or risky situations, stage writers may be able to avoid future problems by tackling the legwork themselves.

(As an aside, interviews, conversations and statements made by others are not owned by the person who writes nonfiction. Transcribing what other people have said lacks originality as required under copyright law to earn protection. These words belong to the *speaker*, and the person gathering such information will typically obtain releases from each person interviewed to avoid copyright liability. If, instead of transcribing, the nonfiction author *reconstructs* a conversation, and in so doing contributes original material, he or she could claim ownership of the new expression. If the author was a part of a conversation, his or her own remarks are copyrightable.)

Adaptors are strongly encouraged to keep diaries when writing about subjects in which others might feel their creativity has been infringed, even if the adaptor has obtained assurances from outside advisors—such as formal legal opinions from legal counsel—that the areas of inquiry and use are not protected by copyright. Keep copious notes of locations visited, resource materials read or used (including public documents such as court transcripts), people interviewed and the like. Hold onto all drafts, notes, copies of documents, etc., long after the work has been created and produced.

If an adaptor finds that she or he is using a fair amount of someone else's factual research, that person should be acknowleged as a matter of professional courtesy. You may not be required by the copyright law to obtain permission, but that person's hard work is obviously worth something to you in the creation of your work, and you would be most gracious to give thanks publicly.

USING OTHERS' SONGS OR LYRICS

The use of others' songs in your theatre piece—entire songs, pieces of songs or song lyrics, sung or recited by characters or used only in the background—may not technically constitute exploitation of underlying rights, but it does fall into the category of using material that belongs to someone else. Assuming that the music and lyrics in question are not in the public domain, they cannot be used without the permission of their owner. As explained in the chapter on copyright, no number of lines of lyrics or bars of music can be used without permission. The song or lyric you wish to use may seem perfect for your purpose, but if the price for permission is too high, or the owner simply denies permission, respect the owner's copyright and move on.

There may be situations in which having to obtain permission seems ludicrous and extreme. For example, if you write the annual thirty-minute skit for the December holiday party of your local community organization, and part of your "gimmick" is to take a popular song and insert your funny lyrics about the past year's events, that technically falls under the copyright law, but *this* author would be hard-pressed to state that you must request formal permission from the copyright owner to write this part of the skit. However, such narrow and isolated exceptions should not be unfairly used or enlarged to justify a real "taking" of something that belongs to someone else. If you want to take other people's songs and write your own lyrics for a legitimate theatre piece, you are advised to read carefully the sections on fair use, parody and satire in the chapter on copyright, and perhaps consult with a lawyer.

Obtaining permission

If you wish to obtain permission to use a work written by someone else, or any parts thereof, the first step is to track down the copyright owner. If that person is well-known, it may not be difficult to find someone who represents his or her work. If the work has been published, you can contact the publisher. If the other work is a song or song lyric, contact the music publisher, which in most instances controls the rights. You can often find the music publisher by looking at the sheet music, or by contacting BMI or ASCAP, which can check their computerized song indices.

As suggested earlier, there are also ways to seek contact information from the U.S. Copyright Office.

Information to provide

Whenever requesting permission to use part of another work, provide the recipient of the request with enough specific information to allow a reasonable decision to be made. Include information about the original work (title, author and publication date if applicable and known) and about the new work (whether a play or musical). Give a brief description of the proposed work, then explain in detail what material you wish to use and how you intend to use it. If you have received an offer of production, provide information about the level of production, the number of performances each week, the seating capacity of the theatre and the like. Be honest and realistic. If all you're interested in is two lines of one song lyric, to be recited once by a single character in a two-hour production, make sure the recipient understands how little of the original material will be incorporated, and be certain to tell the copyright owner the specific lines or other material at issue. If you intend to incorporate bits and pieces from an assortment of works or many songs, make clear to each copyright owner that the monies allocated to pay for these rights may have to be split many ways.

Ultimately, the copyright owner will want to know whether you are seeking exclusive or non-exclusive rights (exclusivity will cost more), whether it's for performance *and* publication (rather than just one or the other), the applicable geographic territory (worldwide? United States and Canada? other?) and whether you seek permission for use in all languages or just in English. The copyright owner will also want to know what billing credit will be promised (for instance, in programs or on a copyright page) and that you will be vigilant about providing the proper copyright notice, as appropriate.

Payment

There aren't any established rules or guidelines about how much stage writers will be charged for the use of others' works, other than general information that has been compiled about first-class productions (Broadway or national touring companies) as enumerated below. Those figures at least provide a rough ceiling. It is possible, given the level of production, the amount of material you want to use and other similar factors, that the owner won't charge anything. For example, if there were going to be a small production of your work for four nights in a town no one has ever heard of, the owner might say, "Permission is granted for this one production without requiring any payment. If you decide to have the work produced again, you must get in touch with us at that time, and we will evaluate each request on its facts." However, if the work looks as if it's going to have a successful life, you will probably want to enter into a longer-term license with the owner, rather than having to go back for permission time after time.

Payment for use of pre-existing songs in a first-class production is structured as either a flat fee (roughly $200 to $500 per week) or a percentage of the gross weekly box office receipts (roughly one and a half to four percent), depending of course on the extent of use and the popularity of the songs in question. Remember, these are the going rates for first-class productions; scale your expectations and offers accordingly.

If payment is required for other levels of production, such payment can be structured similarly, taking the specifics of each request into account. For example, if very little of the underlying work is used, the payment may be minimal. If entire songs are used, the payment would probably be increased. Different payments might depend on the use of a song for background music, as opposed to having a principal character sing it. As always, if the other work is well-known, it may cost more.

It's unheard of for any copyright owner to ask for money as an advance against royalties for such uses except in extraordinary circumstances. If the work you wish to use is *very* valuable, or you want exclusive rights or to attach significant restrictions to the arrangement, be prepared to pay something up front.

PLAYS BASED ON PEOPLE'S LIVES

(N.B.: The following sections provide fundamental information about writing a play based on or about real people. It is not intended to provide a complete, in-depth explanation of this area of the law; indeed, entire books have been written on this subject. These sections are not intended to provide legal advice about any particular situation; writers who intend to do this type of writing need to consult with a lawyer who can provide a formal legal opinion based on specifics.)

Writing plays and musicals about real people (whether they be alive, deceased, historical figures, fictionalized or factual versions, etc.) involves a number of convergent areas of the law that require a complicated balancing act of interests: the right of privacy, the right of publicity, defamation (libel and slander) and the constitutional considerations of the First Amendment. In the most basic terms, the right of privacy is the right to be left alone; the right of publicity is the right to control the commercial use of one's identity or persona; defamation is the right to protect oneself against false statements being made that injure one's reputation; and the First Amendment protects the exercise of free speech and a free press. Within this complex web, different standards apply to people who are public figures as opposed to "private citizens" (e.g., private citizens enjoy far greater privacy rights than do public figures) and to newsworthy issues of legitimate concern to the public, often called the "public's right to know" or "matters of public interest." If it seems that you don't need to obtain permission, then don't ask for it; if permission is denied, you could be creating new problems for yourself where none previously would have existed. If you believe that you do need to obtain permission, don't relinquish control over the content of your work, nor over your standard approval rights. (If you wish to be granted access to private papers, such as letters, to interview the subject's family and the like, you will find yourself obtaining permission to use those materials, a different situation than if you relied on other types of research.)

The rights of privacy and of publicity

These two areas of the law are fairly recent, continuing developments. Because they are still very much in flux, one must proceed cautiously. It can be very frustrating to writers (and all non-lawyers) to realize that the law is so fluid as to make concrete determinations difficult if not impossible.

Both of these areas are governed by state law. Each state decides for itself whether such rights will exist and, if so, to what extent. Throughout the fifty states, therefore, you may find overlapping and/or significantly different standards and interpretations. For example, the majority of states have determined that there is a post-mortem right of publicity, whereas other states have decided that right expires upon a person's death. (It should be noted that the right of *privacy* is always extinguished upon a person's death.)

Some states have placed very clear conditions or restrictions on a person's ability to avail him- or herself of the protections available, while other states have not. Some states have passed statutes to address these issues, while others have allowed these rights to develop through "common law"; that is, through the body of cases tried and judicial opinions handed down over the years. While it might be too harsh to call the current situation a morass, clear consistent rules may not exist.

The right of publicity has generally been applied to cases in which a person's persona is used without permission for commercial purposes; that is, to sell products or services. At various times, the word "persona" has been interpreted very broadly to include such features as a person's distinctive voice, unique mannerisms and characteristics, her or his likeness, and the use of look-alike actors. For example, singers such as Tom Waits and Bette Midler have been involved in lawsuits to stop advertisers from using their distinctive voices in commercials, Vanna White legally contested an advertisement that used a robot dressed and groomed like her in front of a *Wheel of Fortune* game board, and restaurateur Paul Prudhomme sued to prevent the use of a look-alike actor in a television commercial. Generally, however, the right of publicity would not preclude you from writing a biographical play about a newsworthy person. (A related area of the law is unfair competition—unfairly capitalizing on someone else's investment and success as a shortcut to your own work and success—as embodied in federal statutes and state statutory and common law, but it is not addressed here because it is not closely related to the primary issue of writing a dramatic work based on a real person.)

The right of privacy addresses a person's right to protect personal dignity. Such cases typically involve people who are not famous or publicly known and their right to remain private (i.e., the right to be left alone; the right not to have others intrude into private affairs; the right to sue over being held up publicly in a "false light" or over public disclosure of embarrassing private facts). An exception to the right of privacy can be made when a person is involved in an event that qualifies as a matter of public interest; for example, being involved in a crime is generally considered a matter of public interest, and thus if someone writes publicly about that crime, it would not be considered an invasion of privacy. The more public a person is or becomes, the less right to privacy they may have.

Defamation

The core of defamation law is false statements made about a person: lies presented as truth. It also involves state common law with an overlay of constitutional principles.

Defamation consists of two parts—libel and slander—which are essentially falsehoods told about a person either in writing or orally. Different standards apply to public figures and private citizens: For public figures, the question is whether the person who made the false statement knew the statement was false or made it with reckless disregard of whether or not it was true; for private citizens, mere negligence may be actionable. The category of "public figure" is broken down into "all purpose" and "special purpose" public figures, with the latter referring to those people who have become "public" only for a limited range of issues. Every person's defamation claims die, however, upon their death, with no state-by-state variation. Thus when asked about the risks attendant to writing biographical plays, Robert Harris of Leavy Rosensweig & Hyman has been known to respond, "The deader the better."

First Amendment

It has been said repeatedly that the First Amendment's primary function is to encourage and support the free exchange and dissemination of ideas, generally encompassing both the pleasant and the unpleasant. Its protections encompass news and newsworthy events, entertainment, social commentary, politics and science—that is, matters of public interest—as expressed in both fictional and factual works. First Amendment protections are very strong, but they are not absolute. Certain types of speech, in particular contexts, raise countervailing concerns (most famously, shouting "Fire!" in a crowded theatre).

There are many different ways of telling stories: fiction or nonfiction; historical fiction or biography (either authorized or unauthorized); dramatization or documentary; etc. Generally, the right of publicity takes a back seat to First Amendment issues for both fictional and factual works. Although no clear guidelines exist, the relatively few cases that have been decided along these lines seem to indicate that if a work is merely imitative (nothing more than a replication of another person's original "act" or character, such as replicating an Elvis Presley concert), the person being imitated might be able to make a right of publicity claim. However, if the creator of the work in question has made her or his own creative contribution (the work is not simply a replication), it appears that the work would be protected by the First Amendment, even if an impersonation of an actual person is incorporated as *part* of the new work. Similarly, works that are or serve as unauthorized biographies would be protected as factual material (assuming that the biographical information is accurate) and as a legitimate dissemination of information about subjects of interest to the public. The right of publicity cannot be used to squelch a discussion of the life of a public figure just because that person doesn't like what's being said or he or she doesn't wish to be written about. (It should be noted that the ability to make money from one's work—here, a dramatic or musical work—would not convert the issue into one of "commercial use" as that phrase is used in right of publicity cases.)

Fiction/dramatization

Some works begin with facts from which a writer launches into speculation and fantasy. Others are dramatizations based to some extent, whether closely or loosely, on actual events, with fictional elements thrown in: fabricated dialogue; composite characters; composite scenes; altered sequences of events. These methods are generally considered legitimate creative tools suited to a writer's work.

Writers do need to be mindful, however, of certain parameters. Defamation issues can arise when a living person is used in a fictional work, if the writer knowingly or recklessly makes false statements injurous to the subject's reputation.

Some hold this position to be a little odd, though, since fiction is "false" by definition. Debate continues to rage as to whether defamation should be applied to fiction at all and, if so, what standards to apply. One argument is that when a work is labeled "fiction," the audience understands from the outset that the writer is openly manipulating information, exercising his or her imagination in an unrestricted way. On the other hand, some argue that merely calling a work "fiction" doesn't necessarily make it so, especially if a reason exists for audiences to believe the writing is based on actual events. Content might be closer to truth than a writer wants to admit; simply labeling it "fiction" might not suffice to protect against claims of defamation.

Therefore, if you are writing an unauthorized biographical stage work about a living person, be sure it is factually accurate, or at least not defamatory: Also be careful about revealing private information which might be considered offensive and which is not reasonably related to the person's public role. (If your work is generally accurate, minor errors of fact would not be actionable.)

If you've written a biographical work that intentionally contains fictional scenes and dialogue—whether to create greater dramatic or entertainment value or to comment on or speculate about events in a person's life—go the extra mile to make it clear that the events in the work are figments of your imagination, not fiction you are trying to pass off as fact. Whatever you do, don't ever make an audience think a work is factual if it's not.

Sometimes writers simply insert real people into plays or musicals, identifying them either by name or by recognizable characteristics. Your concern here should be whether doing so is merely exploitative of that person's identity or whether it is integrally related to the content and creative expression of the work. To protect yourself, you should perhaps take extra care to add some type of disclaimer or disclosure along these familiar lines: "All persons and events depicted in this story are fictitious. Any resemblance to real events or persons is strictly coincidental." Decisions in the majority of such cases that have gone to court suggest the fictional use of a person's identity (using their real name or a thin disguise) does not involve the right of publicity, and that writers shouldn't be strong-armed legally into creating only characters that have no basis in reality. The minority position is that incorporating a real person into a work is a commercial use of that person's identity to sell a product: the story itself.

The use of disclaimers

All writers should use disclaimers when basing any part of a fictional work on real people, but you should also be aware that there is no definitive answer as to whether defamation claims can be defeated by using them. In other words, it is far better to use disclaimers than not, but using them does not provide absolute protection.

To enhance your defense (should you need one), use strong and clear wording about which there can be no confusion. With a potentially sensitive situation, writers should write a short statement proclaiming the work to be fiction, *not* a reproduction of actual events. Place the disclaimer prominently, particularly if the work is about people or issues that will likely cause a stir. Don't hesitate to use bold letters, graphic or artwork highlights, or a box drawn around the text. Even though it may not provide absolute protection, a well-placed, clearly written disclaimer may reduce your risk of being accused of misleading an audience.

Which state's laws

Although there is no consensus on determining which state's laws will apply to these types of claims should they go to court, these are the best guidelines at this time: In defamation and right of privacy cases, the law favored is the plaintiff's state of domicile (i.e., the residence of the person who is bringing the lawsuit; presumably, the person who doesn't want to appear in your work). In post-mortem right of publicity cases, the courts will usually look to the law of the state where the subject matter was domiciled at the time of death (this involves estate law, as well). For other right of publicity issues, typically the law of the state where the infringement occurred is favored; but, again, there is very little consistency in such cases.

Chapter 4

MARKETING
AND SELF-PROMOTION

LEARNING how to promote your work (and yourself) is not an easy task. There are as many paths to success as there are successful writers, and there are no precise rules which, if followed, could guarantee success. Still, there are marketing steps you can take which will increase the likelihood of success. Self-promotion requires developing skills that might not come easily; however—not to sound glib—marketing your own work is the natural course of things, so every writer must try to overcome these hurdles or, failing that, accept the consequences.

Much of what I suggest requires a significant investment—of both time and money—and it is hard work. The writing field is very competitive, and even though there are many, many areas in which to have your work presented, there are many, many other writers competing for those same opportunities. Understand that marketing your work is not a quick, short-term proposition: If you are not prepared to assume a deep, long-term commitment, you may need to rethink your writing career. To be serious about a writing career, you must approach it with the same level of professionalism and determination as any other business venture.

In conducting research for this book, I found that the most common theme expressed by producers, publishers, agents and lawyers was that writers need to learn and understand how to present themselves in a professional manner. You must show you are serious about your submissions and that you are not going to waste a reader's time. Sending your letters and scripts out into the marketplace, the message you must convey to the theatre community is that you are committed to your work and career, and that they should respond in kind.

It is assumed here that every writer begins his or her career without an agent, and therefore the responsibilities of promoting and marketing the work (to try to secure readings, productions and the like) will fall squarely on the writer's shoulders. A writer's first response to this is, generally, "I'm an artist; I can't possibly do those things!" But you must *learn* to do it. You must start thinking differently and see yourself as someone who can master the basic business skills necessary to navigate the murky waters of the theatre business, because no one else will do it for you.

Writers must be methodical in promoting their work. It is a laborious, time-consuming process that requires careful thought and endless creativity. The theatre is a risky and temperamental business, like any other. A writer must believe wholeheartedly in the value of what she or he has written and of the importance of finding an audience for it.

There is much information available to help you further your marketing efforts as described below. For example, some writers endorse the monthly newsletter, *Market Insight*, which compiles tangible information from other trade publications (a free sample copy can be obtained by calling 800-895-4720). However, it's best to investigate the entire spectrum of tools available for marketing purposes, since no single avenue is likely to make you successful. Use these informational tools to enhance your research, not supplant it.

QUALITY OF THE WORK

There are many subjective and intangible factors in getting your work produced or published: the quality of the writing; the appeal of the subject matter; the likes and dislikes of those receiving your submission; the economic conditions facing theatres; audience preferences; etc. Some of these are within the writer's control and some are not. It is incumbent upon the writer to think carefully about his or her work and the marketplace, and to strategize.

Fairness is not an issue. We all know there are good plays that can't find the right production. One well-known writer keeps a sign above his desk that reads, "No one asked you to become a playwright." Just because you've written a play does not mean you deserve or are owed a production. Do not enter or move through this industry with a sense of entitlement, because that can only cause great frustration and disappointment. In the final analysis, there will always be a significant element of chance in a writer's career. The objective of marketing and self-promotion is to create the conditions that favor success.

The most important trait to foster is perseverance. Attempting to build momentum around your work and your career can be exhausting, but you must keep working at it to make it pay off.

PREPARATION OF THE MANUSCRIPT

Enough cannot be said about presenting your work in the proper, professional manner. Even if you are fortunate enough to meet some producers face-to-face (an unlikely situation given the theatre's national scope), ultimately, the script must sell itself, a proposition which is not limited to your story and writing skills alone.

Learn the proper format. Scripts are supposed to look a certain way, and it's *not* best to stand out from the crowd. If you are not perceived as a professional writer, with an understanding of even the most basic facets of stage writing, you run the risk of being discounted before your play is ever read, or of not getting your play read at all. You will have some choices to make (such as where to place the names of your characters), but most guidelines are essentially standard. If you are unfamiliar with the appropriate format, consider buying the book *Professional Playscript Format Guidelines and Sample* from Feedback Theatrebooks (305 Madison Avenue, Suite 1146, NY, NY 10165, 212-687-4185) or contact Samuel French, Inc. (45 W. 25th St., NY, NY 10010, 212-206-8990) for their recommended format guidelines. There are also many different software packages available to format the work for you, so do some research at your local computer store to find out which will work best for you.

Don't overlook the importance of your cover page. Be sure your name, address and phone number (or those of your representative) are as clearly evident as your title. Do not rely on your cover letter to provide this information; a reader will curse you—even if he or she adores your script—if he or she must dig up a letter in order to contact you.

Invest in a good quality computer and printer, or else be prepared to spend your money at a store that rents time on such machines. Think twice (or ten times) before sending out a manually typed script. The supreme objective in preparing a manuscript is to make it attractive and easily readable. No reader can afford to expend extra effort deciphering illegible characters. An unreadable script soon finds itself on the reject pile.

A script of poor quality and appearance sends a strong message to the potential reader of the work: that you don't take your writing career seriously enough to invest in it, and that you don't respect others' time and energy. You should be mortally embarrassed by faded characters, smudges, white-out and the like, or the reader will be mortally embarrassed for you. Don't even consider sending out a manuscript that is battered, torn or coffee-stained. (Sadly, it's been done.)

Proofread your work until you can't bear to look at it one more time—then put it aside for a while and proofread it again. Have a friend read it through slowly, carefully, word by word. Be sure you have eliminated all typographical, spelling and grammatical errors: The professional reader takes note of such mistakes, and they will likely affect the response to the work.

Use clean paper. No one expects to read scripts printed on 25-pound fancy bond paper, and—given the cost of copying and mailing scripts (including the ever-necessary self-addressed stamped envelope)—you will not want to increase expenses unnecessarily. Nevertheless, a good-looking sheet of paper makes an excellent impression.

Always bind the script. You need not go to great lengths or expense, but never, ever send unbound pages. Imagine this all too typical scenario: The reader has four stacks of manuscripts on his or her desk, all waiting to be read and evaluated . . . and yours slips to the floor, spilling unbound pages everywhere. Even if the reader can find the time to reorder the pages for you, a semi-conscious resentment may color the eventual reading—if it ever comes to pass.

A sturdy cover is recommended, but other types of binding may be preferred, as detailed in a theatre's submission guidelines. A script may be thin enough for heavy-duty staples, but don't cut corners and end up with a script that has its final few pages threatening to fall off (or actually doing so).

Be sure the cover and the script are *clean*. You can't be held responsible for damage occasioned by the postal system, but peanut butter and jelly smudges will not be tolerated, even if cute little hands or paws put them there.

GENERAL RESEARCH AND NETWORKING

Before moving into the submission stage, you are strongly encouraged to do extensive research about the field and about the particular theatres or publishers to which you will be sending query letters or scripts. It is not possible to think effectively or creatively about how to proceed until you have some sense of what is available or possible. Start by educating yourself about the industry nationwide; don't begin with a preconceived, narrow idea of what you're looking for, because you could do yourself a serious disservice by overlooking something wonderful or enticing. As discussed below, this research will serve a dual purpose: In part you will be educating yourself as a writer who needs tangible information to make the best impression; and, as you make contact with other people in the theatre industry, you will be networking and establishing yourself as a writer, an important part of self-promotion.

Begin by going to a bookstore or the library, to see what resource books they have about the theatre industry in particular or being a writer in general. If all else fails, look for books such as *Writer's Resources* (Poets & Writers, 72 Spring St., NY, NY 10012) or *Songwriter's Market*

(Writer's Digest Books, 1507 Dana Ave., Cincinnati, OH 45207), which are oriented more towards other writers than stage writers but nonetheless contain valuable general information as well as information specifically for stage writers. Also contact your state and local arts agencies and the local Volunteer Lawyers for the Arts to see what resource materials they might have for individual use or what recommendations they can make. Contact the theatre companies in your area, whether professional, amateur or educational, to find out if they maintain any resources you could look through.

On the national level, get hold of often-used resource books such as the *Dramatists Guild Resource Directory* (Dramatists Guild, 1501 Broadway, Suite 701, NY, NY 10036), the *Dramatists Sourcebook* (from Theatre Communications Group) and the *Playwrights Companion* (from Feedback Theatrebooks); and check the "Announcements" section of the Dramatists Guild's newsletter, if you are a member. Regionally or locally, investigate books such as the *Writer's Northwest Handbook* (Media Weavers, L.L.C., 1738 N.E. 24th Ave., Portland, OR 97212) or the *Theatre Directory of the Bay Area* (Theatre Bay Area, 657 Mission St., #402, San Francisco, CA 94105), to name just a couple. If you can't find these books where you live (or for some reason they can't be ordered through a local bookstore), contact the publishers directly.

Once you have unearthed information about the various theatre and production possibilities, think honestly about your script and the venues in which it might best attract interest. As discussed in more detail under "Submissions research," the most effective marketing involves submitting the work to those targeted theatres where past work or the mission statement reflects or includes works such as yours. Trying to squeeze your work into a production opportunity that simply doesn't fit will be time-consuming and frustrating, with no real benefits. Draft multiple prospect lists: first, the theatres most likely to be interested in work like yours; next, a fallback list of theatres that *might* be interested; and finally, theatres that wouldn't be interested in your work now, if it's never been produced, but which would be good places to submit once you've had your first reading, contest win or production. (Think ahead and be prepared as long as you're poring over this information anyway.)

Some possibilities will be local (don't overlook opportunities right outside your door!), others will be spread out across the country. Try to have a realistic mix of production opportunities represented on your lists, depending on the work and your career: smaller and larger theatres; lesser-known and well-known theatres; second stage and main-stage possibilities; contests, staged readings, workshops, etc. Strive to create a good cross-section of hoped-for results.

Regardless of where you live, find out about local or regional playwriting groups; they spring up almost everywhere and are a treasure trove of information, both in terms of formal research and for becoming connected to the local writing community. If you live in one of the larger cities, there may be several relevant organizations, some of which are specifically targeted to the stage-writing community and others to the general advancement of theatre or writing, which will encompass stage writers' concerns. Theatre Bay Area, in San Francisco, and the Austin Writers League, in Austin, Texas, are two such resource organizations for people who work in the theatre. Their members include stage writers among other targeted professional groups.

If you are a woman or a member of an ethnic or other minority, consider looking into opportunities that have been created with you in mind. There are theatres, conferences and festivals specializing in Asian-American, Hispanic, Native American and African-American work, works by gay and lesbian writers, works by women, Jewish theatre, venues for and by people with disabilities, and so on. Organizations and associations related to these issues, even those that may not be specifically theatre-oriented, can be good places to hear about opportunities and to network with other theatre professionals.

Check out the university or college near you that may have a theatre or drama department, playwriting classes, resource materials, or even an annual playwrights' conference, workshop or contest. You may be surprised at what you find in seemingly unlikely places. For example, there's a wonderful annual playwriting conference at the Prince William Sound Community College in Valdez, Alaska, that sponsors important events featuring prominent writers and speakers.

Go where other stage writers congregate to learn more about the profession: playwriting conferences and workshops. These gatherings serve many purposes. First, you will have an opportunity to talk with other writers, to network and to share information. Second, seminars, workshops and panel discussions are usually run by people actively involved in the theatre industry; not only do they have valuable information to impart, but you may find yourself talking with someone whom, under ordinary circumstances, you would never be able to meet. Third, these events make you a participant, not just an observer; you will leave energized and motivated.

Join the national community of stage writers by becoming a member of the Dramatists Guild. Consider joining other organizations, too, that will bring you into the information loop, such as Theatre Communications Group; membership in the latter includes a subscription to *American Theatre* magazine, which will help you stay abreast of current issues and developments, as well as personnel changes at theatres that may interest you.

If playwriting groups don't exist where you live, start one yourself, so writers can get together to read their new works, receive constructive feedback and share information. Contact a local cafe, bar or bookstore about starting and running a weekly playreading night. Organize or teach a workshop or a seminar. Get out of the house and get involved.

No matter where you live, consider going online to reach a national network of writers. Most commercial services (America Online, Compuserve, etc.) feature discussion groups for writers, and even chat rooms connecting stage writers across the country and around the world in real time. On the Internet, many Usenet Newsgroups are devoted to theatre and writing, and World Wide Web home pages increasingly provide substantive information. Every day, more theatres, theatre organizations and theatre professionals are joining the online community; even if you are familiar with them in the "real world," it might be worthwhile to investigate their cyberspace counterparts.

PROMOTING YOURSELF

Writing is a lonely profession; to overcome the inherent aloneness, you have to make an effort to be involved with other writers. Groups of writers discussing their craft can be an inspiration, and nowhere will you find better information than with other writers who are also working hard to launch their careers. Not only may other writers be able to point you in the right direction, but they also may keep you from making the same labor-intensive mistakes they did.

Being visible has other, distinct advantages. Once you have become a familiar presence in the theatre community, you gain access to the inside information loop. Don't underestimate how important these connections may be! For example, you might impress another writer who happens to be in touch with a theatre company looking for a writer to commission, and she or he might recommend you. As an insider, you will hear of projects in the planning stages, projects for which others might begin to think of you. It's possible you might hear of an agent who is quietly taking on new clients. That people tend to work with people they know and like is as true in the stage-writing community as anywhere else.

One way to get better known is to develop your own professional "hit list," using simple, tasteful postcards to announce your latest production or reading. This can be organized easily with a computer, using software to maintain your ever-expanding mailing list and to generate mailing labels.

People who work in the theatre often comb through trade publications and press releases for announcements of works being presented, contests won, etc., and if they see a writer's name appearing repeatedly, it may pique their interest, possibly inspiring them to ask around for more information or, if you do submit a script, making your name already familiar. For starters, consider placing announcements in *American Theatre* magazine, the *Dramatists Guild's Quarterly* "Dramatists Diary," region-specific publications such as *Drama-Logue* (Southern California), *TheaterWeek* (New York/eastern seaboard), *Callboard* (the Bay Area) and other local publications and newsletters.

No one can predict what successes might come your way from becoming part of the writing community, but if you do not participate in any of these ways, people won't know who you are. The key isn't that you think of yourself as a professional writer, but that others think you are, too. You can spend a lot of time submitting your work, but without being known in the community—be it local, regional or national—that may not, in many instances, be enough.

PROFESSIONAL PRESENTATION

The script is but one of the marketing materials you must create. Most often, you will first send out a query or cover letter containing a succinctly detailed list of your credentials and information about the work's development or production history, together with an engaging synopsis of the work and important production information such as cast size, set requirements and so on. In your synopsis, describe the work in no more than one page. What's required is an overall picture of the work, not a scene-by-scene breakdown or an interpretation. Your resume must also be succinct and up-to-date. Producers, directors, literary managers and agents are not looking at resumes to see prestigious degrees, but rather to get a sense of who the person they're dealing with is, and to see that the resume has been written and presented in a professional manner.

If the work being submitted has been previously produced, theatres will want to read its best reviews. As the work gathers momentum, you will want to compile an impressive, attention-grabbing (but not gaudy) publicity package containing letters of recommendation and/or reviews. Don't be caught off-guard if an interesting opportunity presents itself on a moment's notice: You won't want to scramble to create and assemble materials—such as reviews—any professional writer could reasonably be assumed to have at her or his fingertips. For example, if someone asks to read the synopsis, don't be put in the horrible position of stuttering an admission that you've never put one together. You will be much happier if the labor required to fulfill this request is simply to personalize a cover letter and place the synopsis in an envelope.

SUBMISSIONS RESEARCH

It cannot be said often enough that writers must force themselves to conduct basic research before submitting their plays. A "machine gun" approach—sending letters to any name you come across—won't do, but writers are also encouraged not to be too conservative. It's good to take a few chances even if they're long shots, but it's best to know as much as possible about the organizations and individuals to which and to whom you submit the work that matters most to you.

Try to find out whether a theatre has more than one space or production method. There may be a second stage or black box theatre for small-budget productions of new works; perhaps the theatre has a new playreading series. Some theatres simply don't produce new works, and a writer will not find it the best use of time and money to try convince one to do so. Some theatres produce only dramatic works, not musicals, so it would be unproductive to submit musicals to them. Many theatres produce a mix of classics, contemporary hits, older favorites and new works; some allocate one slot per season to a new work; others are committed to producing exclusively new works (and even then it's important to know how many slots are available). Some theatres won't produce first-time writers (so it might be best to approach a small theatre first; don't think you have to start at the "top").

Find out your prospective theatre's production history, production budget (if possible) and the facilities (seating capacity; thrust or proscenium stage configuration; etc.) Know the theatre's mission, the specific work they're known for, and the type of audience they attract and hope to attract. Gathering all this information might not be possible, since some theatres have a clearer identity than others; however, if it's available, this information can save frustration on both sides of the submission process.

Focusing on a theatre's mission and production history is especially important when responding to a call for scripts. If a theatre provides a description of what it's looking for, pay close attention. The theatre is not establishing guidelines arbitrarily to limit opportunities available for writers; it wants to produce a particular type of work for its audience, and is gracefully trying to winnow out inappropriate submissions. If you can make a good case for your work relating to a theatre's expressed guidelines, even though the work doesn't fit neatly within the description, it's fair and even encouraged to take a chance and submit the work, since parameters might prove fluid, depending on the works received. However, if your work is clearly outside the guidelines, think twice about the best path to pursue. If, for example, a theatre is committed to producing plays addressing gay themes and issues, don't assume they will seriously consider your play about the nuclear family unless there is good reason to suggest that it in some way involves the gay themes and issues the theatre wants to present.

Inform yourself of each theatre's individual submission requirements. Write to theatres to obtain their submission guidelines, to find out when and how they accept and read scripts. Don't assume that every literary department reads scripts however and whenever they're received. Some theatres don't accept unsolicited manuscripts. Some require a query letter before agreeing to read your work. Some accept scripts only during certain times of the year. Rather than buck the system, understand its rules and make them work for you.

There are so many production possibilities, it makes sense to focus your energies and expenses on those theatres that might actually produce your work. Theatres that accept scripts are always overwhelmed with them; receiving scripts which have no relation to what they produce may eventually compel administrators to create stricter submission criteria. This is not to suggest that all writers must always play within the rules—everyone can think of a theatre which read a work so wonderful they said, "We have to produce this, no matter what"— but that is a rare situation, and probably not the best strategy for first-round submissions.

As mentioned above, there are books which provide production history information, such as *Theatre Profiles*, published by Theatre Communications Group, and the *Regional Theatre Directory* and the *Summer Theatre Directory*, both published by Theatre Directories (P.O. Box 519, Dorset, VT, 05251, 802-867-2223), but not all theatres presenting new works qualify or choose to be included in those compilations. Another suggestion is to obtain a company's season brochure; or, if you happen to live in or near an urban center, there may be generally distributed resource information, such as theatres' press releases, available at a playwrights' center or the library. Sometimes, particularly given the vast range of small productions across the country, this information may be hard to uncover; but, for your own sake, you should make an effort to obtain it.

If you live in the same area as a theatre to which you want to submit your work, you are in a unique position of which you should take advantage. Attend a full season's productions to get a real understanding of the work they produce and their production values. You may uncover valuable information pertaining to the work you wish to submit and, if you are fortunate enough to have a conversation with someone in the literary or artistic department, it will seem unprofessional if you've never bothered to attend a performance.

Consider getting involved with local theatres: Volunteer to work on productions or as a reader in the literary department. Theatres often look for volunteer ushers who then stay to see performances free of charge. As a volunteer, you will gain invaluable information about the inside workings of not-for-profit theatres in general and of the theatres that interest you in particular. However, go in with the appropriate mindset: You're there to learn about the theatre. Don't expect to meet people with the sole purpose of getting them to read your script, a motive which can easily prove transparent and offputting. On the other hand, you might be able to move from volunteering to organizing a new playreading series if the theatre doesn't have one; and, maybe your play might be one of those read. There are many, many possibilities to explore—depending on your ingenuity and creativity—which could benefit both you and the theatre.

In rare instances, pure luck succeeds where strategy doesn't. Don't let the research issue control all actions. While it's certainly best for the writer to be well informed, don't leave the field if the information you seek is not readily available. If you live in an area where resource material is not abundant and you can't afford to invest in a small library of your own, it's possible to proceed without it. Just know that a hit and miss approach really does depend on luck, whereas careful research improves your prospects.

BUDGETARY ISSUES

The vast majority of theatres in this country are run as not-for-profits; they never have unlimited financial resources, and most simply don't have enough money to hire as many staff members as they need. Not-for-profit doesn't automatically mean a small budget—some of the larger not-for-profit theatres' annual budgets reach into the millions—but even not-for-profit theatres must be run as a business. From the largest to the smallest, every not-for-profit theatre must consider how an understaffed, underfunded company can accomplish its goals.

The economics of the theatre have been changing in recent years, and continue to change, and writers must be aware of this. Many theatres have found that the amount of contributed income has been reduced, that the focus for foundation grants has changed, that corporate sponsorship is harder to secure, that fewer people subscribe to their seasons, and on and on. When a community's demands seem to change, the theatres may have to change, too.

A theatre's tighter budget may force it to reduce the number of productions in its season. Perhaps the theatre will maintain the number of productions but reduce each production's budget. It may have to cut staff, possibly in the literary department. In this instance, the theatre will not be able to hire as many readers as before, thereby cutting back on the number of plays that can be read or extending response time significantly. Perhaps the literary manager will have to restructure the department, instituting stricter policies, limiting unsolicited submissions.

Cast size is always a financial issue. Theatre administrators are frequently forced to make decisions based on the number of actors and sets for each production, which in turn affects the type of scripts the literary department can consider. Some seek productions involving unit sets. Some won't consider a large cast (generally, more than seven actors), while others creatively double- and triple-cast. (If a writer wants to work with a truly large cast, she or he might be well served by looking at theatres connected to or closely allied with a university or school; these are more likely to produce large-cast plays than independent institutions, due to the availability of student actors to fill many roles.)

Budgetary concerns can mean that a theatre feels it has to provide popular fare in order to retain or increase its subscriber base. This often translates into a reluctance to take risks on experimental works, or works which are emotionally charged, challenging or threatening in substance. Though the theatre community, in general, believes strongly in freedom of speech, it should come as no surprise that in many communities resistance is equally strong to works which contain certain language, themes, ideas, etc. Some audiences cry out for plays that tackle life issues, and others don't; and, for financial reasons, a theatre may choose its season accordingly.

These reasonable and necessary responses to all-too-tangible budgetary issues can have an unfortunate impact on the writer's art. This is *not* to suggest that writers should always write plays with budgetary and/or community concerns in mind (particularly if that would stifle the writer's creativity); writers should tell the stories that their hearts and souls compel them to write. But in the search for production, these realities may someday confront a writer whose works exceed a theatre's capacity or focus. Theatres themselves express concern that budgetary issues may foster self-censorship, restricting the content and complexity of plays they present.

Theatres have far more to consider than, "Do we like this work?" It's easy to become frustrated by the limitations imposed on submission or to rail against theatres that don't push the boundaries or, perhaps to the inexperienced eye, seem not to care about emerging writers, but theatres *are* looking for good, new material, and they are constantly trying to identify writers with whom long-term relationships are possible. They look at scripts not only for the prospect of immediate production, but also for voices, styles and ideas that would be complementary to the theatre's overarching artistic vision. The bottom line, though, is that theatres also have to think carefully about how to survive in the current political, social and economic climate.

THE NUTS AND BOLTS OF SUBMISSIONS

There is a vast range of theatres; they are not a monolith with one clearly established set of rules for script submission. Consequently, different theatres take different approaches to solicitation and management of the script-reading process. The following is *general* information that has been compiled by surveying many theatres across the country, but writers should always contact individual theatres to obtain information about their current submission policies.

The query packet

A good query packet consists of elements discussed above (a query letter; a synopsis; a cast list; and the writer's resume, which is a *must*: Don't think you can disguise your lack of production experience with the absence of a resume), sometimes between five and twenty pages of the script (any part is acceptable, but the beginning seems to be preferred unless you strongly feel a different excerpt shows off the piece better) and, most preferably, a self-addressed stamped postcard (SASP) for their response. Don't send sample scenes without a synopsis and cast list. Know that query letters are looked at seriously and serve an important purpose.

Keep the response card simple:

_____ Yes, I would like to see the entire script.
_____ No, we have decided not to read the script.

The key: Make responding *easy* for the theatre. It's best to provide a response postcard rather than make the recipient take the time to write a letter. You'll likely hear back from the theatre more quickly, and you'll save a few pennies over the expense of a first-class stamp. (In 1996, the cost of a postcard stamp is twenty cents compared to a thirty-two-cent letter. This twelve-cent difference might seem miniscule, but when each submission can cost seven to thirteen dollars start to finish, every little bit helps.)

Remember to put some return information on the postcard so that you know from whom it's being sent; at the very least, mark the post-card with the theatre's name. (It will be very frustrating to receive a postcard saying, "Yes, send the script," only to realize that you can't fig-ure out which theatre responded!) If you are sending out different works to different theatres, you might want to include a clue for you to tell easily which work is being requested. (Some writers indicate on the back of the postcard the theatre's return address, the writer's address and what work it's for. Others use a simple code.)

It cannot be stressed enough how much presentation means. A well-thought-out submission package presented in the most professional manner will set you apart from the crowd by one notch. The literary department will not be impressed if your submission package screams "amateur."

The don'ts:

♦ Don't be cute: no cute graphics, no computer art, no fancy title pages, no unusual typefaces, etc. It's annoying and considered amateurish.

♦ Don't send overly clever cover letters. What is needed is concrete information about the work and the writer.

♦ Don't send set or costume designs.

♦ Don't request or demand an instant response. Literary departments are continually swamped; you cannot speed up the process, but you *can* make someone dislike you.

♦ Don't call the theatre the day after the approximated response time has expired. Response times are provided with submission procedures as a general guideline; they are never absolute. Understand that people who work at theatres have more to do than time to do it. Since they often must juggle ten different projects at once, they know how and when to squeeze work in; it will not be according to your schedule.

♦ Don't lose patience. You should have many things to do while waiting for a response; for instance, conducting further marketing research or starting a new play.

♦ Don't "pitch" your play: This isn't Hollywood. And don't tell the theatre your play is the greatest work ever written and it will right all the wrongs in the history of dramatic literature. Hype is not necessary or welcomed.

♦ Don't sound desperate. You needn't say, "I really want to get produced at your theatre," because the fact of submission says that already.

♦ Don't fabricate representation by an agent. Theatres know the names of agents throughout the country and they know, generally, whom these agents represent. Don't think that using your spouse, significant other or a friend as your "agent" will fool anyone.

♦ Don't submit plays with endorsements that aren't what you say. For example, don't say, "Glenn Close wanted to star in this play," and then enclose a letter from Glenn Close that's just a gracious rejection letter. Sometimes people write very kind letters that, in essence, actually say they're not interested; by enclosing these as endorsements you indicate your naiveté. (And whatever you do, don't say things like, "Jessica Tandy was all set to star in this play, but then she died.")

Within roughly three to four months of receipt of the information packet, a theatre will decide whether or not to request your script and will contact you. If the theatre is interested in reading the full script, send it promptly and be *sure* to include a large-enough envelope bearing sufficient postage to enable the theatre to return it. (Never expect any theatre to supplement the cost of postage; err on the side of putting a little more postage on the envelope rather than less, and don't cut it close. Be cognizant of impending changes in the price of postage and anticipate this in advance; the theatre will rarely make up the difference if there is a rate hike between the time you first send the script and the time the theatre is ready to return it to you.)

Submitting the script

A significant number of theatres simply will not read scripts if you haven't first sent a query packet (unless you've met someone who's already said, "Send me the script.") Theatres polled expressed emphatically that—unless their guidelines say otherwise—the literary department will not read an entire work unless an information packet has been sent and the script has been requested.

If you want to know that the theatre *received* the script, enclose a "Yes, I got it" postcard (and keep it simple; never, ever ask anyone to type a response just for acknowledging receipt of a script). Keep in mind that during the heaviest submission season (generally speaking, September through January), literary departments can receive an average of ten to twenty scripts each day. Do the math: five months of ten scripts a day equals roughly 1,500 submissions; at twenty scripts a day, the number increases to 3,000 . . . and this doesn't take into account the "slower" months of the year (when submissions continue to flow in at approximately twenty to forty per week), or scripts the literary department or others on the artistic and production staff hear about through the grapevine or solicit themselves.

When you have prepared the script for submission, be sure to enclose a cover letter with it, repeating everything you said in your initial query letter (or enclose a copy of that first letter). Don't expect the literary department to remember what you've already said! (Consider the volume of works submitted: No literary department can maintain a separate record of information on every writer and work.) If the script has a history, tell it. If there are good reviews, enclose the best ones.

Package your script so it arrives in one piece. One writer suggested reinforcing the envelopes with tape, which she learned to do when a theatre sent back the corner of a shredded envelope with a note asking, "Was there anything in this?"

Never, ever send out your original manuscript, and always send an SASE large enough to accommodate the copy if you want the theatre or publisher to return it. (Given the cost of copying, this is advisable financially, except when submitting your script to another country, in which case the cost of postage might be higher than making another copy.) If you don't care about getting your script back, then just tell the theatre to recycle the paper or throw it out.

Remember: If you fail to enclose an SASE, you will most likely never see your script again. Do not hold a theatre responsible for your oversight.

Most important: Don't send a script until it's ready. Read it again. Read it out loud. Have someone else read it aloud to you, or invite friends into your living room to read all the parts. Do everything in your power to be certain you've taken your script as far as possible without a professional reading, workshop or development process before submitting it.

Never send a theatre first drafts, or multiple drafts. Some literary departments *might* read another draft if the first showed unusual promise; but, for the most part, one reading is as many as a theatre can afford to give any script. Certainly, no one will insert new pages and re-read it to see how a later version differs from the first!

If, on the other hand, you revise a previously submitted work in such a way that it significantly changes the character of the work, you might send a new query letter to a theatre that has read the earlier draft and *briefly* explain the situation. As always, enclose a return postcard to make it easy for the theatre to request the new version of your script.

The don'ts:

♦ Don't ever fax a script. A faxed script could be unpleasant to handle and, as likely as not, illegible. (And don't ask anyone to download a script via computer, either. In the future, the Internet *may* be used for script submission; but, at this time, it's a safe bet that this mode of transmission would be equally ill-received.)

♦ Don't harass the theatre after you've sent your work. Reviewing manuscripts takes time and there is nothing you can do to speed up the process. If the theatre wants to produce your play, they *will* get in touch with you. Nagging the theatre to hurry up can only create a bad impression. (One exception: If you have simultaneously made submissions to other theatres—which of course you can and should do as long as you let each theatre know you are doing so—and another theatre makes you an offer, you should contact any other theatres considering the script, explain the situation, and give a firm deadline for their response. This will speed up their reading if it's possible, but don't even think about fabricating another theatre's interest: You don't know who talks to whom about what within the theatre community—indeed a significant amount of discussion takes place at all times and at all levels—and such a "clever" ploy will likely blow up in your face.)

♦ Don't call any person affiliated with the theatre at home, unless they have specifically asked that you do. Someone may be listed in the phone book but that doesn't mean she or he wishes to have her or his privacy invaded.

♦ Don't imagine that a work submitted now will be produced right away or even in the upcoming season. Most theatres choose their seasons six months to a year in advance. It typically takes at least two years for a new work to get produced, even when the writer in question is well-established in the field. (Some theatres even warn writers against writing about hot or topical issues; given the lag time in getting a production, hot topics may turn cold.)

♦ Don't assume your first work will be "it." You might have remarkable talent and show great promise, but rarely does a writer craft a producible work the first time out.

Response time

Having received the script, in most cases you will not hear from the theatre for six to nine months, depending on the size of that theatre's operation and the volume of submissions at that time. Only in rare instances would a writer hear from the theatre in the interim; they simply do not have the time to contact every writer who submitted just to provide an update on the status of the work. And, as stated above, don't watch the calendar, ready to follow up the day after the six- or nine-month period is up. Theatres ask that writers refrain from following up with a note until the theatre has had a reasonable amount of time (in their opinion, not yours) to read and respond to the script. Be patient. Either focus your marketing efforts in other areas, so that you have more irons in the fire, or move on to other projects.

When the proper time comes to follow up, it is considered highly inappropriate and extremely bad judgment to call the theatre; always follow up in writing. And, again, always include an SASP stamped postcard that can be effortlessly dropped in the mail. Don't be insulted or offended if you receive a form letter from the literary department or if it is signed by one of the literary manager's assistants: There simply isn't enough staff in such departments to respond personally to each and every submission requested. The only direct contact writers would probably have with the literary manager is when he or she can make an offer. And if the letter says they'd like to see future work of yours, take them at face value, because they mean it; most literary managers agree that they don't encourage a writer to re-contact the theatre if it's not sincere.

A tangential question often asked is whether theatres will provide feedback on scripts they decide not to produce. Most often, the answer is no, because there's just not enough time; theatres are not set up to provide this service for every writer whose work is not produced. From the writer's perspective, it can also be dangerous, unless you have a clear idea about the credentials of the person giving the feedback. (It's difficult to control, but try not to rely on the advice of every person ready to impart wisdom on what is "wrong" with your play, since you will find as many opinions as there are readers.)

However, sometimes the theatre will send an encouraging letter which states, in essence, "this is a decent work, and even though we're not interested in it, please send us works you write in the future." This should not be misinterpreted as an invitation to send them all your past works. When you've been given a positive sign, don't abuse it.

Resubmissions

It is possible that the person who rejected your work five years ago is no longer the person reading scripts at a particular venue, so you might decide to resubmit the work. However, depending on their ability to do so (considering staff and time constraints), many theatres maintain their own reader reports on every script received, and they will check to see what they have already seen; so, if you decide to resubmit, keep this in mind. And do not confuse this with the admonition above against sending multiple drafts of a work to the same theatre.

The reader

There are usually multiple levels of approval to pass through at each theatre. The specific tiers and order of events varies according to each theatre's internal structure, but the basics don't vary significantly. If a typical route can be traced, it would begin with a literary intern or associate in the literary department. It would move from there to the literary manager, who often has the authority to decide what might receive a reading at the theatre. From there, the script would move to the artistic staff, perhaps to an associate artistic director and eventually to the artistic director of the theatre, who would decide which scripts will receive a production. Depending on the size and hierarchy of the particular theatre, it's possible that the managing director might be involved in the high-level decisions about the upcoming season as well.

The most important lesson to learn, then, is never to assume that people you consider low-level readers lack the ability to reject a script; that is, to decide *not* to pass a script on to the next level. Readers usually have been instructed about the theatre's mission, what their higher-ups are looking for, etc.; precisely because readers are the foot soldiers in the trenches, they've probably been given both insight into what the theatre is hoping to find and the authority to make base-level decisions as a matter of necessity. Sometimes theatres (and contests, too) may be able to afford multiple readers for each script, so that nothing becomes hostage to one person's taste and preferences; but, in the absence of the necessary financial support, the best the literary department can do is to hire qualified readers—preferably people with some background in or understanding of theatre and reading scripts, which is a developed skill—and allow them to make the first cut.

Solicited and unsolicited scripts

A large number of theatres no longer accept unsolicited scripts. What this means is that they've made a decision to winnow the number of scripts received to those that come from or through familiar channels. It's a difficult decision for any theatre to make and usually it's generated by necessity: Most likely the sheer volume of unsolicited scripts became prohibitive and mandated stricter traffic management and allocation of available resources. This could be as basic as not being able to afford as many readers as the volume of scripts requires.

As mentioned above, some writers seem to assume that theatres receive a relatively small number of unsolicited submissions, and resent it when theatres impose submission restrictions. In reality, theatres receive thousands of scripts and cannot possibly give them all the proper time and attention. Theatres acknowledge that in restricting submissions, they may miss out on the opportunity to discover and produce a wonderful new work by an emerging writer; but, they have arrived at a solution, on balance, which allows the theatre to continue pursuing its mission and artistic vision without overwhelming the staff and the budget.

If a theatre won't accept unsolicited submissions, the following is a fairly standard list of sources from which it will still accept submissions: agents; other theatres that may be interested in co-production projects; established writers; writers referred by other known writers, artistic directors, managing directors, literary managers or others on staff in the department; dramaturgs; freelance directors and producers; and possibly other theatre artists, such as well-known actors, designers, etc. Occasionally a persistent new writer will break through via a letter of inquiry, but that is rare and depends a lot on timing, the subject matter of the script and/or a summary that the reader finds especially unique or intriguing.

If you know someone who can get the script to someone at a theatre in which you're interested, take advantage of that. Do not think that the inside contact needs to be in the literary department. This is where the schmooze factor becomes all-important: finding a contact who will enable you to bypass the traditional lines of submission.

Word of mouth

If someone at a theatre reads a work they like but that the theatre can't or won't produce, it is common for him or her to recommend the script to other theatres and theatre artists who are also looking for good work to produce. The theatre community's grapevine is efficient and, for the most part, there are friendly relationships between theatres. Literary, artistic and sometimes management departments are in touch with directors, dramaturgs, other theatres' literary departments and so on. A referral from anyone a theatre knows, not only agents, may be what gets your work read. Consequently, in the cover letter to a theatre accompanying a script submission (*not* in the initial submission package), don't be afraid to ask a theatre to make their recommendations of theatres that might be more appropriate for your script, if they decide not to produce it.

In addition, many literary managers and their associates, artistic directors and freelance directors do extracurricular activities such as jurying various fellowships, contests and the like. They may find works they like in that way, too, so don't think they look only at what comes to them directly through their theatres.

Industry guides to new plays

Literary Managers and Dramaturgs of the Americas (LMDA) is a professional service organization for literary managers and dramaturgs in the United States and Canada. Founded in 1985 as a membership organization, it has expanded its membership beyond working literary managers and dramaturgs; as of this writing, there are three additional levels of membership: 1) performing artist professionals and academics; 2) students of dramaturgy, performing arts and literature programs, and related disciplines; and 3) institutional memberships, open to theatres, universities and other organizations. Included in LMDA's array of activities are a few of particular interest to stage writers. One is the LMDA *Script Exchange*, published five times a year for theatres looking for new works. In each issue, five people affiliated with theatres across the country (including literary managers, dramaturgs, executive directors, associate directors and associate producers) recommend exciting plays, writers or projects they've come into contact with (not necessarily plays they're producing). Recommendations are submitted from all over, with the editor of the *Exchange* making the final decisions for inclusion. Recommendations from each theatre typically encompass many different works, not just one script or any one writer. A brief description of the work is provided along with the author's (or agent's) contact information. LMDA also publishes *Full Spectrum: The Expanded Script Exchange Annual*, which is an anthology of mostly unproduced new plays, alphabetized by author's name and containing contact information.

Another way theatre professionals tell each other about new work is through *PlaySource*, a Theatre Communications Group quarterly bulletin which contains descriptions of new plays that have recently received productions at nonprofit professional theatres, or workshops or readings at major developmental organizations.

Do *not* write to LMDA or TCG to ask to be in *Script Exchange*, the *Script Exchange Annual* or *PlaySource*. These are based on recommendations, not requests from writers. And don't ask someone at a theatre to recommend your work for one of these publications, which would be considered highly unprofessional. The above information is provided only so that stage writers understand three of the many methods used by theatres and producers to exchange information about promising works and writers.

Organization of submissions

Every writer must establish a system for keeping track of all submissions. It doesn't matter whether this involves a handwritten log book, an elaborate cross-referenced system of index cards, a computerized tracking system or some other method of your own devising. Create the system that will work best for you and your idiosyncracies, but know it is absolutely essential that you get organized about your submissions. Certainly there are people whose organizational skills are not as finely honed as others, and obviously this is yet another task you must find time for, but there is no getting around it. You are running a business, and you should conduct your business in a business-like manner. It frustrates theatres to encounter writers who, because they have no record of having done so in the past, submit the same works repeatedly. This is a quick way to become someone theatres won't want to work with. (As an aside, it's also not a bad idea to establish a submission system to be prepared in advance for any IRS audit.)

If you are uncertain how even to begin to create a system, ask your fellow stage writers to describe theirs. You are encouraged to create whatever works best for you, and ideas, suggestions and recommendations from other writers may help you put together the best possible system. Don't listen only to what works for others, but inquire about what *failed* or didn't mesh with their personal styles. The following is one writer's system, intended only as a starting point:

1. Keep a copy of all letters (written to and received from others) in a three-ring binder, with a separate binder for each work. Maintain these letters in alphabetical order according to the name of the theatre, producer, publisher, whatever. This will allow you to turn to a particular section quickly and find all important correspondence.

2. Keep a related index card file, also in alphabetical order by name of theatre, etc., containing a history of all submissions made to that person or organization. Also maintain a written record of the names and address changes of all literary managers and associates, artistic directors, dramaturgs and the like who have been at that theatre and moved on (including where they went if that has been announced), and have clear notations indicating what work was sent to which specific person. If someone responded by saying "we're not interested in this work, but in the future please send us your new material," note that on the card, too. In other words, take the extra few minutes and be thorough with this information. If you are doing a good job marketing your work, it is impossible that you would remember all the details.

3. Maintain a file cabinet with separate files containing information you gather pertaining to each theatre. When you read through industry trade publications or local newspapers, talk to friends, see press releases, flyers, brochures and the like, keep an eye out for information which might help in your search for readings, workshops, productions or publications, including announcements of grants or awards that may underwrite existing programs or create new ones (as well as announcements of cuts, so you don't mistakenly apply for a defunct opportunity). Clip or copy it, and stick it in the appropriate file.

Rejection

Not to cast a pall over the enthusiasm generated so far, but a few words on this subject are in order. First, attend to your organizational system: When you receive a rejection, make an appropriate notation on your index card, in your computer file, whatever. If the letter clearly says, "Thank you, but we're not interested," note it as such. Whatever you do, *don't* send back an angry letter telling the theatre that they have just made a huge mistake by not producing your play.

If the letter says something to the effect of, "We don't do this particular type of play," consider writing back and finding out what types of works they are interested in producing. If the reader has taken the trouble to critique your script, consider whether you find the comments useful and, if so, write back a positive thank you letter, perhaps incorporating some of the comments made. Do not, however, write a defensive, point-by-point response to show the reader that his or her remarks were wrong or off the mark. If you believe the critique is not useful, throw it away, but don't respond angrily. If the critique is simply bizarre, then you might find it useful to note that in your system, too.

If the response is, "We're not interested in this work, but send us other works you've written," and this is the only script you've written that they might be interested in (or perhaps it's the only script you've written), write back graciously and tell them you will send something when you think it's right for them. Maybe keep these notes or cards separated, perhaps out on your desk or in a special folder, to remind you of future possibilities. If you follow up on expressed interest, especially if time has passed, be sure to remind the theatre that it's read your work before and asked to see more scripts.

There are certainly maddening and insulting responses that you must laugh off. Form letters are necessary and to be expected; however, some theatres haven't updated their form letters in years, and you might receive the eight-millionth-generation copy that is faded and illegible. It's offensive to receive "Dear Playwright" letters. Some writers report receiving rejection letters obviously intended for other writers, or rejections that either have nothing to do with the script sent or reveal that the reader didn't actually read the script.

Try not to get discouraged by rejections, which are inevitable; particularly if the submission is your first play. Try not to take it personally if a theatre is not interested in reading or producing your script. It may mean you haven't yet found the right fit for the work, rather than reflect on the quality of your writing.

Unreturned scripts

If you follow the rules and enclose an SASE of the proper size and with sufficient postage, but the theatre neglects to return your script after a *long* time passes—say, a year—write requesting its return. If you are unable to obtain a response to this letter, you can contact the Dramatists Guild (if you are a member) to see if someone in the membership department will follow up for you. If the theatre's response is that they can't find the SASE you sent initially, you will have to decide whether it is worth sending another. If the theatre's response is that it simply can't find your script, swallow your rage and move on. If the theatre doesn't have it, all the letter writing in the world won't make it reappear.

PRODUCTION IDEAS

In researching possibilities, look beyond the obvious choices. Don't limit yourself to chanting "Broadway and Off-Broadway." There are so many different types and levels of theatre going on in this country at any given time, you will regret not at least considering them. If you decide ultimately that your goal is the commercial theatre, go for it, but know that that's not the only path to take, nor are all works particularly suited for the commercial arena. Success can be enjoyed in many different venues.

The point of the following list is not to dissuade any writer from shooting for the Broadway or Off-Broadway markets, but rather to acknowledge that one career path isn't necessarily right for every writer or work, and to encourage more writers to expand their horizons.

Regional/resident theatres

There is a vast network of not-for-profit theatres all across the country. Some are more prominent than others, but collectively they provide a cornucopia of opportunities each season for new works to be done. These productions are generally of high quality and enjoy a loyal audience. Some theatres have both a mainstage and a second stage, and sometimes a black box (essentially, four walls and seats), which may present any number of production possibilities.

To get a clear sense of just how many theatres there are, along with substantively helpful information such as the type of work presented and who to contact, you may want to obtain a copy of the *Regional Theatre Directory* available from Theatre Directories (P.O. Box 519, Dorset, VT 05251), or *Playhouse America!* from Feedback Theatrebooks (305 Madison Avenue, Suite 1146, NY, NY 10165) in addition to the resource directories mentioned earlier. If you want to know what works were produced somewhat recently by the regional theatres (there is roughly a two-year lag time in compiling and publishing the information), consider purchasing *Theatre Profiles*, published by Theatre Communications Group.

Contests

There are many playwriting contests and competitions each year, sponsored by theatre companies, universities and colleges, foundations, for-profit corporations, national, regional or local playwrights centers, and other organizations. Often the winning play receives a full production, and possibly a cash prize or an all-expense-paid trip to participate in the production, in addition to the ability to use the fact of winning a contest, award or prize to enhance the work's promotion in the future.

Competitions are a wonderful way to try to get your material out into the marketplace, because you *know* the recipient is looking for new work. Entries are usually read by at least two readers and sometimes three, if the contest sponsors can afford and arrange that. And they are not looking for "perfect" work: What they want is a script worth developing.

Seeking contest-related productions is encouraged, because they serve several invaluable purposes: to hear the work performed, perhaps for the first time; to be able to revise the work during and after production; and to begin to learn how to participate in the rehearsal and production process, including working with a director, often without high pressure stakes (i.e., great expense) or reviewers, and instead with interested, unjaded audiences.

Various competitions establish their own guidelines and deadlines, which you must review and follow before submitting the work. Generally speaking, they result in quality productions; but, unfortunately, there is no guarantee of quality for every contest. If you are able to discover the names of recent winners, it may behoove you to contact them to find out whether they were satisfied with the experience and, if not, what their particular concerns were.

A word to the wise: Be very clear about what the contest deadline is—sometimes the date provided is the postmark date; others, it's the date of receipt. Don't assume. Contest readers/jurors receive so many scripts they will *not* be sympathetic to a writer submitting a script late. Write for the guidelines early and try to submit early, so there's a better chance the readers are fresh. The closer your submission to the final deadline, the more likely the readers will have been inundated.

Entry or reading fees. Be aware that some competitions charge an entry or reading fee; that is, a flat dollar amount each writer submitting a script must pay in order to have the work considered. This fee, ostensibly, is collected to pay for readers, but not to pay for the production itself. Ideally, these expenses would be underwritten; unfortunately, however, this is not always the case. A competition that charges is not necessarily trying to milk writers—there may be no other way to support the competition—but the reality is that this creates a very difficult situation for many writers, ethically and financially.

Paying a reading fee can become a serious hardship because these fees add up quickly. Fifteen or twenty dollars may not be a large sum to pay to enter a contest, but when a writer enters ten contests, the bill soars, especially on top of the plethora of other unavoidable expenses in which writers must invest.

Writers must decide for themselves whether to pay such fees or to risk missing out on what might be good opportunities. Unfortunately, access will be denied to those who simply can't afford such outlays or who believe it's unconscionable to be required to cover a contest's expenses.

Sometimes a writer will receive a reader's written report in return for paying the reader's fee; that is, the contest's or organization's reader(s) will respond with a written critique of the work, addressing weaknesses and suggesting revisions. Again, think carefully about who will rendering such a critique before assuming that its value will offset the reading fee. For example, if the readers are college playwriting students earning a few extra dollars, beware. If readers have advanced playwriting degrees or perhaps relevant experience making them particularly skilled, then perhaps an individual writer will find the critique worthwhile.

Prizes

Though not really a production idea, this is an important category for writers to consider. Individual grants and fellowships are awarded to stage writers every year—some large, some small; some prestigious, some less well-known. In addition to the financial benefit, there is an important message implicit in winning a prize: that someone else thinks you show talent and promise as a writer. Acceptance into a writers' colony or other residency, while not a prize in the strictest sense, also represents a special feather in your writer's cap that sends an equally important message: I am a serious, professional writer committed to learning my craft.

Nearly every library maintains some type of resource library providing research information about grants available for writers. One of the most comprehensive of these books is called *The Individual's Guide to Grants* by Judith Margolin, the former director of the Foundation Center (Plenum Press, 233 Spring St., NY, NY 10013). (If you live in or near New York, make a point of exploring the Foundation Center at 79 Fifth Avenue.) Perhaps the most timely is *Grants and Awards Available to American Writers* (PEN American Center, 568 Broadway, NY, NY 10012).

University/college productions

Don't overlook university or college theatres and drama departments as a way to get produced. These institutions often have a reasonable amount of money to spend on productions as well as a built-in audience (both at the school and from surrounding communities), not to mention a talented, enthusiastic pool of actors, directors and designers who are looking for new projects on which to hone their skills. As with contests, remember that experience is the best teacher of how to be involved with a reading or a production: how to work with other artists; understanding what your and their roles are in the process; what rehearsals and rewrites are like; etc. For many writers, it's helpful to find a supportive environment in which to learn how to work with others towards a successful production. Keep in mind, too, that universities and colleges often maintain resident playwright positions, whereby a writer might receive a stipend and room and board, enabling him or her to focus on writing, in exchange for teaching playwriting classes. In other words, working on productions at this level might open other doors.

Theatre for young audiences/educational markets

Theatre for young audiences, often referred to as "children's theatre," and the educational market, are burgeoning fields. There are many children's theatres—a good number of which tour their productions nationally and internationally—and countless elementary, junior high and high schools. The growing interest in these areas cannot be pegged to any one source, but it is notable that many children's classics are finding their way to the stage. One reason might be that some classics are finally entering the public domain, as *The Secret Garden* did a few years back. In addition, many of the underlying rights owners of works that remain protected by copyright have realized that stage adaptation is a wonderful way to expose new generations to their work. Just glancing through the 1995-1996 season schedules reveals productions of *Alice in Wonderland, The Magic Mrs. Piggle-Wiggle, Charlie and the Chocolate Factory, Little House on the Prairie, Stuart Little* and a plethora of other such titles. And don't think that adaptations are the only way to get produced in these arenas: There are many original works for these audiences also being produced all around the country. Many writers have created plays for these arenas that focus on issues of importance to young people or to instill a love for theatre in children of all ages.

More information about getting involved in theatre for young audiences can be obtained by contacting ASSITEJ/USA (the International Association of Theatre for Children and Young People), c/o Jolly Sue Baker, Executive Director, 2707 East Union Street, Seattle, Washington 98122. If you are interested in writing for elementary and secondary schools, contact the American Alliance for Theatre and Education (AATE), c/o Barbara Salisbury Wills, Executive Director, Department of Theatre, Arizona State University, Box 873411, Tempe, AZ 85287-3411.

Dinner theatre

Another area brimming with opportunities for writers is dinner theatre, the many examples of which ordinarily present shows year-round, with professional casts. A growing number of writers are beginning to tap into this venue, learning what others, including publishers, have known for years: that there is an entire circuit of dinner theatres, and the theatres share information between themselves about plays they've produced successfully. (There are roughly seventy-five dinner theatres in the United States.) And dinner theatres are beginning to recognize that audiences may be growing tired of seeing the same older works again and again.

Dinner theatres are all highly commercial ventures; they do not operate in the not-for-profit world. The guidelines for writing for this arena are generally the same as for any theatre; the primary difference is that dinner is served before or during the performance. Keep in mind controlling the size of the cast, as well as striving for simplicity of set design. A lot of works done in this venue are musicals (roughly sixty-five percent) and, over the last fifteen to twenty years, in response to changing audience demands, there has been a significant decline in "sex comedies," which used to be their bread and butter, although farce is still popular. In a somewhat related area, interactive plays, such as murder mysteries (to give but one example), have really taken hold nationwide.

The National Dinner Theatre Association can be reached at P.O. Box 726, Marshall, Michigan 49068. David Pritchard is the Executive Director.

Outdoor drama

An often overlooked area of opportunity is outdoor drama, or outdoor historical drama. There are ninety-six outdoor historical and classical theatre companies in the United States (including thirty-six Shakespeare Festivals), where the run of a production can last anywhere from two weekends to six months. These productions have large casts and take place on enormous stages, involving elaborate sets, lighting and costumes. The theatres (actually amphitheatres) are phenomenal, often seating two or three thousand. Works for outdoor drama have usually been commissioned for, and involve historical characters and events related to, the particular location in which they are produced. Sponsor groups are frequently not-for-profit corporations established by local residents, sometimes aided by money from the state and federal government. Successful outdoor dramas can run year after year, often as an integral part of the area's tourist industry.

The Institute of Outdoor Drama has been in existence since 1963. For more information, contact it at the University of North Carolina at Chapel Hill, CB#3240, NationsBank Plaza, Chapel Hill, NC 27599-3240.

Radio drama

As discussed further in the chapter on developing areas, one of the hottest, expanding arenas for production is radio drama, sometimes also called audio drama. More and more people are interested in listening to theatre at home, in their cars and at work, and opportunities continue to be created in response to the growing demand. Radio drama is an enormous industry in Europe where they do more and fuller projects than here, because there's more money available. The United States is slowly awakening to this vast potential market, both in the broadcast and audio cassette markets.

Writers who have worked in radio drama extol its virtues: the caliber of people involved (engineers, directors, actors), which is very high, and the creative possibilities, which seem limitless. This is an exciting arena, which results in an accurate and permanently preserved rendering of the work as intended. In addition, a broadcast can reach many thousands of people simultaneously.

Writers interested in learning more about radio drama should contact such organizations as L.A. Theatre Works in Venice, California, California Artists Radio Theatre in L.A., the American Radio Theatre in San Francisco, the Midwest Radio Theatre Workshop in Columbia, Missouri (which also has an annual radio script contest for both established and emerging writers), New Dramatists in New York, and the Roger Hendricks Simon Studio, also in New York.

International production opportunities

This can be daunting, because it's hard to do research and make connections internationally, not only because of the distance but because there are so many different countries to address, and sending scripts overseas is expensive. Add to that the difference in cultures, which may extend to business, contract and copyright issues, as well as language barriers. However, many stage writers have plowed ahead and been successful with overseas producers looking for American works. While this will probably not be among the first avenues of inquiry, there are many production possibilities available that should not be ignored.

The International Theatre Institute of the United States may be a good place to start your research (47 Great Jones St., NY, NY 10012, 212-254-4141). ITI maintains operating centers in ninety countries, and the New York office houses the ITI International Theatre Collection, a reference library containing a wealth of information, including foreign theatre directories, so that you can find the names of producers, directors and companies abroad, as well as various theatres' programs and policies.

Nontraditional sponsors or productions

All writers are strongly encouraged to think creatively about where works might be needed, produced or commissioned, and to investigate sponsors outside the traditional lists. In these days of tight funding, you may be able to think of interesting co-production possibilities or creating synergistic relationships between people or organizations that may have overlapping interests, but which might not have previously considered joining forces. Just because it's never been done doesn't mean it couldn't, or wouldn't, be a great idea. (If there aren't models to follow, you can always blaze trails.)

There are many areas not touched upon here. For example: short works sponsored by national, state or local governments or corporations (often created to teach employees); industry-sponsored scripts to entertain business people who participate in conferences, retreats and so on; tourist-centered attractions at amusement parks; cruise ship entertainment; summer playhouses; year-round production possibilities in resort areas, such as Branson, Missouri; narration for music or dance; opera; etc. You're a writer: Use your imagination!

PROMOTION AFTER PRODUCTION

A writer's work is never done. Once you've had the pleasure of production, it's time to get back to marketing. Now you have something tangible to offer with submissions. Good reviews are invaluable, and should be used to their maximum potential. If the production is extended, use that, too. It will certainly interest a potential new producer if you could say, "This play was originally scheduled for a six-week run; but, due to rave reviews, it was extended an additional ten weeks."

Think logically and sequentially about what the best next step might be. Be realistic: Don't make the mistake of thinking your work is going to jump from a fifteen-performance run at a ninety-nine-seat theatre to an open-ended commercial Off-Broadway production; absent extraordinary events, there most likely will be at least one or two interim productions as the work continues to gather momentum.

Again, do your homework and be methodical. The frustrations of finding a second production can be formidable, and you must be prepared for yet another excruciating round of submissions.

If you haven't yet created a publicity packet, it's best to do it now, with positive reviews in hand. Your existing query letter can be amended into a letter trumpeting the success of the work. You can either include copies of reviews, if there are just a couple of good ones, or create a composite review sheet containing engaging statements or paragraphs from a number of different reviews, similar to the string of critics' quotes one sees in advertisements. Of course, don't forget to update the production history of the work on any other materials you send out, such as your resume.

Having had a full production may eliminate you from contests and competitions specifically looking for unproduced work. But don't fret, because other doors that previously were off-limits will open for you now.

Send another round of announcements to your computerized mailing list. Talk with your director to see if she or he has any recommendations as to where you might send the script next. Consider grants or other prizes that are awarded only to works that *have* been produced. Publishers may express interest in your work, but be careful about moving in this direction prematurely (see the chapter on publishers for a discussion of this topic). Depending on the level of production, this might be the time to consider talking to agents (see the chapter on representation), but try not to get ahead of yourself. Most likely, you will want to capitalize on your production's success to move to a second or third production, which will only improve your prospects elsewhere.

Chapter 5

PRODUCTION
CONTRACTS

THE FOLLOWING DISCUSSION about productions uses the word "producer" to encompass all types of people or entities producing theatre: all ongoing institutional theatre companies, including any small and midsize not-for-profit theatres, whether they produce entire seasons, annual productions, contests, competitions, festivals, plays in repertory, etc.; and all commercial producers, regardless of location. In some ways, differences in venues and sizes of productions warrant consideration, and I have tried to indicate situations in which that might arise. However, the majority of authors' issues are not affected by the level of production, so most of the discussion applies across-the-board to all types.

Having a production fundamentally requires the existence of a contract, yet writers are often hesitant and nervous about bringing up the issue. The focus of conversations with a producer have probably concerned how much the producer loves the play and both the writer's artistic vision and the producer's vision of the production. The writer may be afraid that if a contract is even mentioned, the producer will become defensive and disenchanted, as if such a discussion implied the producer was untrustworthy. There could also be apprehension that a contract would somehow taint the creative partnership.

Rethink this approach to what a contract is and the purposes it serves. Remember that you are entering into a bona fide business relationship and, as such, it should be treated like all other business relationships in a writer's life.

When you rent an apartment, you naturally expect there to be a lease. When you obtain and use a credit card, you naturally expect there to be written information explaining and confirming the details of the arrangement. If you take out a mortgage, you naturally expect to sign loan documents with the lending institution. And just as naturally, both you and the producer should expect that your relationship is complex enough to necessitate formalizing the arrangement.

THE IMPORTANCE OF CONTRACTS

Contracts are necessary for the purpose of memorializing what has been agreed to by the parties involved. It is a normal and necessary part of the process.

Contracts clarify your previous conversations. Since language is not precise, it is not uncommon for two people to end a conversation with different perspectives on what was resolved; this is often true where they don't know each other well, when each is trying to impress the other, and when the talk is in broad strokes, not focused on details. Each party comes to the relationship with different expectations (and possibly even misconceptions) based on past experience, what friends and colleagues have said of their experience, myths, and so forth. Without the shared language of a contract, misunderstanding is almost inevitable.

Contracts force both parties to focus on the important details of their arrangement, some of which may not be realized until discovered in negotiations. Making a contract provides the opportunity to anticipate and address difficult situations in an amicable fashion, before they become problems. Even small things neglected or understood differently can cause heated discussions, create uncomfortable situations or engender deep resentment if, months or years into a project, writer and producer disagree about who promised what to whom. Most of this can be avoided by a thorough discussion of all details in the beginning.

Contracts underline the import of each party's rights, responsibilities and obligations. People ordinarily enter into contracts only after carefully considering what they are promising; they don't usually sign them with the intention of breaking them. One wouldn't sign a lease for a year's rent knowing he or she would be living there for only two months. Similarly, the relationship between a writer and producer is not to be taken lightly; these are your careers at stake.

In addition, option periods stipulated in production contracts typically run between one and three years. It is natural for memories, motivations and intentions to change over that period of time, but the document remains the same, so it enables parties to look back and remember what they actually agreed. This is not to say that circumstances won't change in the interim, which perhaps may compel the parties to agree to change the document later; but even if that situation arises, the original contract creates something substantive and tangible, a starting point easily referenced.

Given the above, it should be clear that a contract is in the best interest of all parties, and that the *absence* of any memorialization of the arrangement puts parties at significant risk. Consequently, a writer's antennae should twitch a little if a producer balks at the idea of entering into a contract. If a misunderstanding arises and no contract exists, the parties will be left to fight it out, which is certainly not conducive to achieving the best possible production.

Contracts do not taint a relationship. It is far better to address issues, even difficult ones, reach a resolution, commit them to writing and be able to focus on a production and its artistic needs than to try to avoid discussing potential conflicts. Ignoring areas of disagreement will not make them go away, nor will it enhance the relationship.

Remember, too, that silence can be misinterpreted. While you may not raise an issue because you didn't want to "rock the boat" just when everything was coming together, your silence could easily be (mis)read as approval or assent, and that, too, could cause problems later on.

BASIC CONTRACTS ARE BEST

Contracts don't have to be unwieldy and obtuse documents that no one can understand. Certainly there is a list of issues that should be addressed in any writer's production contract and, generally, the bigger the production, the bigger the contract. But, in most instances, straightforward agreements of reasonable length are quite workable.

Strive for plain language that can be understood by the parties; while some "legalese" will be warranted, we've all read contractual paragraphs that leave us scratching our heads, wondering what we're being asked to agree to. However, language is not inherently infallible, so you may have to work to find the right words. If the language is vague, clarify it. If it feels too broad, be more specific. If you are uncertain about the meaning of a phrase, sentence or clause, have each party explain its interpretation of the provision to be sure there is a "meeting of the minds."

No one can anticipate every possible circumstance that may arise after a contract has been signed, and you should try not to look *too* far down the road, because that could turn a succinct document into a confusing mess. Think about what is important to both parties for the immediate production and, if applicable, create a basic structure opening the way to a second production.

Generally, it's not wise to try to work out every detail of a second production before the first gets off the ground. It's virtually impossible for either party to possess enough information to make reasoned decisions that far in advance, so it's best to avoid spending excessive amounts of time focusing on the long-term minutiae. Strive to find a balance between providing the producer with reasonable assurances about the future and allowing the author room to negotiate fair and reasonable terms as the value of the work increases through successful production.

The most important fundamental concepts to incorporate into production contracts are balance and fairness. Look at the underlying issues and focus on what is fair and reasonable. Strive to craft a reasonable, practical document for *both* sides, not just the producer or just the author.

Remind yourself over and over that the first contract proffered is intended to represent a *first offer*. No one expects you to sign that very document; to the contrary, producers often purposely add terms to a contract that they anticipate will be renegotiated or simply eliminated, which is part of the negotiation process. You will perhaps be thought naive if you don't understand this.

It's hard for stage writers, or any writers for that matter, to accept the fact that an offer of production is not a gift, even while acknowledging that there is an inherent imbalance of power in the relationship and, therefore, in the negotiations. But rather than acquiescing to everything the producer suggests, treat reaching this agreement as you would any other in your life.

For example, if you were in the market to buy a house, and you looked at one listed for $100,000, even in a relatively tight market you would never just agree to that figure and sign a contract without looking carefully at the contractual terms and at the benefits and risks of that particular house; you would undoubtedly make a counterproposal, and the negotiation would continue from there. Most likely, the seller of the house would have named a higher price than she or he really expected to get, knowing that she or he would have to compromise, based on the condition of the house and other factors.

A production contract is no different. Yes, producers have lots of work to choose from, and yes, you want a production and don't want to "blow the deal." But trying to negotiate a fairer contract should not put you at risk of losing the production. While you might not win all your points, no legitimate producer should walk away from a deal just because the writer wants to negotiate.

IMPORTANT PRODUCTION PROVISIONS

The following presents the core concepts of an author's production contract. Remember that different levels of production may warrant different terminology and may necessitate addressing additional issues.

REPRESENTATIONS, WARRANTIES AND INDEMNIFICATION

The essential purpose of these provisions is for the writer and the producer to make certain fundamental statements and promises to each other and to allocate responsibility for certain problems that could arise. The writer states that he or she is the sole owner and author of the play, that the work is original and doesn't copy someone else's work (except to the extent that it is based on public domain material or that permission to use another person's work has been obtained), that copyright in the work will be secured and maintained in those countries that have signed the international treaties addressing copyright matters (most notably the Universal Copyright Convention and the Berne Convention), and that producing the work won't infringe another party's rights. The writer also states that he or she has the authority to enter into the production contract and, most important, that if it later turns out the writer was not stating the truth about these assurances, she or he will take responsibility for any resulting legal judgments (or settlements made with the writer's consent). The phrase most commonly used is that the writer will "hold harmless and indemnify" the producer.

Consider the following example: A writer claims to be the sole author of a play and the producer reasonably relies on that statement. After the contract has been signed, another writer appears, with evidence of having co-written the play with the writer who signed the contract, and therefore making claims on the play and the production. The producer would reasonably expect the writer who signed the contract to take responsibility for those legal problems, because they would result from a breach of the representation and warranty made by that writer to the producer.

In a reciprocal fashion, the producer makes certain statements and promises to the writer. The producer states that he, she or it has the authority to enter into the contract, that by signing the contract the producer doesn't violate other agreements or obligations to third parties, and that the producer will "hold harmless and indemnify" the writer against legal judgments (or settlements made with the producer's consent) relating to the production of the play (or any element thereof) not related to the writer's representations and warranties.

It is important that there be reciprocal representations and warranties (running both from author to producer and from producer to author). This is not to say that these paragraphs should be identical, but each side's obligations to the other party should be in the contract.

THE OPTION PERIOD AND GRANT OF RIGHTS

These two provisions necessarily go hand in hand. Essentially, they address what the producer has the right to do within a certain period of time. The contract should state clearly the time frame of the option period, the category of rights being granted from the writer to the producer, and the applicable geographic territory. The contract should also state clearly that if there is no production by the end date of the option period, the rights terminate automatically and revert to the writer. As discussed below, the producer's rights should not be drafted too broadly; ideally, both the option and grant of rights will be specific in terms of the geographic area and level of production the producer will be targeting for production, and the time period will be tailored appropriately.

Most if not all contracts contain both the option and production terms in one document, because no one will want to have to go through another negotiation after six months or a year, especially since what could become apparent over time is that the parties cannot agree on important, fundamental terms. Besides, if the option agreement were a completely separate document from the production contract, intervening events might significantly change each party's position, potentially causing problems in the relationship. And the risk in signing only an option agreement first (which enables the producer to move towards production) is that if it becomes increasingly difficult to compel the producer to resolve the outstanding details as the production gets closer, performances may begin without a signed production contract in place.

The option period

The option period is the amount of time granted to the producer to mount the production. Obviously, no producer can obtain production rights and begin performances the next week. A producer's many responsibilities (which differ somewhat, depending on whether the producer is a theatre company or a commercial producer) include hiring a general manager of day-to-day operations, drafting budgets, raising money, working with the author to select a director, renting a theatre (if there is no home base), helping to hire actors and designers, overseeing weeks of rehearsals, making sure the production elements are realized, designing and implementing a marketing strategy, selling advance tickets, and on and on. All of these things take time, and all are of course dependent on the producer being able to raise the necessary funds. Consequently, the length of the option period will vary with the level of production; for example, it necessarily will take longer to produce a play Off-Broadway (for which the producer must reasonably raise $300,000 to $600,000 or more) than for a limited-run production in a ninety-nine seat theatre.

In essence, by agreeing to an option period, the writer says, "I'll grant you the right to produce my play, and you have one year (or whatever time frame reasonably applies to that level of production) to put it together. If you can't begin performances one year from today, then you will lose these rights." And the producer says to the writer, "I'm going to *try* to produce this play, but there is no guarantee that I will be able to put it all together. I will use this time to the best of my ability, but at the end of the option period, if I am not successful, I will not 'owe' you anything more than the option payment you have already received. You will simply get your rights back. We will go our separate ways, and you will be free to find another producer."

Both parties are taking some risks. If exclusive rights to a particular market have been granted to the producer, the writer takes the play off the market for some period of time, but may not have a production to show for it. (While the writer *does* get to keep the option payment, that's not the production she or he obviously wants, and certainly the amount of the option payment for stage works is never enough to allow a writer to kick back and relax.) The producer works hard during the option period to get the play produced, but may not be able to make all the pieces fit, and thus also may not have a production to show for all the work done and money spent.

It's best to create the option in increments rather than long periods and lump-sum payments. For example, if an option period is going to last for two years altogether, it's best for it to be structured as one year plus two six-month extensions.

There is a fundamental reason for this from the writer's point of view, and *no* risk to the producer. Remember: the option represents a producer's agreement to *try* to put together a production, not a guarantee. For any number of reasons, a producer may not remain enthusiastic about a project for a two-year period; in a worst-case scenario, the producer may lose interest because he or she can't raise the money, has other problems, etc., and the writer will want to retrieve the rights as soon as possible, in the hope of finding a new producer. If the option period were for a flat two years and problems arose early, the writer would be in the uncomfortable and vulnerable position of having to ask for the rights back, or even of having to offer to buy them back. If, however, the option period were structured incrementally, with natural "resting" points built in, the rights would automatically revert to the writer if the producer would not be able to, or would decide not to, continue to make payments to extend the option. Incremental payments can also serve as a perhaps not-so-gentle reminder to the producer to reevaluate the commitment to the work periodically. Incremental payments are not necessarily higher than lump-sum payments, and no producer sincerely interested in producing a work would be discouraged by such payments.

The risk to the writer in this type of structure is that when it comes time for the producer to write the check for the second or third option payment, she or he may opt out. The writer risks a few dollars at that point, but knows, at least, whether the producer is or is not still committed to the project. If so, the writer receives the next payment. If not, the rights revert.

Under either scheme—the flat period or the incremental structure—the writer cannot unilaterally change his or her mind and withdraw the agreed-upon grant of rights, as long as the option payments are made, so the producer's rights remain fully protected.

As mentioned, different levels of production warrant different option periods: For small productions in a ninety-nine seat theatre or comparable arena, six to nine months is typically sufficient, although a one-year period may be reasonable depending on the circumstances. For regional theatre and comparable productions, one year (i.e., one season) is typically sufficient, although some works may merit a two-year option period, which could certainly be negotiated between the parties. For Off-Broadway or comparable productions, the optimal option period runs from one to two years although, depending on the work, three years overall may make sense (incrementally, of course). However, if the work in question has just had a well-reviewed production and is thus gathering momentum, one to two years generally should be all that is necessary for the producer to capitalize on existing publicity and word-of-mouth. For Broadway or comparable productions, the maximum time frame is generally two years for a play and three years for a musical, again structured incrementally.

No producer's options should last longer than two to three years, absent extraordinary extenuating circumstances.

Grant of rights

Be specific. Which rights will be granted is often the subject of much discussion. From the writer's point of view, it's best for the grant to be relatively specific: The writer wants to negotiate for particular levels of production, rather than simply granting "all rights" to the producer, letting the producer loose in the marketplace to put "something" together.

A writer should be able to go into this relationship with certain expectations as to the type of production that might result. For example, if the writer believes she or he has negotiated a deal for a theatre to present her or his work on its mainstage for at least three weeks, but the theatre believes it retains the right to choose instead to produce the work on its second stage for just a few nights, this could wreak havoc. Or, if a writer thinks that a commercial producer will try to produce the play in New York, but the grant of rights language is so broad that the producer could choose to produce the play in Chicago instead, the parties will understandably not be happy with each other later. The contract should state clearly in what arena(s) the producer is granted the exclusive right to produce the play. A producer needs a strategy, and should be able to give the writer a pretty clear idea of where he or she wants to go with the work. (The producer presumably would also need to explain this to potential investors or funders.) The producer should talk to the writer about the production strategy and the contract should reflect this reality.

If a producer has contacts in, experience with and resources for a particular market and will target efforts there, little or no reason exists to draft the contract in broader terms than those necessary to accomplish the intended production. For example, if a producer has the desire and resources to mount a ninety-nine seat production, it is unnecessary to grant that producer concurrent Broadway rights. Later, if it becomes appropriate, the producer can enter into a Broadway contract with the writer.

Here it's important to mention what are referred to as "additional" or "subsequent" production rights, and to distinguish concurrent production rights from serial production rights. It may make sense, as discussed below, to create a structure that allows the producer to move the play from its initial production into a second, presumably bigger and more visible production. Such a structure would appropriately move the relationship through a natural progression of events one step at a time. That is very different from a producer starting out from square one with a broad grant of concurrent rights. (In other words, the writer grants the producer the right to first produce in arena A. If the producer succeeds, he or she earns the right to move to arena B, and so on. No reason exists for the writer to start out by saying to the producer, "Here are arenas A through Z. They're all yours.")

While a producer may have a particular plan, some degree of flexibility may be warranted, because no one can predict what might happen. A staged reading, workshop or backers' audition may be the best possible route to take to a fully realized production, so it's not unreasonable to provide the producer with the ability to decide among them by building such interim steps into the contract. Similarly, while a producer may begin by talking about one level of production, he or she could "hit the jackpot" while working on it and decide to "upgrade" to a different level of production; this, too, can *easily* be anticipated and included in the contract. Obviously, it is in the writer's best interest *not* to tie the producer's hands too tightly.

What is important is to *balance* each party's concerns while drafting the contract. You will want to strive to grant the producer the option needed to produce the play within a specified period of time which allows for reasonable development, but not to go overboard by tying up rights that are not essential to the immediate production.

Exclusivity. Exclusive rights give only one producer the right to produce a play for an agreed-upon period of time. Non-exclusive rights allow a writer to sign contracts with more than one producer for multiple productions that may occur simultaneously or in close proximity, either geographically or temporally.

Granting exclusive rights presents a level of risk for a writer, because it means taking your work off the market for a defined period of time with no guarantee of production. However, acquiring exclusive rights can be very important to a producer, who won't likely want to expend a lot of time, energy and money only to find out there will be another, competing production. At certain levels of production, and at certain points in the work's life, exclusivity is warranted and even necessary, usually for the first series of productions. Once the work has achieved a certain degree of success, then the demand for exclusivity falls off. In fact, after the work begins its journey into the secondary markets around the world—when the goal is to get the play produced as often as possible—exclusivity would be counterproductive.

The following is a common example of such a progression: First, a regional theatre receives exclusive rights to give a play its premiere production; then a commercial producer wants to move the work into the commercial arena and needs exclusive rights to do so; then the work is signed with Dramatists Play Service and released into the stock and amateur market. With stock and amateur licensing, since no one theatre can claim geographic exclusivity, non-exclusive rights are the norm (although the licensing organization will probably grant some limited degree of exclusivity so that there won't be competing productions in the same city or town).

The decisions surrounding exclusivity and non-exclusivity cannot be reduced to an exact formula. There are certainly norms to which the industry adheres generally, but do not look for absolute rules: Evaluate, instead, the circumstances of each work at each stage of its life.

Geographic territory. Geographic territory is also a specific right granted to the producer. Just as a producer cannot effectively try to produce a play in multiple venues simultaneously, neither can it effectively try to produce the play "anywhere in the world."

A producer's strategy must integrate not only level of production but also general *location*. Although it is always possible that a producer's plans may involve road-testing material (and the contract should be structured accordingly), it is best not to grant rights unnecessarily. Do not grant the New York producer, for instance, rights in Chicago, Los Angeles, London or anywhere else in the world *unless* the producer intends and plans to produce your work in these locations within a specified time frame.

The option payment

The phrase "option payment" is often used interchangeably with the word "advance," so don't be confused if you are offered either. (There are a couple of limited-case exceptions in which the writer will be paid both an option payment and an advance, but these are so specific as to be less relevant here.)

Production rights granted to a producer—including every extension of the option period—have value, in return for which the producer should make a reasonable option payment to the writer. This is the quid pro quo: an exchange of rights in return for payment. Usually, the *existence* of an option payment isn't in question, only the *amount*. Even for smaller venues, it is reasonable for a writer to negotiate an option payment; for larger venues, the dollar amounts would simply increase.

An option payment is the writer's "insurance"; if the producer isn't able to produce the work within the option period, at least the writer has received *something* for his or her work. It is also a symbolic acknowledgement of the producer's respect for your work. Be wary of doing business with producers who want free, or nearly free, options. While it's understandable from a human point of view that a writer might be so excited by the prospect of a production that he or she would be inclined to give the option away for free or for so little money that it might as well be free, no writer should ever be asked to do that. This is *not* to say that writers can expect to earn significant amounts of money from option payments or that they should walk away from small offers; that would be completely unrealistic. It *is* to say, however, that value exists in an option on rights granted, and an option payment should be paid.

The exact amount of an option payment is negotiable, so try to speak up for yourself and your work: There is no single dollar amount that automatically applies to all options and venues (though there are customary ballpark figures for different venues; e.g., Broadway option rights will cost more than those in regional theatre, etc.). Artistic endeavors such as plays and musicals don't generally have an intrinsic value—they acquire value as audiences respond—so the industry has established rough figures on which to base negotiations for each level of production as well as other factors enumerated below. Don't get caught up in the myth that an option payment somehow approximates "fair market value" or a "wage" for the time you've spent writing the play.

The amount to be paid will depend on whether the rights granted are exclusive or non-exclusive, the level of production for which rights are granted, the length of the option period, the interest in the play, whether or not the play has been produced previously, and the great intangibles: the respective bargaining powers of writer and producer, and how badly each wants to make the production happen. The writer should *never* have to pay anyone to produce your work, or have to contribute money to the production costs. While it may be tempting to do so—whether out of frustration or desperation about getting the play produced—this is *not* generally considered a "legitimate" way of producing theatre.

The following ballpark figures are just that: ballparks. It can't be repeated enough that any change in a range of issues could easily result in a shift of these figures. With such general guidelines, there is always the risk that some readers will interpret dollar amounts as absolutes rather than as negotiable ranges, so let there be no misunderstanding here: These figures are *not* to be taken as specific amounts producers are "required" to pay.

Consider a one-year exclusive option period for a full-length work. (Obviously if the option period were only six months, the option payment would be proportionately reduced, since the writer would be taking the work off the market for a shorter period of time and thus would be exposed to less risk. Similarly, if the work in question were a one-act that must be paired with another to make a complete evening, the producer would be making *two* option payments—one for each of the one-act plays—and, again, the option payment would be reduced; in this case, probably halved.) For smaller venues, the general range of option payments runs from $200 to $1,500, with the higher figure often unattainable, assuming a small production budget. In a regional theatre, the general range of option payments runs from $1,000 to $5,000, depending on the size of the theatre and its Actors Equity contract classification. Often, a good rule of thumb for negotiating an option payment is to figure out one week's writer's royalty at five percent of the gross weekly box office receipts (six percent for a musical), assuming roughly seventy percent paid capacity as a fair balance between the writer's and producer's expectations.

The general range of option payments for an Off-Broadway production is also between $1,000 and $5,000 for a one-year option. If the work has previously been produced to good reviews, the writer may be able to parlay this earlier success into the higher range, which a producer might accept since such a work already has value attached to it, and the producer is assuming less risk than with an unproduced or untested play.

The first-class arena (e.g., Broadway or West End) works differently. If the writer is a member of the Dramatists Guild, the member will use the Guild's Approved Production Contract ("APC") for a first-class production. These contracts (different for plays and musicals) were negotiated between the Guild and the League of American Theatres and Producers, which is the organization representing first-class producers and theatres. The use of this contract as the basis of the relationship between a Guild member and a producer is not negotiable, and it actually benefits both sides since they don't have to create a new, and complicated, document from scratch. It thus also enables the producer to avoid incurring thousands of dollars in legal fees just to draft the agreement, and the writer and producer can begin their discussions from a position predetermined to be fair and reasonable to both sides.

If an individual author had to negotiate the contract from scratch—as non-Guild members do—he or she would probably not be able to attain the level of terms contained in the APC. Those writers who are not members of the Guild, and who thus are not able to avail themselves of the APC, may find themselves in a difficult and potentially expensive position.

The APC contains both option payments and an Advance (note the capital "A"), which is a lump-sum payment made on the first day of rehearsal *in addition to* the option payments that have already been made. The specific terms of the APCs for both plays and musicals are beyond the scope of this chapter, in part because the document contains extensive quid pro quos and in part because it is quite detailed. If you are approached for this level of production, it is suggested that you contact the Guild so you understand fully what your choices are at that time.

Obviously, not every possible production venue can be addressed here. The best advice for different circumstances is to research similar venues to try to establish reasonable parameters for negotiation, bearing in mind the above-enumerated guidelines. For example: A 225-seat theatre in Tulsa, Oklahoma wants to produce a writer's play for two weeks, with eight performances each week. The theatre is appreciably larger than a ninety-nine seat venue, but the length of the run is shorter than the twenty-one performance minimum of most mainstage regional theatre productions. This first analysis should go a long way towards reducing the range of figures to be negotiated from the outset.

The writer would then try to find out the average ticket price and run some figures to estimate one week's royalties at seventy percent capacity. Assuming a ticket price of twenty dollars, 225 seats and sixteen performances yields a gross weekly box office potential of $72,000, of which seventy percent is $50,400. Given a five percent royalty for a play, the writer's estimated royalty for one week would be roughly $2,500. Depending on the level of production, this might feel like an appropriate option price or it might feel high. The goal is to arrive at a proposed figure that feels comfortable, fair and reasonable to the writer, yet leaves room to negotiate.

Never enter negotiations believing the figure the producer offers is what the writer should accept automatically or that the producer should simply agree to the figure the writer wants. Anticipate the need to make a counterproposal and think carefully about how much less you are prepared to accept.

Timing of payment

Option payments are supposed to be up front money, paid to the writer upon signing the contract. It's best not to agree to wait until the day of first rehearsal, or the day some portion of the production money is raised, or the first performance, or any later time to receive this money, absent extenuating circumstances (such as an advance large enough to cover your royalties for the entire run that is paid in two installments, with one installment still being paid upon signing). Doing so defeats the whole purpose of the option payment which, as indicated above, acts as insurance of sorts, protecting the writer from having the option period expire without a production transpiring or the option payment changing hands. Producers might argue that they just can't afford the option payment out of pocket—that it's "fairer" for them to be able to wait until they've raised some money from others. No writer wants to be accused of treating a producer unfairly, but this is part of the producer's business. Responsible and experienced producers walk into a relationship *knowing* they will have to make the option payment up front.

Recoupability

Option payments are always nonrefundable and, most often, are recoupable from royalties. This means that if the producer is not able to mount the production within the agreed-upon option period, the writer keeps the option payment; but, if the producer does begin performances within the option period, the producer is entitled to recoup the option paid from the weekly royalties earned by the writer.

AUTHOR'S RIGHTS

The writer should always retain certain fundamental rights; specifically, ownership of the copyright in the work, the right to attend all rehearsals, script approval rights and artistic approval participation.

Copyright ownership

The ownership of copyright can be handled in the production contract in a straightforward fashion, along the following lines: "The copyright of the work, including any extensions or renewals, shall be in the name of the author." While this may seem obvious, given the fact that writers own the copyright in their work from the moment it is created, it is important to include this clause to have the producer *acknowledge* that the writer owns the copyright.

Nowhere in the document, here or elsewhere, should there be any language which states, implies or could be construed as granting or allowing a director to make a copyright claim on the script or the production. This includes any restrictive language that would grant so-called "property" or "proprietary" rights in the script to a director (see the chapter on developing areas).

Rehearsals

The right to attend rehearsals is also handled in a simple manner: "The author has the right to attend all rehearsals." This is a crucial statement, because it makes clear that the writer cannot be closed out of the rehearsal process; that is, has the right *not* to be excluded against his or her will. This is different from a situation where the author is unable to attend all the rehearsals. The producer might also add a second sentence, providing that the author will attend rehearsals as needed but will be excused for "reasonable cause." Even if the author's schedule dictates missing some rehearsals, you still want to establish contractually your threshold right to attend.

It's important to focus for a moment on author etiquette at a rehearsal. Having the right to attend all rehearsals does not allow the author to control the rehearsal. To the contrary, the rehearsal is the domain of the director, with the author retaining rights of participation; authors will learn through experience with different directors how each works best in such situations. Ordinarily, it is the director who talks directly to the actors, not the author. The author often sits in the audience, taking careful notes but *not* interrupting the director's discussions with the actors. After each rehearsal the director should spend time with the author to go through his or her notes. The author's concerns are certainly not to be ignored by the director, since the author's vision is of utmost importance; but, the author should be mindful of the appropriate time and place to raise any issues.

The contract should also address the writer's commitment to being available to attend rehearsals (which can easily last several weeks) and to work on the play throughout rehearsals and preview performances, together with the extent to which the producer will pay the writer's travel and accommodation expenses, plus a per diem, for time spent working in and during rehearsals and previews, ordinarily encompassing opening night, too. Note that writers do not receive any extra payment or fee for working on the piece during rehearsals and previews (i.e., for making necessary rewrites); but, rather, for expenses incurred to be at the theatre.

Script approvals

The script approvals clause is lengthier than these others and, in many respects, it constitutes the heart of the stage writer's relationship to the producer and the production, establishing that the author alone makes final decisions about changes in the work (and that the author owns all revisions made to the work), which must be adhered to by the producer, director and actors. Script approvals should *never* be limited by the phrase "not to be unreasonably withheld."

The contract should therefore state that the work is the artistic creation of the writer; that no changes, alterations and/or omissions will be made to the work without the writer's prior written consent; and that any changes which are made (with the writer's permission) also belong to the writer, free from any obligation to make payments to anyone who suggested or made any changes. In other words, there will be no liens or encumbrances placed on the work, no matter what anyone besides the author may have contributed. The producer often also has a further obligation: not to permit anyone involved in the production (the producer's employees) to tamper with the authorship of the play by making claims of authorship or collaboration. (This rather volatile subject is discussed in greater depth in the chapter on developing areas.)

Ultimately, the author's relationship with the director is the primary focus here. A certain amount of friction may be inevitable between an author's right not to have any changes made to the work without his or her consent and the director's responsibility to interpret the work. Obviously, authors don't want their work misinterpreted or bastardized, especially if it's the premiere or another early production to be reviewed; yet, directors are hired for their skills at interpretation, and one cannot expect or demand blind adherence to the author's stage directions. In the end, authors and directors must learn to work together, and to find areas of compromise and flexibility. Listen to the director's view and consider it carefully: Don't reject all suggestions out of hand, but *do* speak up and tell the director why something isn't working for you or is inconsistent with your vision.

There may be a separate sentence in the contract stating that the producer has the right not to accept changes made unilaterally by the author while the work is under option. In other words, the producer is saying, "I optioned a certain work I liked. While I have it under option—meaning that I'm going to be the producer—I don't want you, the writer, to come to me with revisions that haven't already been discussed with either the director or me. You can revise the work any way you want later, but for as long as I hold my option, the only changes you make to the script should be ones we agree on."

The script approvals clause does *not* contain language allowing a writer to argue that the work does not need revision. (Generally speaking, all works need revision.) Rather, the contractual questions should revolve around what those revisions will be, how they will be made, and the establishment of clear rights and responsibilities.

It's important to create a structure whereby revisions can be requested (usually in writing, if the author isn't at the theatre) and either agreed to or denied. This should involve an agreed-upon turnaround time. It's not a good idea to leave this vague, as in "The author agrees to respond promptly" or "in a timely fashion," since the director and author could reasonably entertain different ideas as to what constitutes a prompt or timely response. Most often, this period will be 72 hours from the time the request is received.

The related question, then, is what to do if the author does *not* respond within the established time frame. From the author's perspective, lack of response should be deemed a denial of the request. The producer may not like this, since it means that changes the producer or director thinks are important may not be addressed. Having optioned the play, the producer may feel entitled to have such issues addressed and resolved, not ignored—not an unreasonable position—but, from the author's point of view, it is dangerous to allow changes to be made without the author's input.

As a practical matter, the author should be especially diligent to respond to all requests for revisions, even if ultimately she or he does not agree to make them. One must also distinguish here between the author's responsibility to be available to discuss and make revisions and the author's decision whether or not to make them. An author is not required to make every revision requested by the producer.

Artistic approvals

It is important for the author to be actively involved in the artistic process. Consequently, language in the contract should state either that the producer and author will have "mutual approval" over the choice of artistic personnel or else that the author will have approval over them; mere "consultation" rights are insufficient. Under consultation rights, a producer could discuss the writer's opinion about choosing artistic personnel, but then make a decision that the writer doesn't approve. For true active participation, the author's rights must be those of approval, not just consultation.

It is also important that the author's approval rights should *not* be restricted by the phrase, "not to be unreasonably withheld." In a worst-case scenario, the producer or director could characterize an author as "unreasonable" about any disagreement. If this phrase can't be completely excised from the contract, then it must be applied equally to both parties; that is, both parties agree not to act unreasonably with respect to artistic decisions.

An author's participation in artistic approvals refers specifically to being actively involved in the choice of director, cast, designers and any replacements that may need to be made, and for musicals this would expand to include the choreographer or dance director, musical director or conductor and the arranger. Such involvement should be distinguished from involvement in substantive decision-making about production elements. For example, the author would be involved in choosing the costume designer, but would not have final approval over the designs themselves. A producer may argue that writers don't know enough about designers to make such decisions, and in some cases might be right. It is always hoped that writers will recognize the limits of their experience (or lack thereof) and defer to the producer's expertise; however, it must also be said that not only do writers have a vested interest in the designers chosen, they will learn and grow as artists only by being involved in these decisions, and should be allowed participation in this important area.

A theatre may indicate in the contract that, as a matter of policy, it gives casting preference to actors in its resident acting company, or from its geographic location, or who have worked there in the past, or who perhaps match a philosophy adopted by that theatre, such as nontraditional or multicultural casting. Theatres have a right to establish such policies, and having language to this effect in the contract serves notice to the author from the very beginning that the pool of actors to choose from will not be any actor the author wants from anywhere in the country. This does not mean that the author's likes and dislikes will be ignored; but, rather, that the author needs to work with the theatre within these parameters toward the best mutually acceptable cast. (The same could also apply to the other artistic categories; i.e., the director and the designers.)

Royalties

Except in the case of commissions, an author is not paid to write a play or musical. Until the work is produced, it is a labor of love. Consequently, royalties earned from performances of the work will be the first remuneration an author sees (apart from the option payment) for all of his or her hard work. At some levels of production, this may not translate into much money, but it's very important that the author be paid nonetheless: Payment of royalties is a strong symbol of respect for the work and its worth.

Remember: The relationship between producer and author is a business relationship, with attendant quid pro quos. Production is not a gift from the producer to the author. Peter Franklin of the William Morris Agency wisely commented, "The producer brings the financial capital and the writer brings the creative capital." However good-hearted the producer's reasons for producing theatre, they are not altruistic, and the author should expect—and contract for, from the very beginning—a fair and reasonable royalty once performances begin. A good general rule of thumb: If the producer charges for tickets and thus takes in money at the box office, or charges a fee for the presentation, such as with school performances, the author should receive a royalty. While the specific royalty terms may vary according to the level of production, the act of paying a royalty should never be at issue.

Percentage of gross calculation. An author's royalties are often a percentage of box office receipts, calculated on the gross, *not* on the net (i.e., on *all* of the box office not just what's left after the producer has paid weekly expenses). The phrase to look for in the contract is "gross weekly box office receipts" (GWBOR) which should be followed by a clear definition of those monies that will be included. The producer is ordinarily allowed to deduct from the total amounts collected at the box office certain taxes and commissions, and what is generally thought of as the cost of making money, such as credit card fees, telephone sales commissions and fees, and group sales commissions; however, these deductions should be minimal.

Paying the author a percentage of the gross box office is eminently fair: It automatically adjusts the royalty to the size of the theatre, the ticket price and how many people are in the audience each night. As the audience grows, so will the author's earnings and conversely, on lean nights, the author's royalty will be smaller. If the production is wildly successful, the author should share in that. If belts need to be tightened, the author should tighten his or hers, too. With this structure, neither party has to worry about being underpaid or overcharged; it's fair to both sides.

A reasonable minimum royalty percentage to the author(s) is at least five percent for a play and at least six percent for a musical. For commercial productions, there should always be an increase in the royalty of at least one or two percentage points post-recoupment; i.e., when the show has recouped its production costs. (Licensing of works that have already been produced successfully is a separate issue and addressed in the chapter on publishers.) With these minimums in mind, exact percentages are negotiable between author and producer and sometimes depend in part on the author's reputation and the perceived demand for the particular work.

Flat amount royalties. In some situations (as with amateur productions or when calculation of the GWBOR might be difficult or virtually impossible), the author might instead negotiate flat dollar amounts as royalties rather than a percentage of the GWBOR. In other situations, the author may combine the two types of calculations into one: a flat weekly guarantee against a percentage royalty, whichever yields the higher payment. These scenarios are often found in dinner theatre, where the ticket price includes both dinner and show. Obviously, it wouldn't be fair for the author to receive a percentage of the price charged for dinner, so the author may receive a percentage of just that portion of the ticket allocated to the theatre performance. In such cases, the percentage minimums for newer works are the same as above, with stronger titles—because of name recognition—warranting higher royalties of eight to twelve percent. The portion of the ticket allocated to the show is never more than fifty percent and more usually is roughly thirty-eight to forty-six percent of the overall ticket price. It's also possible the dinner theatre and author will negotiate a fair flat dollar royalty which, depending on the seating capacity—which averages 375—and number of performances per week—generally four to eight—is typically somewhere in the ballpark of $300-$600 per week, or sixty to seventy-five dollars per performance.

A flat dollar amount can be negotiated on a per performance, per week or per run basis. The dollar amounts will vary according to the level of production and other factors particular to that production. Generally, the writer should be advised of the seating capacity, ticket prices and number of performances, which will enable some basic calculations. Ultimately, again, a good general rule of thumb is to focus on the percentage royalty that would be earned at seventy percent of capacity, and to round upwards or downwards as the circumstances dictate. This estimation increases in importance when negotiating flat fees as opposed to option payments, because the allocation of risks is trickier: There won't be a later point in time to make adjustments for mistakes.

When asked to establish flat fees, authors worry immediately about naming a figure that will later prove too low, while producers are concerned about promising payments that later will prove too high. Often, then, a combination of flat fees and percentage payments is best: The author would negotiate to receive the greater of a base flat dollar amount or a percentage of the gross weekly box office receipts. Thus, the author is assured a certain minimum payment for each performance and, if the box office does well, a higher royalty.

This arrangement alleviates the author's fear of being underpaid (the percentage portion takes care of that), so the writer may feel more comfortable agreeing to a relatively low flat dollar amount. At the same time, it frees the producer from concern about overpaying the author, perhaps making him or her more generous in sharing the "wealth" should the show succeed.

Timing of the royalties. Ordinarily, an author receives royalty payments on a weekly basis, within seven days after the end of each performance week (which is usually considered to be Sunday). If the royalty is a percentage of the gross, the contract should provide that the check will be accompanied by copies of the weekly box office statements, signed by someone authorized to attest to the veracity of the contents.

Sometimes a theatre company will want to pay an author at the end of the run rather than weekly. This issue should be approached cautiously. For some theatre companies—often those with many productions running or in rehearsal simultaneously—it's simply a matter of bookkeeping rather than insufficient cash flow; but for others—both individual producers and theatre companies—cash flow may be a serious concern, possibly running the risk that the production will end and there won't be enough money "left over" to pay the author, even if the author's arrangement was to be paid a percentage of gross.

Such a risk should not be borne by the author. Regardless of whether the arrangement is based on a percentage of the GWBOR or a flat dollar amount, the author should not be the last in line to be paid.

Billing credit

Author's billing. The contract should state that the author's billing will appear in all programs, advertising and publicity under the control of the producer, immediately beneath the title on a line of its own, and the type size should not be less than fifty percent the size of the title.

Ordinarily, no one receives larger billing credit than the author (a possible exception is a "star"), and no one except the producer and stars should receive billing credit above the title. If there are multiple authors, the parties must incorporate the terms of the collaboration agreement (see the collaboration chapter).

Mistakes in billing. An important correlative paragraph is one that addresses the producer's responsibility if a mistake is made. In the contract, such a mistake is referred to as a "casual or inadvertent failure" to provide the contractual billing. Normally, the producer has an obligation to rectify the mistake either "promptly" or "as soon as practicable" after receiving written notice of the mistake from the author. Note the use of the word "rectify" rather than the word "correct": Mistakes may occur that can't be corrected without costing the producer lots of money; but, the situation should always be "rectified." For example, if an author's name is inadvertently left out of the program, it may not be feasible for the producer to reprint the entire program because of prohibitive cost. However, the producer can't simply say, "Sorry." The producer would still have an obligation to fix the mistake, which often can be accomplished by printing program inserts containing the correct information.

In the contract, do not use the word "prospectively" in lieu of "promptly" or "as soon as practicable." Prospective responsibility means the producer has an obligation only to fix the mistake *next* time, obviating the need to find a present solution. Using the example above, the producer's obligation would only extend to fixing the mistake the next time programs were printed; but there might not be a second printing, and with the word "prospectively" in the contract, you would not be able to compel the producer to run a correction. The producer may express concern during negotiations that in the absence of the word "prospectively" the author might demand retroactive action or even payment of damages for a mistake; if so, the author should make clear to the producer that that is *not* the intention. The author simply wants to obligate the producer to resolve the problem immediately, not only in the future. Such an agreement compels the parties to think creatively about the best approach to take in case of a billing problem.

Admittedly, some situations are not so easily rectified. Consider a regional theatre that sends its season's marketing brochure to an extensive mailing list. If there is a mistake in the author's billing, reprinting and remailing would be prohibitively expensive, and an insert would not be an option.

There are certainly other solutions to explore, and it may help to call other theatres which have faced similar problems in the past. With creative brainstorming, a solution can always be found, even though it may not be perfect.

Authors need to keep in mind that mistakes do happen. A producer simply can't control every single aspect of a production. No one can or should be expected to guarantee perfection. But an author (and an author's contract) can obligate a producer to find the best solution if and when mistakes occur.

The producer's future billing credit. Future billing credits a play's original producer by name and with the original year of production. If the producer is a theatre company, it will usually include both the managing and artistic directors' names. Generally, future billing credit is granted to the premiere producer; possibly to a second producer, depending on the level of production; and to commercial producers (i.e., Broadway, Off-Broadway, etc.) The obligation ordinarily applies to future productions' programs and publications, and it may be limited to a finite number of years. However, often the obligation is granted on an open-ended basis, depending on the level of the production or whether the work was commissioned by the producer seeking credit.

Some producers may also try to pin down details of the future billing credit; for instance, designating not only the specific page of the program or publication on which it will appear, but also its location on that page, the type size and so on. Since these details necessarily require the consent of an unknown third party (i.e., a future producer or publisher), it may be very difficult for the author to make such specific promises. Future producers sometimes see these promises as not their responsibility since they didn't agree to them. This is especially true for promises made concerning adaptions to other media, such as film or television.

There are four approaches for an author to consider when presented with future billing requests from a producer:

1) Make the future billing credit obligation subject to "best efforts." This means the author must do his or her best to talk future third parties into giving the original producer credit, but the author cannot be expected to refuse the new production or movie/TV project if the third-party producer refuses.

   Be aware that some producers object to "best efforts" since they will not be personally involved in future negotiations. They worry—not without reason—that if the author is not truly obligated, he or she might not make much of an effort.

   To be fair, a first producer has legitimate concerns about billing credit. Future billing credit is an important marketing tool with which to attract other authors, to raise money for future productions and so on.

2) Establish clearly the basic obligation as mandatory ("The author shall provide the producer with billing credit on the

title page in programs and publications"), but keep *specific details* subject only to the author's "best efforts." This binds the author to the fundamental obligation—which should satisfy the producer's future publicity needs—yet affords the writer the necessary flexibility in negotiating with a subsequent producer or publisher. This approach represents a compromise.

3) Use mandatory language throughout to lock in not only the basic obligation but also *all* specific details wanted by the producer. Obviously, this is the least desirable solution for authors, leaving no room to maneuver.

4) Use mandatory language for basic obligations and specific details, but include an additional paragraph stating that if in the future the author finds that the producer's billing credit has become a substantive issue in negotiations, said producer will agree to changes in the billing. This approach represents a compromise.

Keep in mind that if a subsequent producer wants to produce your play, a previous requirement of future billing credit rarely would become a "deal breaker," but it might force the author to bargain away something else. And in negotiations with the first producer, be prepared to balance the importance of this issue against others on the table.

Ownership and control

As stated earlier, the contract should contain two related provisions: first, that the author owns the copyright in the work throughout the world; second, that he or she represents and warrants that he or she is the sole owner and author of the play and that the material contained in the play is original with the author. This may seem redundant, but these two distinct provisions serve different purposes: Think of the representations and warranties provisions as the author providing certain assurances the producer cannot confirm independently and which thus must depend, legally, on the author's statements; by contrast, the copyright ownership paragraph makes the producer acknowledge that the author, not the producer, is the copyright holder.

A related clause is referred to as the "reservation of rights." This statement makes two ideas clear: first, that of the "bundle of rights" owned by the author, only the ones clearly enumerated in the contract are granted to the producer, with all other rights remaining under the author's control; second, that the author won't sign other contracts conflicting or interfering with the rights being granted by *this* contract.

An author should not be forbidden from continuing to market a work as long as no *competing* contracts or productions result. A producer deserves protection from circumstances that could hurt a production's chance at success. (For example, a geographically proximate production, or a film version released simultaneously or before the stage production.) Each situation must be evaluated on its merits, but the goal is balance: Authors don't and shouldn't want to grant rights too broadly without compelling reasons to do so, and producers should not seek more than is fair and reasonable in the given circumstances.

Subsidiary rights participation

The term "subsidiary rights" generally refers to the dispositions of rights the author makes *after* the premiere production. (The contract itself will contain a more specific definition.) Subsidiary rights income, and the idea of sharing some of it with a producer, is complex. A number of interdependent variables must be understood and evaluated separately and together. It is also important not to confuse the author sharing future income with the fact that the author alone continues to own and control the work and thus makes all decisions about future dispositions.

The threshold question is whether the producer's level of production warrants sharing *any* percentage of the author's subsidiary income: The answer is not automatically yes, as addressed below.

If the answer is affirmative, the next level of analysis examines the following factors: 1) the triggering number of performances that sets the obligation in motion; 2) the percentage(s); 3) the period of time during which the obligation will be in effect; 4) the time the obligation begins; and 5) the specific categories or types of dispositions encompassed in the obligation, including the applicable geographic territory. And while not a factor per se, it should be noted that the producer should be in full compliance with the contract (e.g., a producer who has defaulted on monies owed to the author can't fairly expect to participate in the author's subsidiary income).

Level of production. The philosophy underlying subsidiary rights participation is that a successful production substantially enhances the future market value of a work and, consequently, monies that flow to the author because of that level of production should be shared with the producer(s) who first took the risk in producing that work. If Producer A produces a work and Producer B sees the show and wants to take it to a higher level of production, should Producer A receive a percentage of the author's money made from Producer B's production? This may seem eminently fair as stated, but the concept is not without gray areas and complications; not all situations will be that clear.

From the first discussion of subsidiary rights participation on, it has always been understood that an author should not cede a share of future earnings unless her or his show receives a level of production that truly could enhance market value. Some levels of production may provide the first production of the work that helps the author examine and rewrite it, but those are different considerations.

It is impossible to guarantee in advance any production's contribution to market enhancement; at the same time, no one can deny that certain levels of production—for example, Broadway and Off-Broadway, to name the two most obvious—do launch work very visibly, and can substantially help to create a viable market for the work in stock and amateur licensing, foreign productions and film or television adaptation. Consequently, it was decided long ago that instead of trying to *prove* the precise cause and effect relationship during the negotiation of each and every contract, the theatre industry would eliminate the guesswork and would create certain structures which provide the *likelihood* of enhancement at specified levels of production.

Thus, should a production fit into one of these structures, the author could assume the producer would "qualify" or "earn" the right to share in the author's subsidiary income. This provides balance: The author doesn't pay a percentage on non-qualifying productions, but the producer receives appropriately earned percentages.

Currently, it is generally accepted practice that Broadway, Off-Broadway or regional theatre mainstage productions, receiving different degrees of national (or, in some cases, international) attention, qualify for sharing in an author's subsidiary income, but with very different parameters applying to each of these arenas. On the other hand, there is an ongoing debate as to whether and to what degree producers of smaller productions should share, especially considering that if a work subsequently moves into the regional theatre, Off-Broadway or Broadway arenas, the new producer will reasonably want his or her share.

Still, even a small production might enhance the future market value of the work. Depending on the situation, a limited arrangement might make sense (involving very small percentages, brief periods of time and restricted geographic territory).

The following discussion assumes that a production has qualified for *some* degree of subsidiary rights participation. Suffice it to say, the larger, more visible and more marketable the production, the larger the percentage share; however, all factors must be analyzed.

Number of performances. In the vast majority of cases, the minimum number is twenty-one paid public performances of a full production. (No more than eight previews count, and there *must* be an official opening.) If the show isn't scheduled to run that long, the parties can agree to adjust the number of performances; but, as the number of performances shrinks, so too may the value of the production to the author. While the level of production might still qualify the producer for subsidiary rights participation, a reduced number of performances might result in a proportionately reduced share. A reading or a workshop production should not even be considered. Similarly, a short run (less than twelve to sixteen performances) ordinarily would not qualify.

The percentage. The percentage share varies according to the level of production. Within each level the industry has established general ranges which actually benefit the author by providing both a floor and a ceiling within which to negotiate.

For a regional theatre premiere mainstage production that runs at least twenty-one performances (again, with no more than eight previews and an opening night), the generally accepted share in the author's sub-sidiary income is as much as five percent. On occasion if the author's royalty percentage is higher than five percent of the box office, the the-atre may ask to receive that same percentage back in subsidiary rights income (e.g., if the theatre pays a six percent royalty to the author, it could try to negotiate for a six percent share of the author's subsidiary income; but, if the theatre pays only the standard royalty it should not expect a higher subsidiary rights participation). If the original pro-duction was a co-production between theatres (not unreasonable given today's economics) or, depending on the circumstances, if a second regional theatre production follows, the first theatre should agree to make room for the second theatre so that collectively they receive the agreed-upon percentage of the author's subsidiary income. Note, too, that commercial producers may agree to assume responsibility for this prior obligation to the not-for-profit premiere producer.

The structure for Off-Broadway is very different. Because commercial runs are open-ended, the percentage share is allowed to increase up to a cap, depending on the number of performances presented. And the per-centages are higher because the impact of a commercial Off-Broadway production on future markets, both national and international, has his-torically been markedly higher than that of a regional theatre production.

A standard example follows:

From 21-35 performances	10%
From 36-50 performances	20%
From 51-65 performances	30%
Over 65 performances	40%

The ten-percent figure should *never* kick in for fewer than twenty-one performances, and the forty percent should *not* be triggered by fewer than sixty-five.

It should be noted that there is strong disagreement as to whether this same broad structure of participation should be used for the lim-ited subscription runs at not-for-profit Off-Broadway theatres. If there is an open-ended commercial Off-Broadway production after the lim-ited subscription run at the not-for-profit theatre, the author needs to have a reasonable subsidiary rights participation to offer the commercial producer, without going beyond the standard forty percent maximum share. Some not-for-profit theatres have incorporated the full Off-Broadway participation into their contracts, but the writers' community is not happy about it, and an answer has not yet been found.

For Broadway, subsidiary rights participation is handled completely differently. Broadway productions obviously significantly enhance a work's reputation worldwide. The Dramatists Guild's APC provides producers with a number of methods for sharing subsidiary rights income according to the different types of dispositions, such as audiovisual media; stock, amateur and ancillary rights; revivals; etc. Each producer must choose between several alternatives by estimating which type will generate the most money from a particular work. The general range of percentages is similar to those found Off-Broadway, although at times the highest percentage might be fifty percent for audio-visual production rights (film, television). Unfortunately, a complete detailing of the choices a producer faces is beyond the scope of this discussion.

Again, if a writer is *not* a Guild member, and therefore cannot use the Guild contract, these terms are freely negotiable. Some producers have been known to name participation figures as high as fifty percent across all categories.

At the opposite end of the spectrum, if a writer decides that a small production warrants *some* level of participation, two or three percentage points would do, but not more. However, writers are again warned not to agree to any such terms precipitously. Many small theatres do not ask for such percentages, and most authors do not agree with smaller producers who believe they are entitled to something.

Basis of percentage calculation. Percentage of what? In almost all cases, the answer is the author's "net proceeds." Net proceeds are the sums received by the author minus his or her representative's commission, if the author has representation.

There might be times when a regional theatre company wants to carve out a very limited exception to a calculation based on the author's net proceeds. In the case of subsequent commercial productions, the theatre might wish to receive a percentage of the gross weekly box office receipts in lieu of a percentage of the author's earnings. For this to occur, the contract should state clearly that the percentage of the box office receipts would be *instead of* the general sharing arrangement, *never* structured as a second payment on top of the first. A reasonable percentage of the GWBOR would be *much* smaller than the percentage of an author's subsidiary rights income—perhaps one-half to one percent pre-recoupment, increasing by at most one percent post-recoupment. The vast difference in these percentages is due to the fact that the pool of money on which it's calculated—gross weekly box office receipts versus the author's royalty *share* of the box office—is very different.

To illustrate: Assume gross weekly box office receipts Off-Broadway of $100,000 (and, for purposes of simplicity, no representation). An author's royalty of five percent would be $5,000. If a regional theatre were entitled to five percent of the author's net proceeds, that would be five percent of $5,000, or $250. If, however, the regional theatre instead were entitled to half a percent of the GWBOR, that would be $500.

Consequently, a regional theatre might prefer to negotiate a percentage of box office receipts. This is a good arrangement for the author, too, who would not have to share his or her royalties. However, keep in mind that the commercial producer would then have to pay both the playwright and the regional theatre. The author's bargaining strength comes from the fact that the commercial producer has been saved a great deal of money by the regional theatre production, since an expensive first try-out is no longer necessary. Nearly every commercial producer accepts this argument, and the arrangement is very common; most producers *do* assume responsibility for paying the regional theatre so long as the percentage remains low and within the normal industry range.

It should be clearly noted that even if a small production results in a limited subsidiary rights participation, it should *never* involve a percentage of the GWBOR, which is a special arrangement reserved solely for larger productions.

Duration. How long the subsidiary rights participation should last is important, with different levels of production having established different norms. The shorter the time frame, the more likely that a first production is related somehow to the next production; the longer the time period, the greater the likelihood that intervening events (e.g., other productions) actually attracted that subsequent producer's interest.

For example: Assume a regional theatre mainstage production that closes on August 1, 1996, and therefore, a subsidiary rights participation that begins the next day, August 2. If a commercial producer signs a production contract with the author within six months, one could assert with certainty that the commercial producer's interest was directly linked to the premiere production. If a commercial producer signs such a production contract with the author within one or two years after the mainstage production, one could still assert with reason that the commercial producer's interest was directly linked to the premiere production. Up to five years after the production closed, an argument can still be made (with decreasing assurance, but still reasonably), but jump ahead ten, fifteen, twenty years: Is the commercial producer who signs a contract on August 1, 2006 (or 2011, or 2016) excited about the work because of the original production? Probably not.

Since no one can determine absolutely when influence peaks and declines, the industry has established, based on years of history, what it has found to be generally reasonable and fair periods of time for a producer to share in an author's subsidiary earnings. The values assigned to each level of production may seem arbitrary, but at least the same amount of arbitrariness applies both to authors and to producers.

For regional theatres, five years after the last performance is appropriate. For Off-Broadway, it's closer to ten years. As discussed above, Broadway is usually structured as per the Guild's APC. Depending on the alternative chosen, the applicable time period can run as short as five and as long as forty years (although shares in audio-visual production rights may last in perpetuity). And if you decide to grant a participation to a small production, only eighteen months to two years would be reasonable. Understand, though, that a producer earns a percentage of the author's subsidiary income on *contracts signed* within the specified time frame, not on money *received* during it. This was established so producers would not have to worry that an author would make a deal with a new producer to delay payment beyond the sharing period in order to circumvent his or her obligation.

Categories of disposition. The categories or types of dispositions that are encompassed in subsidiary rights participation, and the applicable geographic territories, should be defined explicitly in the production contract. A producer's participation is *not* calculated on "all monies earned by the author" and, again, depends on the level of production.

The normal definition of the types of subsidiary rights dispositions is generally: motion picture, television, videocassette and videodisc rights, audio and audio-visual recordings, radio, first-class, Off-Broadway, second-class and stock and amateur performances presented by someone other than the producer and its licensees and assigns, condensed and tabloid versions, so-called concert tour versions and stage performances of any musical comedy, operetta or grand opera based upon the Work, as well as foreign language performances, all within the appropriate and contractually designated geographic territories. (Note that if the regional theatre is receiving a percentage of the GWBOR from first-class and Off-Broadway productions, instead of a percentage of the author's net proceeds, as discussed above, these two categories would then be deleted from this definitions list to avoid double payments.)

For musicals, the cast album will also be lumped into the general subsidiary rights definition, unless you are negotiating for a commercial production. There, the commercial producer is also granted the rights to produce the cast album (defined as an audio recording of the cast of any production presented by the producer). Although the terms of the cast album agreement are beyond the scope of this book, if the producer does in fact produce the cast album, the musical writers and producer share in the proceeds received from its worldwide exploitation, with sixty percent going to the authors and forty percent going to the producer, in perpetuity.

With respect to geographic territory, motion picture dispositions are handled differently than other categories. Regardless of the level of a first production, motion picture deals (selling the rights to make the play into a movie) enjoy a worldwide geographic territory—which obviously represents a potentially large chunk of money. For regional theatre premiere productions (or any other noncommercial production level), the list of all other dispositions is generally limited to the United States and Canada. Other English-speaking countries (primarily the

British Isles, but possibly Australia and New Zealand) are *sometimes* included; but, the market impact of these productions outside the U.S. and Canada has been questioned repeatedly by authors and agents.

A regional theatre presenting an original mainstage production will not share in foreign stage royalties earned by the author (with only the aforementioned English-speaking countries being possible exceptions). Thus, if the author receives a royalty check from a U.S. stock production, he or she will share that with the regional theatre. If, however, it's a check from a production in Argentina, the royalties will not be shared, absent extenuating circumstances. Obviously, every geographic distinction made will have a direct impact on the author's bank balance.

On the other hand, a Broadway or Off-Broadway producer *will* share in foreign royalties, because these production levels historically result in high visibility and tangible marketing impact around the world, although the percentages may be reduced for the foreign territories. This is not to suggest that regional theatre productions aren't "good"; but, rather, to recognize the fact that foreign producers tend to scout out commercial venues for new works to produce abroad.

ADDITIONAL PRODUCTION OPTIONS

In some situations, a producer may wish to option additional productions of a work should the first production prove successful. This might take the form of extending the run of the first production with no hiatus, but such an extension is usually incorporated into the basic grant of rights. More often, the producer would like to be able to produce the work a second time, presumably in a bigger venue and perhaps at a higher level of production, to try to capitalize on the initial success. There are ways to structure these additional options protecting both producer's and writer's interests, as detailed below. Often granting these rights makes sense, as when the producer has the experience and resources to produce in other venues, but it may not be a good idea to grant these additional production options if the producer's real intent is simply to hold onto valuable rights, thereby usurping the author's place in the "driver's seat" as regards future deal-making. With some productions, producers actually want someone else to move the show while they remain in control of the property, so that they can negotiate themselves into the deal. While this may not be offensive, necessarily, writers must be careful that their best interests are not given short shrift in such negotiations, with the original producer's desire to profit financially taking priority.

If a producer expresses interest in obtaining several different options on a work, authors would do better to grant these options concurrently rather than serially. With concurrent options, a producer's rights run simultaneously; with serial options, one option period follows the next. If options run serially, a producer could tie up your work for years, possibly preventing an author from taking advantage of other opportunities at the best time.

For example: If a work is produced Off-Broadway, its strongest value in other markets—commercial tours, foreign productions, stock and amateur venues, etc.—will be within roughly two to three years of its opening. As time passes, the clamor for that work will gradually subside, as other successful productions hit the market. However, the Off-Broadway producer might want to continue to option and produce the work in a market-by-market fashion (i.e, optioning the work for a particular market and, by producing it there, earning the subsequent right to option the work again for a different market, and so on). The substantive problem is that each option, once exercised, runs for about a year and possibly longer, depending on the market. If an author has to grant one-year options on a market-by-market basis, having one production open before the next one-year option begins to run, productions may not begin in some markets within a reasonable time frame. (And remember: an option is never a guarantee of production—so with serial options, an author might not find out that the producer won't exercise the option in a particular market until third-party interest abates.)

This is why authors and their agents want producers to choose options and territories in which they truly believe they have the ability to produce, leaving the author or agent to maximize other production possibilities during the period of the work's greatest marketability. This can be a difficult point to press with producers, who are understandably nervous about relinquishing any rights which might help them turn a profit.

Another consideration: It's not a good idea to have one contract apply to all productions. Given the difference in levels of production, and the fact that a successful first production improves an author's bargaining position, particularly if that author was previously unknown, an entirely new contract should be negotiated for each production, containing terms appropriate to the new arena.

There *is* a way to create a fair structure for such situations in the initial production contract. It would: 1) specify the types of venues to which the work being optioned *could* be moved (typically one, two or three choices that make sense based on the initial level of production); 2) give the producer a small window of opportunity in which to decide what to do and actually exercise the next option; 3) state the length of this next option period (i.e, the time in which performances in the new venue must begin); and 4) detail the option payments for each possible level of production. The contract would also state that the parties agree to negotiate an entirely new production contract, in good faith and in accordance with industry customs and standards, once the producer has committed to a new production by exercising an option.

After an examination of each of these elements, an example will clarify any confusion.

Levels of production

The producer and the writer need to think realistically about what the next level(s) of production could be. Very few ninety-nine seat productions move right to Broadway, and yet some small theatre producers will try to include this option in the production contract. (While it's understandable to want to protect one's interests, doing it in this fashion seems unrealistic.) Typically, such a production would move to a slightly larger house—perhaps with 150 to 300 seats—either in the same city as the original production or maybe in New York or another major city. Depending on the particular work, a tour might be the next feasible step, or perhaps the producer has contacts in regional theatre and could best expect a second production in that arena.

This is not meant to suggest that each producer needs to exercise four different options simultaneously, securing all possible rights. To the contrary, it suggests that each producer should take an honest look at the work, the initial level of production, the producer's own experience and contacts, the *reasonable* possibilities for a next level of production, and the money necessary to support such a move. Only then can the parties negotiate a fair and reasonable option clause in the original production contract.

The window period

From the date the first production closes, a window period of thirty to ninety days is a fair amount of time for the producer to decide whether to move the production into a different, contractually specified venue. Thirty days is better for an author, but a producer will usually negotiate for sixty or possibly ninety days. The producer doesn't pay extra for this window period.

If the producer decides not to proceed with the work or simply fails to exercise the next option before the window closes, the production rights in question automatically revert to the author. If the producer does want to proceed, either independently or with other producers (subject to the terms of the assignment clause, discussed below), the option can be exercised and a new production contract negotiated.

Length of option period

The length of a subsequent option period will typically be consistent with the customary option periods discussed above. The length of such an option period shouldn't be longer than normal; in fact, depending on the circumstances, a case sometimes can be made that this option period should be shorter (within reason), since the work in question will presumably have had a successful first production and should not be allowed to languish.

Amount of option payment

The ballpark dollar amounts for option payments discussed above remain relevant when negotiating additional option payments, as do all the other factors for balancing risk.

An example

Assume a regional theatre production closes on September 30, 1996. Beginning October 1, the theatre then has sixty days in which to decide whether it wants to and reasonably can exercise an option to move the work to an Off-Broadway theatre. During this sixty-day period, the theatre administrators will evaluate the production's success and will contact commercial producers who might be interested in getting involved in the new production. The regional theatre must make its decision by the sixtieth day. If it decides not to exercise its additional option, it either notifies the writer or simply does nothing, allowing its rights to lapse and revert to the author. If the theatre decides it does want to exercise the additional option, it must notify the author in writing and make the option payment before the sixty days expire. If the original production contract specified an initial one-year option period for this new option, with subsequent extensions, the new option period begins to run when the theatre notifies and pays the writer. Then the parties negotiate a new contract, which will govern their relationship for the Off-Broadway production. This new contract could include its own subsequent production options after the Off-Broadway production. Should performances of the new production not have begun within the new one-year option period, the theatre must send another letter and check to the writer, exercising its extension rights under the original contract.

Other considerations

It is possible that a producer might also want to add two clauses to the initial production contract: one addressing the author's royalty at the next level of production and the other concerning the producer's new subsidiary rights participation should it successfully produce the work in a new venue. Some argue that this defeats the purpose of this structure, since the author would not have a new opportunity to negotiate these important terms; others argue that since each venue dictates the general parameters of these terms, it is questionable how much would actually be gained by subsequent negotiations, even if the author's bargaining position *has* been improved. Although it would be best for the author if these clauses were *not* included, an adamant producer might be accommodated so long as the numbers are fair and reasonable; excessive or one-sided arrangements should be further negotiated before signing. Remember: The work will have had to prove itself successful for the parties to find themselves seriously talking about the next level of production.

In a related vein, the author should be sure the original production contract states clearly that the second production contract will supersede the first contract in its entirety (preventing the producer from picking and choosing from among the most favorable terms in the old and the new), and if the producer "vests" in (i.e., earns) the subsidiary rights participation from the second production, the new sharing arrangement supersedes the old one (so that the author does not owe the producer two separate shares of his or her money).

Whether the additional options you grant are concurrent or serial, be sure each geographic territory stands on its own, with the author receiving an option payment for each one. For example, no producer should try to lump together all English-speaking countries as one territory with one option payment: Australia, New Zealand and the British Isles should be treated separately. As with any other options, if the producer doesn't make the payment on each of the individual territories, the rights to that particular territory would automatically revert to the author.

ASSIGNMENT

Often overlooked or underestimated, the assignment clause is deceptively simple: "The producer shall not have the right to assign or license its rights under the contract without the prior written consent of the author."

What this means is that if the producer wants to bring in other producers—not an unlikely occurrence if the producer moves the work into the commercial arena—or if the producer wants to license the work to an unrelated third party, the author's interest in those transactions cannot be overlooked, and the author retains the right of prior written consent.

This provision serves a very important purpose. When an author enters into a contract with a producer, it is intended to be an agreement with that particular person or company. If the producer later wants to change this relationship, the rights to the work should never be treated as fungible goods that can simply be passed from producer to producer for the "right price," a concept based on the unfounded assumption that authors would be just as happy with one producer as another. The relationship between an author and producer is more personal than that, based in part on factors such as artistic vision and trust, not just who has the biggest bank account. Indeed, there may be a producer with access to money who just doesn't feel right as the producer of a particular work, or other authors' negative experiences with that producer may come to light. Authors do not want to find their work traded like baseball cards.

Some producers believe that since they have taken the financial risk of the first production, they should have unfettered rights to do whatever it takes to capitalize on that investment. This views the work only in terms of dollars and is *not* in the author's best interest. Alternatively, a producer will often want to add to this clause the phrase "not to be unreasonably withheld" as regards the author's prior written consent; but, it's best *not* to agree to this restrictive language. If necessary, a better modification would be to add a statement that *both* parties have to agree not to act unreasonably with respect to any matters that arise under this clause.

It's certainly in an author's best interest for the producer to have access to other producers who can increase the ability to get a new production on its feet, so it is difficult to imagine an author who would arbitrarily or capriciously withhold consent. Actually, the reverse situation is much more likely: An author might be tempted simply to say "yes" to any such request the producer makes.

Last, the producer will also want to add a sentence which states that the author's consent need not be obtained if the producer's formal structure is changed simply for legal or tax purposes—which may be necessary to secure investors—as long as it remains the active producer on the project. For example, the producer may form a limited partnership, a joint venture, or a corporation. An author is not put at risk by such an assignment. It is necessary simply to switch the right to produce the play from the producer named in the contract to a new legal entity which may have been created to receive the capital necessary to produce the play.

ARBITRATION

An arbitration clause states that if a dispute arises about terms of the contract, the parties agree to submit the problem to arbitration rather than litigating the matter in court. Arbitration is an alternative means of dispute resolution, and while it has its attendant costs and pitfalls, it is far better, faster and cheaper than going to court. However, arbitration must be clearly elected in the contract. Regulation varies from state to state but, often, in the absence of explicit election the parties cannot avail themselves of this remedy.

The arbitration clause should state the name of the city in which the arbitration will take place and should incorporate by reference the rules of the American Arbitration Association. There should also be appropriate language providing for the ability to affirm the arbitrator's award in the higher state or federal courts.

If arbitration is sought because one side hasn't paid the other money owed (e.g., author's royalties or a producer's subsidiary rights participation), it's in each party's best interest that the clause include a sentence that compels the arbitrator deciding the case to order the losing party to pay the costs of the arbitration, including the arbitrator's fees, and reasonable attorney's fees. This will eliminate a situation in which one party knows the other owes it money but the cost of the arbitration itself precludes its invocation. This premise is usually accepted, since the nonpayment of monies is ordinarily not an area subject to interpretation: Either one party owes the other money, or it doesn't. Besides, this provision applies to and benefits both sides, since it tends to inhibit frivolous or nuisance arbitrations.

COMMISSIONS

A producer (or, theoretically, anyone) may commission an author to write a work for the stage, based on the producer's ideas or a particular subject or an underlying work to which the producer has already obtained the dramatic or musical rights. Or a producer might just want to commission an author's next work, whatever it may be. Regardless of their source, the way commissions are handled is the same.

The contract for a commissioned work will look substantially like any other production contract, except for the opening provisions addressing the creation of a work rather than one already written. It's generally preferred to negotiate the whole contract—commissioning, option and production terms—up front, rather than waiting to negotiate the production terms after the commission has been filled. With just one contract negotiation, it is assumed that all tough issues will be resolved before the author begins to write.

If the parties prefer, it is possible to sign just a commission agreement, and then to negotiate the full production contract when the producer has reviewed the completed work and is determined to move forward. Just be sure the commission agreement expressly obligates both parties to negotiate a full production contract once the script is delivered and accepted.

The issues particular to commissions are the commission fee and the payment schedule, the schedule for writing, delivering and revising the manuscript (which includes time for any necessary research), and the option payment and option period once the work has been accepted by the commissioning party. As discussed in the chapter on copyright, the writer always retains ownership of a commissioned work. The producer receives the exclusive right to produce the premiere production of the commissioned work, never ownership of it.

Commission fees

The dollar amounts paid as commission fees enjoy a much wider range than option payments. Some commissions are underwritten by grants from foundations and corporations; some theatres and producers tend to commission new work from writers they already know and trust; sometimes a producer wants to "lock in" a certain writer's next work and will pay up front for a commission to avoid a possible bidding war later. Not-for-profit theatres may pay more for a commission than an option, since commissions may interest funders and thus add value to grant applications. Philosophical considerations exist, too. Many theatres committed to advancing the future of American theatre commission at rates that underscore that commitment. And from the writer's perspective, you are being paid to write a work you might not otherwise have written.

The general range of commission fees runs from $2,000 to as much as $13,000. (Depending on the fee and the amount of research that may be necessary, some writers may be able to negotiate travel expenses, though one shouldn't go overboard here.) Even though the commission fee is not considered a "wage," writers should think carefully about how much work is involved in fulfilling the commission. Negotiating a commission fee that reflects the time actually spent on the work is far from likely, but writers shouldn't automatically accept commission fees so low they may feel resentment. It is not unreasonable, however, for emerging writers or those being commissioned for the first time also to evaluate the less tangible benefit of breaking into this sought-after area.

Commission fees are treated differently than "regular" option payments. They, too, are nonrefundable, but they are generally *not* recoupable from first royalties since they represent payment for doing the actual writing. In some situations (typically when the commission fee is large; for example, $8,000 to $13,000), the parties may decide that twenty-five to fifty percent of the commission fee is recoupable from royalties.

Payment schedule

The timing of commission fees is structured differently, since the producer doesn't have a finished product in hand that would start the option period clock ticking. The writer always receives some portion of the commission fee upon signing the agreement—typically half—and the rest when the completed work is delivered. Often the writer receives half of the commission fee upon signing the agreement, one-fourth when delivering the first draft of the work, and the final fourth when delivering rewrites. Note that paying the balance of the commission fee is not conditioned upon acceptance of the work for production, but rather on completion of the work commissioned. It is always understood that the writer will undertake necessary rewrites; do not assume your work will be ready for production "as is." Thus this structure should not be interpreted as paying for rewrites, but rather, as a form of protection until the producer knows she or he has the completed work in hand.

Writing schedule

The writer and the commissioning party need to establish how long the writer will have to research and write the work, exactly when the completed script will be delivered to the producer, how long the producer will have to discuss revisions with the writer, and how long the writer will have to make revisions and deliver the final script to the producer. There is no single answer to this, since every writer works at a different pace and producer's plans and needs will vary. You need to think carefully about your personal writing habits, how quickly you can churn out a new work under pressure, how much research there might be to undertake, and—given the immediate circumstances of your life, such as whether or not you also have a full-time job—when you reasonably think you can finish it.

The producer might want the work finished earlier than you believe possible, so don't agree to a delivery schedule you may not be able to meet. But be reasonable, the producer can't be expected to agree to an excessively long schedule, and you serve no one's best interests by agreeing to a truncated writing schedule. Try to find a middle ground.

Some writers find it useful to create a structured writing schedule, including interim deadlines for segments of successive drafts. This is a personal choice, and you should do what works best for you. However, you might ultimately decide to set these interim deadlines for yourself, rather than obligating them contractually with the producer.

The option period and payment

Once the completed work, including rewrites, has been delivered to the commissioning party, the producer and writer may enter into a normal option period, as described above. Understand that the producer is under no obligation to option the commissioned work, which may not turn out as expected, or which may no longer suit the producer's interests or abilities.

Obviously, this would be very disappointing to both parties. Everyone strives to avoid such occurrences, but in a small percentage of cases, it just happens. Happily—because the author owns the copyright—the author may approach other producers with the work; unless, of course, the work is based on underlying rights still controlled by the commissioning party, in which case the author may be out of luck.

Assuming the producer does want to option the work for production, the writer receives the normal option payment to support the normal option period. In fact, from this point on, the production contract for a commissioned work should look generally the same as any production contract.

Chapter 6

REPRESENTATION:
AGENTS AND LAWYERS

AGENTS are an important part of an author's career; yet, representation is not a mandatory step to success: There are many authors whose careers prosper without it. Do not fall into the trap of thinking that having an agent is the only path to getting your play produced, or even that having an agent means you will have a production. Depending on your work, the type of venues sought and the stage of development in your career, you could find yourself pouring precious time, energy and money into a premature or even unnecessary agency search. Having an agent does *not* mean you can stop marketing the work yourself. Many authors dream of the day they will have an agent so they can just turn over the work and have it marketed by someone else, but that is not consistent with the reality of representation.

WHEN TO LOOK FOR AN AGENT

It's difficult to pinpoint the best time to conduct the search for an agent, but it probably won't depend on when *you* are ready. As frustrating as it may be, there are many factors to take into account and, of course, each situation will be different. However, the following should provide some guidance. Some of these guidelines may sound obvious, but experience has shown they are not.

Keep in mind that the number of experienced theatre agents is relatively small in comparison with the number of writers seeking representation. Most agents receive hundreds and even thousands of submissions each year. At the same time, agents' existing clients continue to write new works that need active representation. Consequently, agents must decide how many new clients they can sign while still providing quality service to their entire client list.

Put your best foot forward the first time you approach an agent, because you generally won't have a second "bite at the apple." Agents are very busy—representing clients already signed; attending readings and productions of works by existing clients, emerging writers and others; reading unsolicited submissions—too busy, in fact, to afford most authors more than one focused reading. There are no trial runs, so try to quell the natural instinct to panic and think your work is doomed if an agent isn't attached immediately. Instead, try to build your career methodically, creating a solid package that an agent will likely find attractive.

On the most basic level, make sure your script is readable and looks good. As discussed in the chapter on marketing and self-promotion, no excuses will be entertained for an unattractive or illegible script.

Here are some guidelines to consider:

A. The work should be completely written, and you should feel it is ready to be shown to prospective producers. In other words, show agents only polished works; this applies to both form and content. Never send anyone a first or rough draft; some agents even question whether you should send out the *second* draft. Work through the play over and over and over until you believe you've got the best possible product; it would be rare to find an established writer who believes that the early versions of a work were good enough.

A few agents would go so far as to say authors shouldn't look for representation based on their first play, but that is not a generally accepted position.

B. Test the waters before submitting the work to an agent. Have the play read before an audience, preferably one comprised of more than just family and friends, if that's possible.

C. If possible, a personal recommendation to an agent is a very good—although by no means the only—approach. This makes simple human sense: A personal introduction is always received differently than a blind solicitation.

D. An author must take responsibility for marketing the play, perhaps for quite a while, before approaching an agent. Part of being a playwright—throughout your career, but particularly in the beginning—is being the work's cheerleader and business representative. The days are long over—if they ever existed—when an author could say, "I'm just the creative person; I can't handle the business side." As terrifying as it may be, the author is a work's best, most effective marketer, and it is a rare author who can avoid responsibility for representing the work in the marketplace.

E. Agents are generally reluctant to represent works that have no history; that is, completely untested works. Most agents have expressed a desire not to be approached until the work has some tangible credit behind it. This typically means works that have at least enjoyed a staged reading, a small production or which have won a contest. The importance of such is threefold: It indicates to the agent that someone besides the author believes in the work; the agent will assume that the author has learned from experience and has rewritten the work to make it stronger; and it sends a strong signal about the author—that she or he understands that authors must believe in and market their work, and that she or he has already begun to do it.

A caveat: A few agents prefer that writers show them their work before making submissions to the more visible theatres (e.g., LORT theatres). Their position—clearly a minority opinion—is that if the play has already been submitted to and rejected by a long list of those theatres, the agent may be left with few outlets for marketing the work.

However, there are far more success stories by agents who found a production through their network of contacts even after a play had been turned down. It seems somewhat unrealistic for writers to wait until they are represented to submit their works to those theatres, particularly given how hard it is to secure representation.

These two positions are difficult to reconcile, and in the final analysis they come down to an agent's personal preferences that no author can anticipate. No matter what, if an agent is interested in representing your work you should then tell her or him where the play has been submitted, in part so that the agent can have a reasonable amount of information with which to evaluate the representation, and in part so that if the agent does decide to represent the work, she or he can prepare the proper marketing strategy and avoid inadvertent future embarassment.

APPROACHING AGENTS
Research and protocol

It's not easy deciding which agents to approach for possible representation. While it's a good idea to submit simultaneously to multiple agents, it's not a good idea to adopt the machine gun approach of mass mailings to every agent in New York, Los Angeles and elsewhere.

Think carefully about your work and whether it can be characterized. For example, who and what are your influences? Do you feel that you write in the style of any well-known playwright? This doesn't mean you should pigeonhole your work, but sometimes it's helpful to anticipate questions that you may be asked or to find an angle or a hook for intriguing an agent.

Read trade publications so you're in touch with what's being produced, what's hot and what's not. Agents are impressed by authors who understand, or are trying to understand, the marketplace.

If possible, do research into the authors various agents represent. No one knows at a given time what particular agents are looking for, but if an author knows who else an agent represents, it may help in deciding how to pitch your work to that agent. Look at published versions of plays that have been successful, that you particularly like or that seem to be marketed well in order to find out who represents the authors. The Dramatists Guild may be able to provide you with the names of a few well-known writers represented by a particular agent or tell you whether that agent is well-versed in theatre contracts and issues. Call all your friends who are writers to see what they know. Contact the Association of Authors' Representatives to find out if a given agent is a member. The majority of agents *are* members, but some good ones aren't, so don't make this one factor dispositive. Dig for as much information as possible.

Some people believe it's good to submit your work to the agent who represents a writer whose work has influenced yours or who writes the way you do. According to this theory, if you write like Mamet, you should submit your work to Mamet's agent. A second school of thought suggests that if you write too much like that other writer, the other writer's agent (if he or she took you on as a client) would naturally favor one over the other (usually the more famous—i.e., more lucrative—client). This position is difficult to confirm or reject, so it highlights the best strategy in your uphill battle for an agent: Do the best you can with the information available to you, and base your choices on gut instinct and opportunity.

In general, agents represent works they like, and even with thorough research, there is no way for writers to know exactly what that means in any given case. As frustrating as it may be to accept this, at least no one else has any advantage in this area.

An author writes the work in his or her heart and head, and hopes an agent will be intrigued by it. Don't lose hope: It's possible that an agent you solicit might not be actively looking for a new comedy, drama or whatever it is you have written; but, if you can get an agent to read your script, it might change his or her mind. So—although you should learn as much as possible to improve the odds—don't enter the process intent upon figuring out *exactly* what each agent is looking for. It's simply not a scientific process, and it's pointless to end up frustrated by your inability to pinpoint the answer.

There are many issues of protocol of which to be aware: What to say to an agent and what to send? How many agents to submit to simultaneously? What is considered a reasonable response time? Are exclusivity agreements normal or fair? Is it usual to pay a reading fee? Must I sign a release just to get someone to read my play?

Let's take these questions serially.

The query letter

The query letter an author sends to an agent is of utmost importance. (Never just cold-call an agent!) Sadly, many agents complain of receiving letters containing typographical errors, poor grammar and repeated misspellings, from writers using old typewriter ribbons or worn-out computer printers. Some writers try to be too clever, funny, wacky or just plain bizarre, and some are obnoxious. Although you might wish to stand out from the crowd, there is a difference between being intriguing and over-the-top. Research indicates agents rarely respond to outlandish gimmicks. So don't begin your inquiry letter with, "You have just won the lottery and now you get to represent my play!" On top of everything else, it's been done.

One writer shared what he considered to be the most important advice he had ever read about query letters (and it worked for him): "This letter is one of the most important things you will ever write. Don't rush it. Do several drafts, then put it away for a week. Come back to it fresh and revise it further. Then put it away again for three to seven days, then come back to it for fine tuning before mailing. The time spent is a crucial investment in your future."

What you are selling is you and your work. Agents are looking for clarity and a convincing use of language. Write a good, solid, straightforward business letter which contains relevant information: a brief description of your background and credentials, including any playwriting grants, awards or fellowships you may have received, as well as readings, workshops, publications, etc.; any referrals or personal recommendations that may help; a succinct synopsis of the play; and a short history of the play's development. If reviews sing your work's praises, include excerpts. Think carefully about how to present this information in the best possible light. This is your chance to shine, without appearing to brag. And remember: if you don't have substantial credentials, there's no need to apologize for yourself or for your work.

If possible, try to give an agent insight into the piece, and if there's a hook, spell it out. Think about what's distinctive and special about your work and help the agent see that. Don't say, "It's just like *Hello Dolly*," because that's unlikely, and anyway, the agent's first thought might be, "But there's already one *Hello Dolly*. Why should there be two?"

Some agents like to receive a few pages of dialogue with a letter of inquiry, just enough to get a sense of the writer's style; other agents don't find this useful and, if your letter elicits their interest, would prefer to read the entire script rather than see a few pages out of context. There's no way for you to know how a particular agent feels about this, so there is no right or wrong answer; but universally, agents focus on the quality of the letter of inquiry, so if you are going to obsess about your submission, focus your energies on the content of your letter rather than on deciding whether or not to include sample pages.

Try to think of ways to make the process easy on the agent. Keep in mind that each year agents receive thousands of letters and scripts from writers seeking representation and, fair or not, they've created a personal checklist of ways to sort through them without wasting time.

One good general rule is always to include a postage-paid, self-addressed postcard with your letter, with a few simple lines allowing the agent to check off a response and send the postcard back to you. Possible responses to include might be: "I'm sorry but I'm not looking for new work right now"; "This work has potential, so get back in touch with me after you've had a[nother] production"; and "Yes, I would like to read the script." Don't offer too many possibilities; the keys are *simplicity* and *convenience*. Don't try to elicit career encouragement here; the point is to make it easy for the agents to see the script if they want to, to allow some room for future discussions if they are not currently interested, or to learn that this agent is not interested so that you don't waste any more time or money on this particular pursuit.

Here are some "don'ts" concerning the query letter:

- ◆ Don't send what are obviously form letters.
- ◆ Don't use the salutation "Dear Agent," don't spell the agent's name wrong and don't get too personal by using only a first name.
- ◆ Don't handwrite the letter; that definitely sends the wrong message.
- ◆ Don't tell an agent how he or she will feel about your play; talk about the work briefly, then let it sell itself.
- ◆ Don't tell the agent, "This work is great!" or "This play will make a lot of money for you!"
- ◆ Don't just say, "It's easy to produce"; provide the number of characters and the set requirements if they're a selling point.

The bottom line: You are a writer seeking representation for your work. If an agent thinks you can't write a strong letter—especially one about you and your work—then the agent may wonder about your writing ability in general. One can argue that the ability to write a business letter and the ability to write a play are unrelated, and this may be so, but the letter sends a strong message about you, the writer, regardless, and if it's inarticulate or sloppy, you are asking the agent to make a giant leap of faith to believe that your "real" work is better. Fairness aside, first impressions count.

Multiple submissions

The majority of agents actively encourage writers to submit their work to a number of agents simultaneously. Depending on the volume of submissions and the everyday workload, an agent may not be able to respond promptly, and agents realize it's unfair to expect writers to write to each one serially, because it could take years to send out your inquiry letters and wait for responses one at a time. Agents differ widely as to whether in the inquiry letter you should mention that you're pursuing other agents or just leave that as an assumption, with the majority leaning towards the latter.

If you send your work to multiple agents and one responds positively, you should immediately contact the others to let them know that your situation has changed, giving them a reasonably short period of time to expedite reading your work so they can decide whether they wish to pursue you as a client before it's too late. Don't simply ignore the agents who haven't yet responded and move ahead without them; you may damage your own interests in the process. After all, the fact that one agent is interested in your work may make another agent take notice (but *never* pretend another agent is interested, because this manipulative ploy could easily backfire).

Response time

What is a reasonable response period after you've sent your script to an agent? Generally speaking, anticipate at least two full months, depending on that person's workload and schedule (unless there is a buzz about your work, in which case you might be able to expect a shorter turnaround time). For example, if you happen to send your play out just when every theatre agent is attending the Humana Festival of New American Plays in Louisville, Kentucky, chances are good that it will take longer to receive a response. Agents are like octopi, with full lists of clients who need attention and a thousand matters to take care of; if they are a little late in responding, it's probably not out of arrogance, but rather lack of time. Do not hound an agent to whom you have submitted your work, even if two months have passed. You *must* be patient, no matter how hard it is for you.

Don't just sit around waiting for a response; keep hustling the work and trying to get your name into the active information loop. An agent might be sitting on your play when suddenly someone raves about you. *That* might pique the agent's interest!

Exclusivity agreements

Exclusivity agreements are no longer common, but a couple of agents still prefer them. Essentially, such an agreement means the agent is asking you to give her or him sole (i.e., exclusive) "first look" rights for a certain period of time. Whether this way of doing business is "reasonable" and "fair" is two different questions: From the writer's point of view, the fewer limitations placed on a play's marketing the better, so exclusivity agreements may not seem fair; from the perspective of agents inundated with scripts, it feels unreasonable to ask them to compete with other agents, thereby putting them under pressure to read faster.

While exclusivity agreements inevitably tie your hands (and tie up your work), they cannot be evaluated without considering the amount of time involved. If you have to wait thirty days for a response from a particular agent, it might be worth the gamble; but, if an agent wants more than thirty days, you should think twice about agreeing. If good things are happening pretty quickly with your work and you need to maximize the momentum, agreeing to exclusivity for a lengthy period might thwart your work rather than enhance it.

Each situation needs to be evaluated on its merits—for instance, if you are anxious to work with a particular agent, the wait might be a risk worth taking—but know that exclusivity agreements are not mandatory and only a small number of agents appear to use them.

Releases

Releases are not commonly used in theatre (although, by contrast, they are standard practice in the film and television industries). A few agencies, generally the larger ones, have decided to require signed releases before they will read unsolicited material from writers they don't know. So even though the use of releases is not prevalent in theatre, sometimes an agency will ask for one.

A release is essentially what its name suggests: You release the recipient of the script from any future liability regarding it; most notably, from copyright infringement. The underlying premise is that there is a finite number of ideas in the world and since agents read thousands of scripts, an overlap of ideas is inevitable. The agency's fear is that if an agent receives two scripts written on the same idea or containing similar material and chooses to represent only one, the rejected writer might later claim that the agent helped the competing writer steal from the rejected writer's work. Of course, as discussed in the chapter on copyright, what's protected is the *expression* of an idea, so the rejected writer's concern is that the agent will show the work to another writer who will write his or her own version that may be uncomfortably similar to the original work. But the release represents an extra precaution, and may help stave off so-called nuisance suits.

The downside to releases is that they are usually overdrafted; since they are created specifically to protect the agent's interests, not the writer's, there is a tendency to incorporate language that exceeds what is reasonably necessary to allay the agent's fears. Be aware of releases that protect agents from both "similar and identical material." Even if you believe it's reasonable for an agent to seek protection when reading multiple scripts containing similar material, it is quite another thing for her or him to seek protection when scripts contain *identical* material. Two writers may decide to write plays about corruption in contemporary politics, so there may reasonably be some similarity; however, if two writers write *identical material* on the subject, someone's antennae should go up regarding copyright infringement.

The bottom line in deciding whether or not to sign the release is that releases, if required, are not negotiable. If you want your work to be read by that agency, you will have to sign their release. But perhaps take some solace in the fact that all writers are treated the same by that agency. And remember that signing a release does not preclude a writer who believes another writer has infringed his or her work from pursuing a claim of copyright infringement against the other writer; the release protects the agency from being in the middle of that dispute.

Reading fees charged by agents

Reading fees are a definite "no-no." Authors should *never* have to pay an agent to read a script. If an agent is too busy to read every script, she or he may hire a reader to provide a synopsis and perhaps a recommendation, but paying that reader is the agent's responsibility. The fee should not come out of the writer's pocket. As of January 1, 1996, the Association of Authors' Representatives instituted a total ban on reading fees by its members—they are not permitted to charge reading fees to prospective clients. However, not all agents are members of the AAR.

Remember: All writers have business expenses—computers, printers, paper, photocopying, postage, telephone, travel, copyright registration, research and resource materials, and other miscellaneous expenses; if you write musicals, there are also recording costs, tape duplication, lead sheets and the like. Marketing your work is not inexpensive, but those costs are appropriately the writer's responsibility; paying agents to have your scripts read is not. Even nominal fees—say fifteen to twenty dollars per agent—would quickly add up to a lot of money.

Unfortunately, there are one or two agents who charge hefty fees for reading scripts. Their justification is that they have their readers critique the script for a writer (a critique of perhaps questionable worth, depending on the credentials of the reader). Consider, too, that it takes roughly the same amount of time for an agent to read a script whether or not he or she will represent it (and possibly less time for rejected scripts; since they may not be read in their entirety). If agents got paid for every script they decided *not* to represent, they could make a lot of money just from reading.

The bottom line: Reading scripts is part of an agent's job.

WHAT AGENTS DO AND DON'T DO
Responsibilities and expectations

It's very important to discuss openly with any potential agent the expectations on both sides. Agents will do a lot for you and your work, but they don't do everything, so it's important to enter the relationship with reasonable expectations.

Agents don't "sell" manuscripts or musicals; they *create opportunities* for a work to sell itself. Generally, they actively market and solicit interest in your work and submit it to people who may not consider unsolicited or unagented plays (including but not limited to producers, artistic directors and literary managers). If they are able to obtain a solid offer, agents are responsible for negotiating appropriate contracts subject always to the author's approval of the terms; the author should never relinquish decision-making power to the agent, and the author should remain the person actually to sign all contracts. Once the contract is negotiated and executed, the agent is responsible for monitoring it to make sure its terms are adhered to. If the production that results is one important theatre people should be invited to, that's an agent's business too. While a production is running or just after it closes (depending on the contract terms), the agent is responsible for collecting royalties and box office statements, checking that the proper amounts are being paid and intervening if there are problems. Once one production closes, the agent is responsible for starting the cycle again, using that production as a foundation from which to launch the work to its next level of production.

Unless a particular agent is interested in doing so, agents are generally not financial or investment advisors, personal or business managers, editors, banks, travel agents, therapists, dramaturgs or landlords.

Interaction

First and foremost, you will need to learn how to work with your agent. This differs depending on the two people involved, but communication, trust and the ability to consider carefully the other person's opinion are essential. Each of you brings something unique to the relationship (authors sometimes hear things agents don't, and may have nurtured valuable contacts; a good agent is privy to conversations and information authors never hear). See yourselves as a team to make your work successful.

Then there is the human part of the relationship: The agent is there to talk to about your career, giving both professional and creative advice; to strategize; to give ideas about directors, actors and designers; to fill in the gap; to be a pipeline for information; to toss ideas back and forth. Sometimes an agent just listens, encourages, or holds your hand during frustrating or difficult times.

One thing all agents should do is return your calls, respond to your letters and make time to see you if you feel a face-to-face meeting is truly necessary to discuss something pressing but be fair and reasonable; don't abuse this relationship; remember you are one of many clients. Agents should follow up on leads you bring to them, and they should keep you generally informed as to any progress they are making. This does not mean daily or weekly phone calls, but it's not unusual for an agent to stay in touch with a client to provide periodic status reports about submissions and responses. A lot depends on the agent's workload, of course, so even if you find yourself chomping at the bit, try to relax and be flexible. Things simply don't happen at your desired speed. The agent will certainly let you know if something important happens.

Questions to ask

If an agent is interested in representing you, think carefully about whether that person is right for you. The list at the end of this chapter will help you focus on issues and questions that will assist you in thinking this through.

Have an honest talk with the agent, in person if possible, and get feedback on your work. Talk about your artistic vision and, ideally, where you would like to see the work go. Elicit from the agent her or his ideas about marketing the work, including initial thoughts about the best place to send it for consideration. Think about how aggressive or assertive you want an agent to be since she or he is supposed to get out and solicit interest in your work, and about how personable she or he is since your agent will be talking with a wide variety of people on your behalf, across the country and probably around the world.

Find out how many writers the agent represents. If the answer is none (i.e., you will be the first), think carefully about whether you want this person to learn the industry through your career. Remember that it's important for an agent to have a network of contacts and to know to whom to submit the work. If it turns out the agent already represents forty other writers, talk about how he or she can fruitfully add another client to that list; speak honestly about where you will fit into the agent's scheme of things. Most agents represent "name" writers as well as emerging writers, and it's only natural that they must spend a significant amount of time on the more established writers. This doesn't automatically mean that you will be completely ignored, so don't panic, but do talk it out.

Sometimes emerging writers sign with an agent understanding that her or his plays might not receive priority attention; but, since the fact of representation itself does carry weight, particularly to producers who only want to read agented scripts, the relationship may still be valuable. In these situations, then, the author may remain the primary marketing person for a while, contacting the agent to say, "I would like you to send my play to these places I've contacted." This is not necessarily terrible if it's what the author understands the early stages of the relationship will be; what's terrible is if it's not discussed, and the agent later tells the author, "I'm sorry, but I don't have time for your play."

In your conversation, focus on the personal relationship. In the best-case scenario, yours will be a partnership for the rest of the life of the work, so it's important that you be comfortable with each other. Trust your gut instincts. The agent is a person in whom an author must place a lot of trust, and if you feel you will have a hard time getting this person to respond to a phone call or letter (assuming you don't become the type of annoying client who calls every week), don't ignore that feeling. Remember, too, in the initial interviewing phase, that the agent is evaluating the writer as well, to see what kind of client he or she will be.

Another question you may want to ask will not be directed to the agent. Before deciding to have an agent represent your work, it is not unreasonable to contact one or two clients currently represented by that agent to ask, "Are you happy with the representation and the relationship?"

Most agents have assistants who are also agents, sometimes agents-in-training. Don't be insulted if the agent assigns some or even a lot of the work to an assistant. You will still be receiving good representation, but this is definitely an issue to discuss with the agent in the interview stage, so that later you don't feel you've been misled. Especially when working with smaller agencies, it's not possible for one person—the lead agent, whose name is on the letterhead—to handle all matters for every client. However, if your interest in the agency is conditioned on having the senior agent handle your work, put that on the table early on. But also understand that this might not be realistic.

Scope of representation

From the beginning, talk with the agent about whether she or he will represent all of your works or just individual pieces. There is no right or wrong answer here—different agents handle different matters for their various clients—but you should strive to find the best fit for you and that particular agent.

Be clear about whether the agent will represent you in theatre alone or also in the film and television industries. The unfortunate economic reality is that few agents limit their business to theatre anymore; to sustain an agency, most have branched out into film and TV. Many theatre agents are well-versed in the film/TV industries, but more often than not the reverse is not true; that is, film/TV agents aren't usually well-versed in the norms of the theatre industry. If you want your theatre agent to represent you in these other markets, talk about her or his experience in those other areas. Sometimes you might discover that the theatre agent has forged an alliance with a film/TV agent whereby together they cover all industries and split commissions. If you receive quality representation, how the agents share the commission should not matter to you, as long as you are not asked to pay twice. Some authors have a separate film/TV agent, but theatre agents tend to object strongly to this bifurcation, since film/TV money may be important to them, too.

Agents' risks

Agents assume significant risks when they sign clients, especially emerging writers, because of the percentage commission structure outlined below. It can *easily* take at least two or three years to build a writer's reputation: to get the work seen by theatres, producers, etc.; to obtain a commitment for production; to get to the opening night and so on (see the chapter on production contracts). During this period, agents invest a substantial amount of time, energy and resources with no guarantee of return on that investment.

Try not to underestimate the amount of work it takes an agent to get an offer of production. A good agent will work conscientiously and methodically to find the best place for your play. She or he will think about which theatres produce certain types of work rather than submitting the work blindly; will talk to literary managers, artistic directors, freelance directors and many other people involved in the decision-making; will send letters and make calls following up on leads; will do anything and everything to nurture the play along. While not every agent is this dedicated, agenting is not easy work when it's done right.

Some people say, mistakenly, that agents just send out scripts, wait for the offers to roll in, spend a few minutes negotiating the contract and then take a big chunk out of the writer's earnings. Even if there are a few agents who fit that bill, the reality for agents—particularly those still working in theatre—is nothing like that. It takes skill, fortitude and perseverance to bring together the right play, producer and creative people to make a quality production. So much of what an agent does happens in such subtle ways, it might not be obvious to the author. In some ways, agents are susceptible to the same misunderstandings authors endure. No one sees the years of hard work.

Of course, a lot of what transpires in the entertainment world involves timing and luck as well as hard work. Often an agent will find a producer to option a work, but ultimately the producer isn't able to put together the production. There are false starts, dashed hopes and fifty phone calls for each one that counts. Good agents work hard and risk much, emotionally as well as professionally.

FINANCIAL ARRANGEMENTS

Be sure you understand the ramifications of agreeing to representation. There are two financial issues to address: the agent's commission and expenses.

The agent's commission

An agent makes money when his or her client makes money, and not until then. The agent receives a percentage of the money that the writer makes from any market (assuming for purposes of this discussion that one agent represents the writer in theatre, film and television markets), excluding grants and prizes. The typical commission is ten percent for everything except amateur and foreign markets. In the amateur market, the commission is twenty percent, perhaps because royalties are not as high in the amateur market as elsewhere and the agent is offered more to offset that. For the foreign markets, the commission is typically between ten and twenty percent, since the U.S. agent often has to work and share the commission with agents based in foreign markets.

A few agents charge higher percentages; for them, the overriding issues are what they feel they offer their clients and what the market will bear. While there are no rules or laws that prevent this practice, nor is it unethical, writers would obviously rather pay the lower commission percentages, if given a choice.

Given the percentage commission structure, it's in the agent's best interest to try to find well-paying productions and commissions for the client. Conversely, it's in the agent's best interest to sign works she or he believes will make lots of money. There's nothing wrong with this; it's important to bear in mind that this is a business for agents, a career as well as a passion. Agents make their livings from commissions (as well as pay agency overhead, business expenses, etc.); the commissions are not a "bonus." One agent commented that clients don't contest percentages in the beginning of the relationship, before the work is done; they wait until the money starts coming in—and their checks reflect the agent's commission—to register complaints about how much the agent is keeping. When an agent works hard to market an author's plays or musicals and secure paying work for that author, it is considered bad taste at the very least for the author to begrudge the agent his or her commission.

Commissions should be the same for all authors represented by an agent; emerging writers should not be asked to agree to a higher commission arrangement. Authors who make more money naturally pay greater sums to the agent. Don't turn this on its head and try to convince an agent that emerging authors should somehow be able to negotiate a smaller percentage. Percentages are eminently fair because they automatically adjust to the amount of money made by a particular author.

Expenses

Responsibility for an agent's expenses—typically marketing-related, such as postage, fax charges and long distance telephone bills incurred in getting your script to potential producers and others, and which can also include such items as travel to attend an author's production—needs to be addressed. No author should be asked to pay for such basic overhead expenses as an agent's rent, utility bills, insurance and the like. Expenses incurred specifically in the course of marketing a particular property also should remain the agent's responsibility, although not all agents agree and some will try to negotiate these. The size of the agency might have some bearing. Smaller agencies may feel the need to ask for shared responsibility more than larger agencies do, but that's not universally true.

If an author does accept responsibility for some expenses, he or she is entitled to receive a detailed accounting of the charges plus support documentation such as bills or receipts. Even if an author does *not* accept shared responsibility for an agent's regular expenses, it is normal to pay for script-copying and extraordinary expenses, such as the use of messengers or overnight delivery. However, incurring extraordinary expenses should always be subject to the author's consent, since these types of expenses can add up easily.

DECISION-MAKING

The author makes the final decisions, typically those concerning contracts, not the everyday decisions such as where to submit the work. The author is the client (the "principal") and the agent works for the client. But remember that agents are skilled professionals who should not be expected to follow orders blindly. Since their experience in the market will, in most instances, be *much* broader than the author's, authors are advised to weigh an agent's advice carefully.

Since she or he retains final approval, the author needs to remain open to ideas. Don't set your heart on one particular path to success; stage works take so many, it's impossible to chart them. Stay open to all possibilities and opportunities raised by your agent. Certainly you don't have to accept all suggestions, but don't foolishly reject any out-of-hand.

LENGTH OF RELATIONSHIP

If an author wants to sign with an agent but either person is uncomfortable starting off with an open-ended commitment, the contract could explicitly stipulate a finite period—say, two to three years. A separate provision could allow for each party then to decide whether to extend or terminate the contract. There is nothing unusual about such an arrangement, particularly for emerging writers, although it can increase the agent's risk of losing a client after years of hard work, so it is a much less common arrangement and many agents will not consider it for this reason.

Keep in mind, however, that such limited-term contracts necessarily, and fairly, give the agent the same level of flexibility as the author. If an author feels more comfortable not locking up a work for an unlimited term, she or he must also be comfortable with the risk that the agent might terminate the relationship. Either both parties agree to an open-ended relationship, or both agree to a limited term.

CONTRACTS WITH AGENTS

In most instances, you won't actually sign a contract directly with the agent, even though colloquially people talk of "signing" with an agent. As much as authors are encouraged to have written contracts, the agency relationship is generally handled differently. However, the absence of a signed contract does *not* mean you can suddenly deny the relationship exists or end it abruptly. The fact of the agent actively representing you in the marketplace with your knowledge and approval is generally sufficient to ratify the existence of this relationship.

What ordinarily takes place is that the agency's standard contract clause, including the specifics of your agreement, is inserted into any contract you sign with third parties, such as a producer or publisher. Below is a fairly typical agency clause; the terms contained therein are essentially the same regardless of whether you sign a contract directly with the agent or simply confirm the relationship in a production or publication contract.

> The Author hereby appoints The XYZ Agency irrevocably as the Agent in all matters pertaining to or arising from this Agreement and further declares that this appointment shall be binding upon the Author's heirs, executors, administrators and/or assigns. Such Agent is hereby fully empowered to act on behalf of the Author in all matters in any way arising out of this Agreement, and is hereby designated as the Author's Agent upon whom notices regarding this Agreement may be delivered. Notwithstanding the foregoing, the Author retains all power to sign documents. All sums of money due the Author under this Agreement shall be paid to and in the name of said Agent, whose receipt thereof shall constitute full and valid discharge thereof. The XYZ Agency shall retain a sum equal to ten percent (10%) of all money collected from dispositions in the United States and Canada and not more than twenty percent (20%) from the marketing of rights in all other countries, except that the commission for amateur licenses shall be twenty percent (20%) throughout the world, and it shall be payable to the account of the Author under this Agreement.

It is important to note that the agency clause typically will not (and in this author's opinion should not) contain any mention of the agent being entitled to represent and collect full commissions on any of the following: "sequels, prequels, spinoffs, or any related forms of this project, including such additional projects as may be created using the same or similar character or characters."

The perpetuity clause

It's very important to notice the perpetuity language in agency agreements: that the appointment as agent is binding on the author's "heirs, executors, administrators and/or assigns." Regardless of whether this exact language is used or other similar language is drafted, the intent remains the same: In return for the work performed by the agent—presumably involving a significant investment of time, energy and money—the author agrees to leave the work at issue with that agent even if the author later leaves for a new agent (which is discussed below, in the subsection on termination).

The perpetuity clause has angered a substantial number of writers who argue that the predominant reason for leaving an agent is that the quality of representation has declined to the point the author believes termination is necessary to retain or revive his or her career. If the author terminates the agency relationship because the agent isn't performing the duties and obligations originally assumed, the author might legitimately ask, "Why should that agent continue to represent my valuable work and, tangentially, why should I remain obligated to pay his or her commission?"

A work thus left behind might not only injure an author because its value isn't fully exploited; it might be the very work that would entice a new agent. Without that "jewel" to offer, an author's newer works might not be enough to acquire the new agent's services.

But agents don't focus on the "declining services" scenario, as writers do. Their concern is their devotion to a work, often for years, without seeing much if any income generated, which may finally hit as a result of their hard work, at which point the author might decide to move on to another, perhaps more powerful, agent.

It's not unusual for an agent to spend more money than a work brings in at first. For example, at many good regional theatres, an author may make $10,000 in royalties on a premiere production, of which the agent's commission is $1,000. In order to market the play intelligently, the agent may have to *see* that premiere production, which could easily mean the agent's commission is eaten up in travel costs, not to mention monies expended in obtaining that first production. In return, the agent wants to know that recompense is at least a possibility even if it's spread out over ten, twenty or thirty years. There's no guarantee of a real payback, but with the perpetuity clause, at least the possibility exists. And if the future income turns out to be far greater than mere recompense—as with a hugely successful work—then the agent has earned such a healthy return because he or she made the initial investment in marketing the work.

Sometimes the problem isn't a decline in representation. Sometimes another agent will try to entice a client away, perhaps by subtly denigrating the current agent ("He did what? Oh, I would never have handled it that way!") A would-be agent might make any number of promises about improving the author's career. It can be rather heady to be courted in this fashion, and authors are certainly subject to temptations. Consequently, agents believe that if an author wants to shop for a new agent, she or he should do so only with new work, not with a piece that has become valuable due in some measure to the original agent's labor.

What is interesting and disturbing about these opposing perspectives is that they address different circumstances. Authors want protection from agents who don't represent them well enough, which sometimes happens. Perhaps the agent has taken on too many clients, or more powerful clients demand an enormous amount of time. An agent may have trouble marketing a particular work or may experience a rash of bad luck and not have a hit for some time, so that producers and theatres may respond unfavorably to his or her submissions. An agent may have personal problems which affect his or her professional life. Authors need and deserve protection from agency relationships that—for whatever reason—simply don't enhance the writer's work or career.

The agents' issues are equally valid. Authors may not always act in a reasonable and fair way, or may not entertain reasonable expectations. Agents will not be able to take on the risks inherent in working on commission if they cannot protect their labor.

Where does the solution lie? Perhaps somewhere in the middle. Someday fairer language could be drafted that addresses the very real concerns and risks on both sides of the equation. The best possible solution would be win-win-win: a win for the old agent, a win for the new agent and, of course, a win for the stage writer.

Termination

When two people decide to work together, both hope and believe that the relationship will work well. But sometimes it doesn't, and a writer may be faced with the very difficult decision of whether to proceed with that agent.

Termination is never easy. An author needs to think carefully and honestly about his or her underlying motivation. It's not enough to say that an agent hasn't found work for you or hasn't been able to secure a production. As discussed above, and as painful as it may be to hear, for any number of reasons some works just don't sell.

Strive to avoid making your agent the repository of your frustrations. Agents cannot compel producers to like a particular work. They can only create opportunities, and they shouldn't be blamed reflexively if they are unable to generate interest in the marketplace.

However, after a reasonable period of time (at least two or three years), an author may feel an agent simply isn't doing what she or he promised. If an agent doesn't submit a work often, or if interest is expressed but the agent doesn't follow up, there is a problem. Or the author may feel the agent simply isn't interested anymore, and instead of actively soliciting interest in the work he or she just waits to field offers the author's efforts generate. Perhaps the agent isn't sharing information anymore, or doesn't bother to respond to the author's phone calls or letters.

If something has gone wrong with the relationship, the first step is to schedule an appointment with the agent to talk about your feelings, in person if possible. However, if you find that too difficult, send a well-considered letter. No matter what, you must air your feelings and give the agent an opportunity to respond. It is possible you don't fully understand the situation or that you've misread signals. Before jumping to the drastic step of termination, give the relationship every chance to succeed. At a bare minimum, do the decent thing: Be honest with your agent, treating him or her with the respect any person deserves.

If the agent's response is simply to refute your concerns, you have the right to request some type of proof. For example, if you believe your agent isn't submitting your work aggressively or even regularly but the agent insists she or he *is*, asking for a list of submissions over the previous six months to a year is not an unreasonable request. If the agent refuses, or becomes defensive or insulted, this may confirm a problem.

If your agent admits that he or she hasn't done everything possible for you and your work but promises to rectify the situation, discuss openly what the next steps will be. Try to establish a fair period of time in which to see if things change and, again, be reasonable. It's not fair to your agent to say, "If I don't have a production within two months, I'm leaving." Agents can't and don't promise results and, as mentioned above, they are not the insurers of a work's success. But it *is* reasonable to say, "Let's both work on communicating better, and let's talk again in six months to see how we feel about this." An agent who is serious about retaining an author as a client will work hard to respond to the author's concerns. If the situation doesn't change in the specified time, the author will know at least that he or she gave the relationship its best shot.

If, after all this, the situation hasn't improved and you don't believe it will, communicate clearly to the agent not only the fact that you are terminating the relationship but your reasons. After all, you will want to leave with your reputation intact. At some point you will probably look for a new agent, and since the theatre community is close-knit, you must try to terminate your soured relationship gracefully.

The two substantive issues of termination concerning your work— continued active representation of existing works and whether the agent will (passively) continue to receive future commissions even if not actively representing the work—must be addressed in terms of *any* agreements (production, publication, etc.) that you have signed. Having signed an agreement containing the agency clause does bind you to that agency. What happens next is a negotiation that depends on what has already taken place during the representation (length of time, success, etc.), and how the individuals handle the situation.

It would be hard to argue that a work should remain with an agent who has done virtually nothing to promote it in the marketplace. In the absence of a perpetuity clause, the author may terminate the agent's active representation of that work. Even if there *is* a perpetuity clause, the author can ask the agent to renegotiate the clause's terms, particularly if the author has done everything possible to salvage the relationship.

In the more complicated situation, the agent *has* worked to market the play or musical—sometimes a lot and sometimes not as much—but the author is unhappy or dissatisfied and wants out of the relationship. In negotiating a termination, there are three variables to consider for the future: 1) the scope of an ongoing representation; 2) the commission percentages; and 3) the applicable period of time. Different writers and agents find different combinations appealing, so play with the variables to find the right fit for you.

For example, sometimes an author has several works represented by an agent, and can convince the terminated agent to retain representation of only one or two, allowing the author to take the others to a new agent. Sometimes the terminated agent will release active representation of all works, but will want to retain a full or half commission on them for services already rendered even as they're represented by someone else. There the parties involved might agree to a simple joint commission arrangement for a finite period of years, with the percentages either remaining static for the entire period or perhaps shifting a few percentage points at a time until the author's obligation to the terminated agent expires.

Thus, the three basic choices are to: 1) terminate the relationship completely, leaving absolutely nothing behind and having no future commission obligations; 2) terminate the relationship as to new works but leave some or all of the existing work with the terminated agent, which she or he will continue to market and earn commissions on; or 3) terminate all active representation of your works, so you can take them all to a new agent, *but* reach a financial compromise with the terminated agent with respect to her or his commission on your existing works. A common resolution is for the terminated agent and the new agent to share commissions, each often agreeing to receive half of what they would ordinarily expect. This arrangement acknowledges the terminated agent's previous efforts, the new agent's ongoing efforts and the author's concern over paying double commissions.

However, the terminated agent may not agree to reduce his or her commission or a new agent may not be willing to work for less than a normal commission. In such situations, an author may find him- or herself paying double commissions and, depending on the circumstances, that might just be the price of extricating yourself from the contract/relationship; in the long run, one would hope you would decide it was worth it to find happiness in the new representation.

Remember this: You will not be the first author to have terminated a relationship with an agent, nor will you be the last. It's not what anyone wishes would happen, but neither will it destroy anyone's career. Even well-known authors change agents, and life goes on.

LAWYER VERSUS AGENT

Should a writer have a lawyer rather than an agent? Why do some writers have both lawyers and agents? Lawyers and agents serve different functions, with some overlap in the area of negotiation, and needing to choose between the two usually occurs when an unrepresented writer obtains an offer for a production requiring more complex negotiations (as for a commercial production).

As discussed previously, agents represent either one work or multiple works by a writer for the life of the play or musical, not just individual negotiations. In contrast, lawyers are typically hired, or "retained," on a case-by-case or deal-by-deal basis. When the deal has been concluded, the relationship can be terminated with no further obligations. Keep in mind that the majority of lawyers do not do more than negotiate particular deals; i.e., they do not market works in any way, etc.

Usually a client pays a lawyer's hourly rate for all hours (or portions thereof) spent on the negotiation, plus all expenses incurred on the client's behalf. A lawyer's time can be expensive ($200-350 an hour for entertainment lawyers in major metropolitan areas is not unheard of, although there usually are also those who would charge $150-200 an hour). Consequently, if the writer is not going to make a lot of money from a production, he or she may have to consider how quickly charges can add up in a negotiation.

For example, the option payment for an Off-Broadway production could be $2,500. If the lawyer charges $300 an hour, a negotiation of roughly eight hours duration would eat up the payment. This could be a worthwhile gamble, since the lawyer would have no claim on future royalties, subsidiary rights, etc. However, the writer must also weigh this cost against the complexity of the contract. It may be well worth the investment to know you protected your rights to the work at an important juncture. Don't be penny-wise and pound-foolish.

Understanding the contracts offered in the theatrical arena requires a certain level of expertise, and one would normally want to retain a lawyer who has had some experience in this area, since the client doesn't want to underwrite the lawyer's education. If the lawyer you're talking to doesn't have much experience in this area but is very interested in working on the deal, you might be able to cut a deal of your own, allowing the lawyer to "practice" on you, in a sense, in return for reducing your overall costs.

It is not a good idea to use the same lawyer who represents the producer, even if it is the least expensive option. The lawyer you retain is supposed to be *your* advocate—in your corner—throughout the negotiation. Some lawyers disagree, but it is not possible for one lawyer to represent clients on opposite sides of a transaction equally, to the best of her or his ability. While the producer and the writer share a common goal—the production—their interests naturally diverge on any number of points. It may sound cynical, but if forced to favor a producer with money or an emerging writer, a lawyer may not find it difficult to choose. This can have a direct, negative impact on the writer's contract.

Some writers may find an agent's financial arrangements more palatable, since the writer doesn't pay the agent until the money comes in and the monies owed an agent never exceed the monies flowing to the writer; whereas, with lawyers the possibility always exists that the bill will exceed the offer. However, when signing with an agent, a writer must be willing to commit to a long-term relationship, even for just one work. (While termination is possible, as addressed above, no writer should enter into a relationship with an agent thinking about termination as a way to conduct business.)

Some lawyers will offer to handle negotiations on a percentage, rather than an hourly fee, basis. Even though this may sound attractive, keep in mind the limitations of the type of work rendered by the lawyer compared to the long list of responsibilities an agent assumes. Over time, the writer could end up paying a lawyer far more than the hourly bill would ever have been. Also, there's a reason lawyers generally don't work on a contingency basis, since that gives them a vested interest in the outcome of their clients' business arrangements. (In other words, the concern here is that a lawyer might be inclined to push for a deal that gives higher immediate financial rewards, since that would yield a greater sum to the lawyer, possibly giving in on terms which would be of greater ultimate advantage to the author.) Finally, note that later in a work's life, the writer may have an agent who will take the usual commission percentage, and a producer who earns a share of the writer's subsidiary rights income. A worst-case scenario would be for a writer to have written a work that generates decent income, but a large chunk goes to the agent, the producer and the lawyer. While the agent's commission and the producer's share of subsidiary rights monies are the norm to be anticipated in the theatre industry, paying a lawyer's percentage on top of that may someday prove onerous.

Having considered these caveats, however, it cannot be denied that if a writer can't afford to pay a lawyer's hourly rate, and therefore has a choice between being unrepresented in a complex negotiation and being represented by a lawyer who has offered to charge a percentage instead of an hourly rate, it's more important to have a representative than not. If you find yourself in this situation, first be certain that the complexity of the contract is such that you *need* a representative, and be clear about the possible long-term ramifications of the arrangement, so that later on you don't kick yourself.

FINDING A LAWYER

If you do need a lawyer, the best way to find one is through recommendations from people in the theatre industry: other writers, writers' organizations, theatre companies, producers, directors; in other words, anyone you know who might know someone else. Some well-known lawyers will be the top in the industry, meaning those with the most experience and best reputation, but you may find yourself paying top dollar to work with them, particularly if they are partners in their law firms.

To reduce the hourly rate, look into working with the associate lawyers who work with those partners. The hourly rates of associates are usually far less than those of partners, and associates have at least a minimum level of experience, have learned from the partner, and can talk to the partner if there is a snag in negotiations. Even partners in law firms started out as associates (usually for about seven years), because that's how all lawyers learn their craft. If you don't know the names of associates, ask the partner to recommend one; they should be happy to help keep business within the firm rather than have a potential client go elsewhere.

If the cost is still prohibitive, try to locate a lawyer who is a sole practitioner; that is, one who has his or her own firm. Often, a smaller office means lower overhead, which may translate into a lower hourly rate.

Yet another possibility is to find a lawyer who has worked on similar negotiations in the past and is eager to gather more experience in the theatre field. This person won't be a complete beginner, but may be more flexible about hourly rates.

A final idea is to contact the local Volunteer Lawyers for the Arts, if you think you qualify for low-income assistance. There are many lawyers in any community who volunteer their legal services on a pro bono (i.e., free) basis. They might not be "theatre lawyers" per se; often they are lawyers who practice mostly in other areas and who take on negotiations for writers and other artists because they love the work and want to diversify their workload (or perhaps want to add some excitement to an otherwise drier practice).

Once you have several names to consider, write or call each lawyer, explain your situation and ask to set up a consultation. It may be easier to write to a lawyer than to get one on the phone, but if you need to move ahead quickly, or have a personal referral, you might try to call. When you speak with the lawyer's assistant, be clear about why you are calling, and if you have a referral, be sure to mention it.

A consultation will not last long; typically, thirty minutes at most. The purpose of the consultation, whether in person or on the phone, is to describe the situation and get a feeling for the lawyer and his or her ability to handle the negotiation, so that you can decide whether to retain him or her. In addition to trying to sell the writer on the lawyer's ability to handle the matter, the lawyer will be interviewing *you* as a potential client, deciding whether she or he wants to spend time on you and your project. It's also generally a good idea for the lawyer to glance through the contract, if one's been proffered and if she or he is familiar with such documents, but it's up to the individual lawyer to decide whether or not that is properly part of the consultation.

Absent extraordinary circumstances, the writer should not have to pay for the consultation, but you should inquire about this in advance to avoid an unpleasant surprise. After the introductory letter or phone call, the lawyer should be willing to invest a little time in assessing the project and the potential client and, one hopes, in selling him- or herself to the client. Remember that in this situation the client is the "buyer" and the lawyer is the "seller," and thus the lawyer should act accordingly; that is, not be condescending or arrogant, or act as if the writer is wasting his or her time. If the lawyer wants you to pay for the consultation, think carefully before agreeing to do so, particularly if you are hoping to meet with two or three lawyers before making a final decision. There is usually a choice of lawyers, so don't feel obliged to pay for the privilege of meeting one.

The interview is the beginning of a business transaction, so the writer should feel free to ask any questions. This includes finding out the lawyer's hourly rate, whether the lawyer will require a retainer (upfront money) and, if so, the amount, and how expenses will be handled (usually the client pays for virtually everything).

If the consultation goes well and you are seriously considering retaining the lawyer, also consider asking for the names of other clients you could call to talk to about their experience with that lawyer. Obviously, no lawyer will give out the names of clients who were unhappy with their representation, but it will probably be helpful nonetheless to hear about the lawyer from someone else. Even if you're sold on a particular lawyer during your first consultation, it's always a good idea to consult with others before reaching a final decision.

Once the lawyer is retained—and assuming you're paying an hourly rate—keep in mind that every time the lawyer works on this negotiation, she or he writes down the amount of time spent. This means that every time you dial the phone to talk with the lawyer (and vice versa), the clock is ticking and the lawyer's bill is mounting. Consequently, prepare a carefully considered list of the questions or issues you want to discuss before you pick up the phone. Don't just call for an update or a pep talk. Negotiations often drag on for a long time, so learn to be patient. It may be nerve-wracking, but it's cheaper to call a friend.

LAWYERS AND AGENTS

Some writers have both an agent and a lawyer. For the most part, these are writers who have achieved a certain level of success and who can afford the luxury of having two representatives handle matters simultaneously. It's often said that two sets of eyes are better than one, and different people will focus on different issues. This is particularly true with agents and lawyers, since agents look primarily at how to make certain terms better (not only financial terms, but also matters such as script and artistic approvals, attending rehearsals, travel expenses, etc.), while lawyers are more accustomed to drafting and interpreting the language of contracts.

If you already have an agent, don't panic and think you also need to retain a lawyer. Agents may not be lawyers, but they have usually seen many, many theatre contracts and are very accustomed to the issues and language involved; so, a lawyer's input, while helpful, may not be desperately needed. In addition, many writers don't realize agencies retain lawyers to assist them when questions arise; this cost is *not* passed on to the writer in the absence of truly extraordinary circumstances.

A reminder: If you are a member of the Dramatists Guild, a call to the Business Affairs hotline, while not providing legal counsel, may provide the "second set of eyes" you need to set your mind at ease. The Guild staff often works closely with both agents and lawyers, providing a completely different perspective: They look at documents with an eye towards how all stage writers are treated at a given level of production, rather than focusing narrowly on one client's needs.

LIST OF QUESTIONS FOR AGENTS

The following is a summary of some of the areas writers might want to discuss with agents who are interested in representing their work. Feel free to add any questions of your own, since this list consists of frequently asked questions and is not intended to be an exhaustive list of a writer's concerns. The responses will vary from agent to agent; there are no right or wrong answers.

1. How long has the agent been in business? How large is the agency? How many stage writers does the agent/agency represent? Would the agent be handling your work personally and, if not, who would be, and what is their experience? What happens to you as a client if the agent dies? If there's a long client list, how does the agent plan to add another client, and where will you fit into the existing structure?

2. What services does or doesn't the agent provide to clients? Will the agent give you advice on how to reshape and revise your work? Will the agent provide you with career counseling?

3. Does the agent also handle film and television, or is there someone else in the agency or perhaps affiliated with it who will?

4. What about your work interests the agent? Does his or her feeling for it somehow fit with your overall artistic vision? What initial marketing ideas does the agent have?

5. How does the agent see your role in the relationship? Is it understood that you will still be out marketing and promoting your work, too? What does the agent expect of you and, ideally, what would your relationship be like?

6. Will the agent provide periodic updates of those who have been sent scripts? When an offer is made, how will you proceed? Does the agent fully appreciate that though you value

his or her advice, all final decisions will ultimately be made—
and papers signed—by you?

7. If you are interested in working in a venue that is not considered mainstream, is that okay with the agent? If you already
do, or wish to, work in radio drama, how does the agent feel
about that?

8. What are the commission percentages in all possible venues of
work? Who pays what expenses? Which expenses are considered normal and which are extraordinary?

9. Does the agent handle foreign rights? What are her or his relationships with agents abroad?

10. Will you sign a contract with the agent, or will she or he simply add the agency clause to contracts you sign with third parties? Will the agent sign a contract for an initial finite period
of time, such as two or three years, or will the agreement be
open-ended?

11. Does the agency have an attorney on retainer for any special
needs of the client? If yes, what is the scope of that representation? If you already have a lawyer, will the agent work with
him or her?

Chapter 7

PUBLISHERS

Publishers associated with the theatre industry are an important part of authors' careers. This chapter focuses specifically on publishers of the acting editions of stage works (the inexpensive copies of scripts intended for use in rehearsals) who also license the stock and amateur performance rights, such as Dramatists Play Service, Samuel French and Music Theatre International. These organizations typically are referred to simply as "publishers," without reference to their licensing function, but don't be misled by the name. All publishers of acting editions also license performing rights. This chapter does not address trade publishing (clothbound versions and mass-market paperback editions for the general reading public), which falls instead within the normal trade publishing industry.

This chapter looks first at the publisher's functions, then at the writer's contractual relationship with the publisher, and finally at the question of choosing a publisher.

FUNCTIONS
Primary versus secondary agents

For the publisher of acting editions, licensing is the primary business; such publishers openly admit that their publications are not in and of themselves profitable, whereas the licensing may be. The licensing organization is typically known as the secondary agent for a work, handling the secondary markets of stock and amateur theatrical productions all around the world, in all languages, as opposed to the primary market of premiere and commercial productions, which typically are handled (as discussed in the chapter on representation) by the writer's primary agent (normally just called the "agent").

Neither primary nor secondary agent is "better" than the other; to the contrary, they each fulfill different purposes and are more like two sides of a coin, working together to exploit a work to the fullest. A successful work will often enjoy both an agent and a publisher. The publisher is typically a complement to, not a substitute for, an individual agent.

Definitions of stock and amateur rights

Stock: any and all performances given by any theatre or group using a cast which consists entirely, or of a majority, of paid actors and production staff and/or that has normally been known to handle stock pursuant to one of the Actors Equity Association agreements governing employment of actors in productions so classified, including Council of Off Loop Theatres (COLT), Council of Stock Theatres (COST), League of Resident Theatres (LORT), dinner theatre, repertory productions or other resident or regional not-for-profit professional theatres, but *not* including Broadway, Off-Broadway, first- or second-class out-of-town and touring productions, or Off-Off-Broadway.

Amateur: performance rights for little theatres, community theatres, drama associations, colleges, universities, high school or other school groups, churches, clubs and amateur organizations, regardless of whether any of the above performances are given by paid or unpaid actors or production staff.

The publisher's marketing

The publisher's primary marketing tool is the annual distribution of an updated catalogue listing each play or musical that it licenses, together with a brief description of each work. Usually an author's contract with the publisher will contain only a simple provision along these lines: "The publisher shall list the work in its catalogue and shall use its best efforts in good faith to secure productions of the work." Sometimes, in addition, the contract may also state whether the work will be highlighted in some way (large advertisement, prominent placement, multiple notices) within each catalogue.

Unlike the agent, the publisher does not actively submit works for consideration or solicit productions, nor does it typically market works individually, as would an author's agent. In other words, it doesn't talk up each work, it doesn't cajole people to read the script, it doesn't unearth productions. Once in the publisher's hands, the work itself is supposed to fill that role.

Publishers license many works simultaneously; some catalogues contain a few hundred titles, while the larger publishers each represent 7-10,000 works. Under the best circumstances, their catalogues are distributed to tens of thousands of theatres, schools and others interested in presenting plays and musicals, with total distribution depending on the size of the publisher. In most instances, the publisher then waits for presenters to choose works from the catalogue and request stock or amateur licenses. Each publisher uses its own standard forms for stock and amateur rights dispositions; these contracts are, for the most part, not individually drafted and negotiated as those described in the chapter on production contracts would be. As a practical matter, it is simply not possible to give each play in a catalogue individual attention; this is not to criticize but simply to recognize the publisher's contribution for what it is and to encourage reasonable expectations about such a relationship.

All marketing decisions remain within the judgment of the publisher, unless specific promises have been made during negotiations. This extends to the style and manner of the marketing, including advertising, the number and distribution of free copies, and every detail of the manufacturing process, including book design, if applicable.

THE PUBLISHER/AUTHOR RELATIONSHIP

There are roughly five basic tenets of the publisher/author contractual relationship: 1) copyright ownership; 2) grant of rights and publisher's responsibilities; 3) scope of representation; 4) financial terms, including advance, royalty structures, script publication and the publisher's commissions; and 5) the author's rights, including script approvals (of both the manuscript before publication and the integrity of the script during performance) and appropriate billing credit (again including both the published version of the script and in performance-related materials, such as programs).

Copyright ownership

As always, copyright ownership in the work remains with the author. No publisher should ever try to claim ownership. The publisher will assume responsibility for making sure the copyright notice appears on any printed copies of the script, and may also take on the task of filing the copyright registration form with the U.S. Copyright Office; but, all filings and notices should remain in the author's name. The contract between the publisher and the author grants the publisher the right to publish and license the work (two of the "twigs" in the bundle of rights that comprise the copyright), but these rights never require the publisher to own the copyright in the play. One or two publishers have claimed that to market a work well, they "needed" to own the copyright; this claim has *no* basis in reality, although it may speak to paternalism (i.e., those publishers believing that since they know better than the author how to market a work, they therefore want the author "out of the way"). This is specious. Historically, publishers have worked very effectively and have made good deals with licensees without *ever* owning the copyright in a work, but only having been granted licensing authority by authors. Thus, authors are strongly advised never to sign contracts that assign or sell the copyright to a publisher (or anyone else in the theatre).

Grant of rights

Typically the grant of rights to the publisher is fairly specific, and the language should be clear and concise: 1) to license the stock and amateur performance rights in the work, including public readings and recitations; 2) to publish an acting edition of the work within a specified time frame (no more than 18 months is considered normal); 3) to authorize and license reprints of the work, or parts of the work, by other publishers; 4) to authorize translations of the work into foreign languages, lease or license performances in foreign countries around the world, authorize the licensing and publication of the work by foreign publishers, and make transcriptions of the work into Braille (it being understood that the author also retains ownership of the copyright in all translations); and 5) to authorize the publication of the work, or excerpts of it, in anthologies or textbooks. The publisher should not be granted broad, vague rights such as "the right to license the work in all venues anywhere." The rights granted usually last for the term of the copyright and all renewals.

In return, the publisher assumes complete responsibility for: 1) publishing the acting edition of the work and all attendant costs (after receiving the final version of the manuscript); 2) selling copies of it; 3) licensing stock and amateur performances; 4) registering the work for copyright in the author's name; and 5) paying the author the agreed-upon percentage of royalties collected for leasing and licensing rights and for retail sales of the acting edition.

Scope of representation

Stock and amateur licensing. The scope of the agreement, meaning the range of representation by the publisher, should ordinarily be limited to stock and amateur licensing—the areas publishers know best and are best-equipped to handle—leaving commercial productions and dispositions in other media to the author's primary agent or other representative, such as an entertainment lawyer. Usually, the areas excluded from the agreement are commercial stage productions, film, television, video, radio and all computer-related dispositions. In other words, if a film producer wants to make the work into a movie, or the author receives an offer for a Broadway or Off-Broadway production, the author's individual agent should handle those negotiations, *not* the publisher.

From a purely financial point of view, the publisher would like to be able to share in these other, potentially large sums of money. There has been a recent trend on the part of some publishers to broaden significantly the scope of representation to include many of these other areas. For the author, however, the bottom line is that these additional types of dispositions are not really the areas of the publisher's expertise, and the publisher will sometimes require the author to pay much more substantial commissions than agents for licensing rights—as much as thirty to fifty percent. Particularly for film, television, video, radio and the like, contractual arrangements are very complex and industry-specific; consequently, a publisher should be able to show hands-on, significant experience in these areas, including commercial stage production, before authors consider granting them such rights.

Electronic/computer rights. The topic of electronic rights is discussed further in the chapter on developing areas. However, it needs to be mentioned here that at this time, contracts should not include any mention of licensing electronic or online transmission, CD-ROM, or computer/video rights. These are all very new and rapidly developing areas, and thus there are two major concerns: first, that the publisher is unlikely to be equipped to license such rights, but may only want to be sure that no one else will obtain them; second, it is too early for market standards of use, payments and protections to have been established, so costly mistakes can too easily be made by authors getting locked in prematurely and, tangentially, publishers may not actually negotiate deals in these areas with third parties until their value becomes more apparent. Rather than joining with the author to try to find a reasonable solution to the question of rights in this rapidly changing market, some publishers are moving ahead quickly simply to secure rights and specific terms from the author, inserting *very* broad grant-of-rights language into their contracts and being reluctant even to discuss these terms.

Authors are thus encouraged to proceed cautiously and to refrain from granting these rights precipitously, although this may prove difficult to achieve. The ideal contract would not include these types of rights yet; second best would be to get the publisher to agree that this clause will be negotiated when the publisher is actually ready to enter the electronic rights market, and would include language providing for "terms to be negotiated in accordance with industry standards at the time of the license." If the publisher is unpersuaded, a third possibility is to negotiate the electronic rights clause as specifically as possible in terms of the grant of rights, remuneration, reversion issues and copyright protections.

In all of the above, be certain that there exists a strong reservation of rights clause in the document, which might read: "All rights not specifically granted to the Publisher in this Agreement are expressly reserved to the Author." With this reservation of rights, if there is no explicit mention of electronic rights in the agreement, those rights arguably would remain within the control of the author.

Financial terms

The advance. There should always be an advance against future royalties paid to the author. This is not to suggest that the size of the advance will always be large—depending on the work's production history, it could even be as little as seventy-five to one hundred dollars—but the publisher should offer *some* advance to the author. Sometimes a single dollar may constitute the consideration supporting the contract, which may be legal but is not very fair to the author, even for a work with little or no production history. Since the publisher obtains exclusive stock and amateur licensing rights from the author, the publisher should, in good faith, make some type of real, not merely token, advance payment in return.

The advance should be paid when the contract is signed; that is, in advance of publication or licensed performances. It is the publisher's responsibility, not the author's, to assume any risk involved in not being able to publish or license the work.

Royalty structures. There are different royalty structures for the stock and amateur markets, based on what the publisher intends to charge the various licensees. The author's share of those monies is covered more extensively in the subsection on the publisher's commission, below.

STOCK PRODUCTIONS Arrangements for stock production licenses generally use the common percentage of gross box office receipts calculation for authors. This is typically at least seven percent for any plays written after roughly 1970. If the piece has had a New York production (typically Off-Broadway or Broadway) with good reviews, the royalties would likely be eight to ten percent, with very successful works receiving as much as twelve percent. Musicals generally receive higher percentage royalties, usually starting closer to eight to ten percent with, those in the greatest demand commanding twelve to fourteen percent of box office receipts.

It's important to note that this information will most likely *not* be contained in your contract with the publisher. It might not even state that the publisher will charge a percentage of the gross box office receipts; but, if it does, it will probably also provide that the publisher retains the ability and discretion to negotiate deals based on specific circumstances, which is addressed further below.

AMATEUR PRODUCTIONS Amateur licensing is ordinarily done on a fee-per-performance or per-production basis, often with a certain dollar amount established for the first night and a slightly lower dollar amount established for each subsequent performance. (While the figures are not set in stone, it is not unusual to license a play for fifty to seventy-five dollars the first night and twenty-five to fifty dollars for each subsequent performance, with more well-known works commanding higher fees.) Musicals are treated differently than plays in this regard, and for them the following factors are usually taken into account before a fee is established: size of the theatre, length of the run, number of performances, and ticket prices.

The contract will usually state the minimum dollar amounts the publisher will try to obtain; but, as addressed below, there will ordinarily also be language enabling the publisher to accept lower amounts if a particular situation warrants. Here, the author must trust the publisher's experience and discretion, and believe that the publisher will always try to negotiate the highest price possible (since doing so also benefits the publisher).

LICENSING MUSICALS The licensing of musicals is different due to the existence of a score, which will also be rented to a licensee. Generally the authors are responsible for providing the publisher with a clean, camera-ready copy of the *master materials* comprising the work, which would include a stage manager's script and unmarked, legible, reproducible deshons (the manuscript original) or copies (including computer disks if available) of the music and lyrics for the piano/conductor and orchestral scores of the work although it depends on the authors' bargaining power. The cost depends in large part on the condition of the score when it comes out of the orchestra pit; it may need to be cleaned up. The author should *not* have to pay for this out of pocket. The publisher should advance the money and then recoup it out of royalties. (It's important to note that if the publishing contract raises the issue of who will be responsible for items such as any fees or charges to orchestrators, arrangers or copyists, those usually have been addressed previously by the producer in its contracts with the respective persons, with the producer being responsible for their payment. Those relationships are structured as work for hire as employees of the producer, and the individuals thus relinquish ownership of the scores, so that the authors can own them.)

Once the authors have provided the master materials, the publisher is responsible for paying all other costs: copying, printing, binding, warehousing, maintaining the library, etc. This is a tremendous investment, generally the most expensive part of running the library. Thereafter, the publisher charges rental fees for the use of the scores, and even though the authors are responsible for providing the master materials, they do not share in the income generated by their rental; the authors receive the performance royalties (after deducting the publisher's commission), but the publisher retains the money received for the rental of the scores, since its investment in their creation far outweighs the authors'.

PUBLICATION The contract will often establish the minimum retail sales price that will be charged for the acting edition; but, again, the final decision remains the publisher's. With little or no variation, the author's book royalty is ten percent of the catalogue retail price on all books sold. Royalties are not paid on complimentary copies given to the author or provided at a discount, copies given away for purposes of eliciting reviews or aiding in the sale and licensing of the work, or on copies sold below cost. Typically, the author receives a number of books free of charge (ten is a common figure) and then has the ability to purchase additional copies for personal use at a discount, often forty percent off.

PRODUCER'S DISCRETION As stated, in both the stock and amateur markets the publisher retains the discretion to set fees and percentages charged to theatres and others to whom they grant licenses, as well as the book's selling price, but also assumes the obligation to use its best efforts to maximize the work's exposure and to obtain the greatest number of productions on the best possible terms. Consequently, if the publisher receives multiple requests from one city or region, it would first turn its attention and energy to securing the largest production in that location which will yield the best financial results.

For example: Assume Kansas City has three theatres suitable for a particular play—a regional theatre with 750 seats, a smaller theatre with 300 seats and an amateur community theatre with seating capacity of 150. If the initial request for performance rights comes from either the 300-seat or 150-seat theatre, the publisher would ordinarily first contact the 750-seat theatre to find out if it is interested in the play. If the larger theatre wants to present it, then the publisher will license it the rights, since that would maximize the yield to the author.

Some smaller theatres have objected to this practice, since they stand to lose productions to larger theatres even when they make the first inquiry or offer. While their objections are not unreasonable, it conflicts with the publisher's primary purpose: to exploit the work to the fullest extent possible. The larger theatres admittedly are granted certain privileges and priorities, since they can bring in more visible and lucrative productions.

Publisher's commission. The commission is the percentage of the royalties and fees that the publisher keeps for itself. The greater the commission, the smaller the author's share of the earnings.

Historically, the norm for publisher's commissions has been ten percent on stock licensing royalties (paying out ninety percent to the author), and twenty percent on amateur licensing royalties (paying out eighty percent to the author), and the norm for royalties on all sales of the acting edition is a payment to the author of ten percent of the retail price. These commissions comport with the norm for individual agents, as addressed in the chapter on representation and, also as stated there, the higher commission on amateur licensing offsets the fact that amateur royalties are typically lower than those paid for the stock rights.

In recent years, unfortunately, some publishers have significantly increased their commissions—often establishing one flat percentage for all performance royalties regardless of venue—with the rates in some instances (usually less well-known writers) climbing to twenty-five, thirty-three, even fifty percent. This situation is aggravated further when such high percentages are coupled with a broadening of the scope of representation beyond stock and amateur licensing, as discussed above.

This "trend" does not bode well for the author. To the publisher, these higher commissions seem logical, since they result in more money flowing to (or, rather, being retained by) the publisher; but, they blithely ignore the fact that these higher percentages are not at all consistent with the tradition. Smaller publishers have argued that higher percentages are necessary to enable them to stay in business; after all, they depend on smaller catalogues and perhaps less well-known works, so they don't have the substantial cash flow of the larger companies. At the same time, we can assume that a smaller company's expenses are significantly smaller, too, but the publishers posit that if writers want smaller publishers to exist—so that there are more than just two or three choices of publishers—these commission rates may be necessary.

To be fair, some authors feel passionately that smaller publishers *do* provide a necessary service by taking chances on newer works, untested works, "niche" plays and works for which the artistic value is evident but the money-making potential might not be high. Viewed this way, smaller publishers' higher commissions could be seen as both reasonable and justifiable, given the risks they assume and their commitment to publishing and licensing less overtly commercial works.

But there are problems with these arguments. First, there is a tremendous difference between ten and fifty percent commissions; some have argued that publishers which charge fifty percent are gouging vulnerable writers. Second, the bulk of the services provided by the publisher (e.g., placing the work in the catalogue, fielding requests for licenses, issuing standard license forms) remain the same regardless of the rate of commission. Third, the issue of how to remain competitive should rest primarily on the shoulders of the people who run the publishing company, not on the artists who create the work that provides the basis for such a business.

Consider two other factors: first, that publishers know how important their services can be, and thus writers will do almost anything to establish a relationship. (Some publishers have taken this imbalance of bargaining power to such an extreme that a few actually *charge* writers for the "honor" of "contributing" to the publication—one company charges each writer $300 for the acting edition of a full-length play.) Second, as the smaller publishers push hard enough and establish such high percentages as "normal," other publishers—that is, those that do *not* need to charge higher commissions in order to stay in business—have begun to realize that they, too, could underwrite a larger share of their costs by charging higher commissions. (When challenged, one such larger publisher argued that it cannot "afford" to take chances on emerging writers without receiving a higher commission for their efforts, disregarding the success of its existing catalogue.) In sum, what some publishers large and small are saying is that established or well-known writers (presumably with more bargaining power) are charged smaller commissions than emerging writers (who may be more desperate). This is unpleasant, and does not compare favorably with primary agents' commissions, which do not fluctuate with the author's "market value."

Authors sometimes say, "I don't care about the money; I just want to get published. I can stand on ceremony for a larger royalty, but ninety percent of nothing is less than fifty percent of something." The feeling this statement expresses is completely understandable, but rather than dispute the inherent imbalance and unfairness of high percentages, as it should, it provides an all-too-easy personal justification for paying them.

Remember, too, when evaluating these higher percentages, that stock and amateur licenses are part of the author's subsidiary rights. As discussed in the chapter on production contracts, this means that the producer(s) of the work might have earned a share in these monies. For example, if a work is produced Off-Broadway for more than sixty-five performances, the commercial producer ordinarily receives forty percent of the author's stock and amateur royalties. If the producer(s) receive forty percent of the author's net proceeds and the publisher takes fifty percent, not much is left for the author. (The number of authors who fall into this specific example may be small compared to the total number of authors whose works are published each year, but it remains a scenario every stage writer should consider carefully.)

Theoretically, at least, these commissions are freely negotiable between the publisher and the author (see "Negotiating the contract," below), and all authors are urged at least to explore other possibilities before agreeing to high commissions.

Author's rights

The author's rights of script approvals (including music and lyrics) and billing credit should, but sometimes don't, appear in the publisher's contract. It is strongly recommended that authors try to get these obligations in writing, since the author will never have a direct relationship with the licensees of the work. Including such language in the author's contract obligates the publisher to include these requirements in the contracts it signs with the licensees. This remains the only possible way to enforce such terms, and thus it is important that the publisher be required to take a firm stand on these issues. Most publishers will tell you they *do* stand firmly on these issues, as a matter of course, but just don't mention it in the author's contract. But if, in fact, this does comport with their existing business practices, publishers should have no legitimate objection to saying so in a binding legal document.

Script approvals. As stated above, the issue of script approvals concerns control over the published version of the work and ensuring that in production the work is presented as written and published.

THE MANUSCRIPT, MUSIC AND LYRICS The author typically has an obligation to provide the publisher with a complete copy of the work in final form, together with a description of the characters, a property list, a set design (i.e., stage diagram), perhaps a costume plot and, if possible and necessary, a photograph of the set. The publisher might also ask for other materials to assist in the exploitation of the work, such as reviews, publicity photos, etc.

The author should always have the right to review proofs of the work before it is printed. Since time is usually "of the essence," the publisher and author should establish a clear turnaround time in their contract. It's best to avoid using ambiguous terms, such as having the author return the proofs "promptly," since that word could reasonably be interpreted differently by different people. For example, to the publisher with a clear understanding of the entire publication process, "promptly" could mean one week, while to the author who is busy at work on other projects, it might mean two weeks. Any inadvertent misunderstanding could cause the author to miss an important deadline, and it's unnecessary to take such a risk when it's so easy to establish a clear turnaround time. This does not mean the author can demand that the publisher accept a longer period of time based on the author's busy schedule— the turnaround times are established with an eye to all subsequent deadlines—but a clear statement in the contract will benefit all.

In addition, never let the publisher's editors have final approval over editing the work, including music and lyrics, even if the goal is to occupy fewer printed pages. This right should be retained, and changes should be made, only by the author. If time is a critical consideration, the author can be required to make such decisions, and changes, within a reasonably short time.

LICENSED SCRIPT APPROVALS The script approvals clause should state: "No one has the right to make any changes in the Work without the prior written permission of the Author, and any changes that are made also remain the Author's property." The publisher should then be required to insert this sentence into all licensing agreements for the work.

Some authors have expressed surprise that this would even be an issue; but, unfortunately, the author's right to have the work produced as written is sometimes questioned by licensees in the stock and amateur arenas; authors may find, too late, that the text, context, characters and/or setting of the play have been changed without the author's permission. It is generally thought this happens because there is a fundamental lack of understanding about an author's rights and copyright law, rather than any illegal or malicious intent on the part of the licensees. Some people believe that when works become popular, they are transformed somehow, "belong" to the public, and thus may be rewritten. In addition, while not in the majority, there are some presenters who believe they have the right to delete portions of a work that their local audiences might find offensive; "bad" language often falls into this category, but it can also include items such as gender or character traits. For example, a presenter may be worried that its audience might not respond favorably to a gay character, so the presenter simply changes that. Another presenter may believe it has the right to make cuts in the work to shorten the running time, or because in its opinion the cuts make the work play "better."

These and any other reasons given for changes made without advance, express authorial consent are utterly and completely without merit, so an author's rights need to be established clearly. "Simple" changes often violate the integrity of a piece and the author's artistic vision (not to mention the copyright). *No* presenter should assume that such changes are *ever* acceptable.

Presumably, the presenter *reads* the work, or at least knows what it is about, before actually licensing it for production. If a presenter believes that some part of a particular work will offend its audience (sidestepping the issue of whether theatre should ever be sanitized, and assuming the presenter knows its audience), the presenter should be encouraged either to contact the author *before* licensing the work to find out if the author is willing to make the proposed changes; or, if the author is unwilling, to produce the work as is or choose a different work.

If a presenter signs a licensing agreement containing script approvals language, but still makes unauthorized changes in the work, it raises breach of contract issues the publisher must address.

Billing credit. The most obvious, and simplest, billing credit will be in the published script itself. Ordinarily, there is a paragraph in the contract which details the publisher's obligation and includes a sample of the billing credit to appear wherever the title appears.

Next comes the author's billing credit in materials related to performances and, as with script approvals, the author will not have any ability to enforce billing credit provisions directly with licensees. Ideally, the publishing contract will contain an obligation to include proper billing requirements in all licensing agreements, with the publisher then assuming the responsibility of making sure the presenter fulfills these obligations; however, not all publishing contracts contain this language. As always, the author is advised to try to get what she or he wants and deserves in writing.

The publisher's policing of the author's performance billing can be accomplished in a number of ways; for example, by requiring the presenter to provide the publisher with a copy of the program and all publicity and/or advertising materials. Each publisher has established its own system of policing licenses granted and punishing contract violations, but there should be *some* enforcement mechanism in place.

In addition, if the author has a billing obligation to a previous theatre or producer, that information needs to be included in the publishing contract, too, and the publisher would assume responsibility for policing that billing in the same manner as described above.

NEGOTIATING THE CONTRACT

Even though publishers use form contracts with authors, they should be proffered as generally negotiable documents. Note that raising issues you would like to discuss (i.e., negotiate) with the publisher is considered reasonable and normal business behavior as long as it's done in a polite, gracious manner. As with any contract, the publisher may respond with its own reasons for wanting to retain certain provisions in question, and it may not be persuaded by the author. Be prepared for the fact that all of your positions might not be adopted.

However, if a publisher responds to your legitimate request to negotiate by abruptly withdrawing the offer, something strange is happening. Since negotiating is a normal part of the process (of most business transactions, really), such behavior belies any semblance of good faith or fair dealing, and authors are well-advised to reconsider working with publishers who treat you with such disdain.

CHOOSING THE PUBLISHER

Don't lock yourself into thinking there are only two or three publishers. There are many publishers across the country, and you should take the time to do your own research rather than submitting your work or even inquiry letters blindly. As discussed in the chapter on marketing and self-promotion, it is wise to invest in some of the more popular resource books for stage writers, including those that list publishers together with the types of work they are interested in and the ways they recommend you approach them. There are many different publishers to consider, so think creatively.

If a publisher has already shown interest in your work, it is a good idea to ask to see their catalogue and a sample copy of a script they've published (if you haven't already seen one). You might also consider privately contacting a few writers whose works are listed in the catalogue to ask for firsthand information pertaining to their experience with that particular publisher.

WHEN TO SIGN WITH A PUBLISHER

Inevitably the question arises: At what point, both in terms of a work's life and an author's career, is it best to look for and sign with a publisher?

First, as a general rule, it's safe to say publishers scout for works which have been produced at least once. A couple look primarily at works that have been produced specifically in New York City, but most are not so limited. Some even extend offers for previously unproduced works; their willingness to do this could depend, in part, on the size and success of their existing catalogue.

The work's arc

In trying to answer the "when" question directly, it is often suggested that authors try to visualize a work's life as an arc (or multiple arcs; here, let's focus only on the first one). Ideally, authors would not sign publishing contracts until the work has reached the apex of that arc—once the primary markets have been explored and the work has enjoyed its "highest" level of production. Just as the work crests and would begin its downward turn, the publisher steps in and begins a second upward movement, expanding the work's life into the secondary markets of stock and amateur licensing to the maximum extent possible. (Simultaneously, the author's primary agent will probably actively market the piece into other subsidiary markets, such as commercial foreign productions and other media, such as film and television.) Assuming an "upward sweep," it is generally considered premature to sign with a publisher before the work reaches its apex.

More simply, an author generally waits to sign with a publisher until the work has gotten on its feet—whether through a regional theatre, Off-Broadway, Broadway or other full-scale production—and it's time to try to reach a broader audience.

Exceptions

There are some situations in which you might actually want to sign with a publisher either before the work has been produced or after its first production. Some publishers look for works that target a certain market, fill particular niches, or are especially timely. For example, some publishers look heavily for works aimed at the high school and junior high markets, and for works that fill the growing demand for good roles reflecting racial and gender diversity. Or maybe you just know that your work isn't going to attract commercial productions or film offers (or possibly even a primary agent) and there is no question in your mind that the best marketing route is to get your work into the catalogue and thence into stock and amateur presenters' hands. Or perhaps a publisher has made its focus certain types of works—such as yours—that otherwise have not previously found their way into the public consciousness.

Signing prematurely

The risks and frustrations for an author in signing with a publisher too soon lie in: 1) the possibility of the publisher insisting on representing rights outside the stock and amateur arenas, thus positioning itself to act as the work's primary agent, even if it does not have extensive experience in other areas and it intends to do nothing more than include the work in its annual catalogue; and 2) the fact that if the publisher takes a larger commission than the agent's customary ten to twenty percent, the author will receive significantly smaller royalty checks than she or he would if the work were represented by a primary agent.

But it's the best offer

It's possible, however, that the publisher's offer will be the best one received by an author who, unfortunately, has not had success obtaining certain levels of production. Obviously, such an offer could be very beneficial to a work, since it is arguably better for it to appear in a catalogue than to lie about unseen. And having your work chosen to appear in a publisher's catalogue can be an important step in your career; just as with a production, it confirms the work's value, since someone besides the author is willing to risk money on its future.

However, some writers take a different approach. If the work is beginning to gather momentum, for example, with staged readings, contests or even small productions, an author who has developed methodical marketing and networking efforts may decide to wait.

Taking risks

Try not to accept a publisher's offer just to have something tangible to hold onto, which is very easy to say but not at all easy to do. If you're feeling conflicted—not ready to commit—remember that if a publisher is interested now (i.e., if the publisher thinks it can make money with the work), then the chances are pretty good that the publisher would still be interested in a few months (or after the work has been produced). Admittedly, however, there are risks inherent in waiting: There are no guarantees that the offer will remain open indefinitely; and it is also possible that a production won't elicit the response you envisioned and, instead of heightening demand for the work, dampens it.

If you are a person uncomfortable with significant risk, it may be best to accept the publisher's offer, even with not-so-good terms. On the other hand, if you are a person who believes that without risks there can be no significant gains, then timing and circumstances will help you decide which direction to take. After that, you just have to trust that you made the best possible decision given the information you had at that time. It's a personal choice.

The point here is not to push you in a particular direction, but rather to encourage all authors to explore the full range of possibilities and to discover a direction that makes the most sense for each individual and his or her work, and—perhaps equally important—what feels best in the course of mulling over an important and difficult decision.

Chapter 8

DEVELOPING AREAS

AUTHORS' RELATIONSHIPS WITH DIRECTORS

The relationship between directors and writers is one of the most volatile topics in theatre at this time, and the turmoil shows no signs of abating. Writers believe that directors too frequently, and inappropriately, impose contractual demands on the writers with whom they work, and at earlier and earlier points in the life of a play or musical; put on the defensive, they are fighting back furiously to protect their position, rights and earnings. Directors argue that authors are making greater demands on *them*, asking directors to assist them in the development, revision and marketing of their works; believing that both their direction and the suggestions they make constitute an important and tangible contribution to the work, directors are asking for various types of compensation in return.

Sometimes it feels as if these two groups of artists are operating in two completely different universes, so different are their perspectives on what is to be expected from the writer/director relationship.

Background

Historically, writers signed contracts only with producers, not with anyone else working on a production, and the same was true of all other artists and personnel involved. The author did not sign contracts with the director, the actors, the designers or anyone else, and those artists typically didn't sign contracts with each other, either, only with producers.

A producer's obligation to a director includes financial compensation and, in some instances (depending on union contract requirements), the opportunity to direct one or more additional productions of the same work, assuming the producer has optioned the rights to such subsequent production.

But in recent years, an increasing number of directors have become frustrated with the inherent limitations of having a contractual relationship only with the producer and have turned to the writer to "relieve" those frustrations. (Remember: The writer is the only constant in the life of a work, since the writer owns the copyright. Some directors have determined that there is more security in attaching themselves to the work itself—to secure a longer-lasting guarantee— than only to the producer.) Unfortunately, this is *not* in the best interests of writers.

Roles and responsibilities

Traditionally, the fundamental roles of the writer and the director are separate and clearly delineated; writers create the work, and directors interpret that work. Even during rehearsal, when a director makes suggestions to the writer concerning ways the work might be revised or reshaped, it is the writer who actually makes the changes he or she decides to incorporate. Directors contribute what they might call the "primary visual element," by taking the work from the printed page to live performance. (The use of the word "primary" here acknowledges the contributions of the other "visual" artists—not only designers but also actors—whose work may leave a lasting impression on the audience.) The director's contribution, necessarily, has *always* entailed providing advice and guidance to the writer in shaping the work for production, most often in terms of structure and character development. These services were not considered "bonuses" but part and parcel of the director's responsibility; that is, such advice was expected by writers from their directors.

Direction and suggestions for revisions can occur during readings, staged readings, workshops, small or medium-sized productions, regional theatre productions and so on. Suggestions might even be made outside of any formal context; that is, whenever a director works with a writer, even if there's no producer anywhere in sight.

Sample director's request

To create a common understanding, the following is a composite sample of the types of arrangements sought by many directors. For this discussion, assume the director is someone with a few credits under his or her belt, but not with a track record like that of Tommy Tune or Mike Nichols, who are definitely not the norm.

The director first hears the show at a reading put together by the writer, likes it and arranges with an acquaintance to direct a staged reading. Many regional theatre representatives are expected to attend this staged reading. The director works on the play with the writer for four weeks before the staged reading, giving suggestions as to how the writer can improve the structure. Before directing the staged reading, the director puts his or her demands on the table: the right to direct any regional theatre production; six percent of the author's subsidiary rights income; and a right of first refusal on any future productions, including a full director's fee if *not* hired for the Off-Broadway or first-class production. When the writer balks at these demands, the director states plainly that he or she is not going to spend time and energy on a production (in this case, the staged reading) and have his or her contributions become part of the work for the rest of its life without professional and financial participation. If these demands are declined, the director makes clear he or she will simply move on to another piece.

Typically, then, the director's demands on the writer for "compensation"—including both money and job security—will encompass any of the following in any combination:

1. The unqualified right to be the director on certain future productions.
2. The right to be offered the position of director for certain future productions, with the understanding that the director will be paid a buyout fee if the future offers are made to others; commonly referred to as the "right of first refusal."
3. A percentage of the writer's future subsidiary rights proceeds, perhaps two to five percent or higher, sometimes even double digits.

From the director's perspective

Three positions. Many directors adhere to the traditional view: Because writers begin with blank pages and directors are not writers, some directors do not make contractual demands on authors for their services. These directors assume and understand that future offers of work depend on the quality of their directing and their ability to work well with others on a production. This traditional path is obviously the best avenue for writers and provides them with the greatest protection.

At the other extreme, some directors argue that they should be compensated by the writer for *any* work they do with him or her at any point in the work's life (from a reading to full production) and, as discussed below, regardless of whether this work takes the form of script suggestions, actual direction or both. This represents the worst position writers can find themselves in, affording them maximum exposure and no protection.

For these directors, the question isn't whether or not their contribution falls within their "job description"; but, rather, whether or not they are acknowledged and compensated for their "contribution to the work" in any circumstances. These directors believe that the visual component inexorably becomes a part of the work and contributes significantly to the future success of that work; thus, it is axiomatic to them that if they perform *any* work they earn the right to continue to be the work's director and to receive a percentage of the writer's subsidiary rights income. This position is focused primarily, although not exclusively, on the "hallmark" or premiere production of a work; that is, the production which provides its definition or true launching pad into the marketplace. However, in cases of readings, staged readings and workshops, the persuasiveness of this "visual component" argument is weak, and the same could certainly be said of small productions for which the visual component will not leave an indelible print on the work if it moves to a different arena.

Some of these directors believe that they are the crucial link between writers casting about blindly for a production and the theatres with which the directors have worked previously, another reason they feel they should be compensated: for tapping into these contacts. However, this belief fails to take into account the logistics of how directors typically exploit those contacts: In private conversations with persons at those theatres (conversations to which the writer will not be privy), the director makes a self-interested pitch not only for the production of the work but more specifically for *that director* to direct that work. (As an aside, directors may approach theatres with more than one work in hand, focusing on themselves directing as the first concern; there is no guarantee that a director is attaching him- or herself to only one work at a time.) If the theatre agrees to hire that director to work on the production, then the theatre will pay the director for her or his services. If the theatre does not want to accept the director's conditions—that is, does not want to hire that director—the author should not have to compensate the director for simply making this contact.

Still other directors hold that—depending on circumstances—a few directors *might* deserve to negotiate certain contractual promises. For purposes of this discussion, this will be referred to as the Limited Position.

In the Limited Position, threshold issues are analyzed to winnow out "undeserving" directors. The first and apparently most important issue is that only directors who have achieved a significantly high level of professional recognition should even be able to raise the question of contractual demands with a writer. Emerging and midlevel directors need to work on new plays and musicals to advance their own careers, and therein lies an equitable quid pro quo with writers.

Another possible concern might be whether or not the director is choosing between multiple projects, and therefore must turn down one or more to work on yours. (This could be more complicated emotionally if the director works in industries outside of theatre—specifically, film and television—because a director's devotion to your work might therefore entail financial sacrifice; but, be careful of assuming responsibility for the director's choice and for the disparity in earnings between the various industries.) Another consideration might be whether the writer approached the director to help get the work off the ground or the director approached the writer to work on an exciting project that could prove valuable to the director's professional development. (Indeed, the director could be attaching him- or herself to any number of exciting projects, hoping one will pay off.)

Equally important is whether the director is being hired "just" to direct the work or will work with the writer over a significantly longer period of time than rehearsal; that is, to provide extensive dramaturgical services beyond the normal range made by directors. In the latter situation, directors ask themselves and the writers with whom they work, "Why should I spend so much time on your work without receiving a commitment from *you?*"

Additional factors: What stage of development has the work reached when the director is brought in? What marketing has the writer already done and how much will she or he continue to do? If a well-known director helps develop a new piece for three or four years, meeting with people, trying to get the work seen and heard, the Limited Position suggests these efforts be accepted as substantial and worthy of contractual promises.

Even though there are no clear rules about how to weigh the various factors, an argument could be made that a director should be compelled to make a strong case for him- or herself before making demands. While not providing complete protection to the writer, and certainly not as good as declining to sign a contract with the director, at a minimum the Limited Position would dramatically reduce the number of directors who would seek contractual commitments from writers.

Job security. Those directors who support having contracts with writers also argue that it is unfair for unknown or lesser-known directors to be the first director of a work only to find themselves replaced by "name" directors when the work moves to higher levels of production. Not to defend that practice but to put it into context, one cannot deny that the entertainment industry depends on reputation and name recognition; ours is a society that clamors for "stars"; opportunities and salaries alike rise and fall on this basis. Whether this is fair or not, perhaps the *real* question is whether writers should be required to provide the safety net for directors in these situations. Is a director's vulnerability greater than that experienced by others—say, actors who have worked on a play's development—and is it so great as to warrant extraordinary redress from the stage writer? Who protects the writer's vulnerability in the industry to the same issues of name recognition and reputation?

From the writers' perspective

Stage writers react very strongly to the notion that they are somehow "scribes," merely transcribing a director's thoughts and suggestions. They also object to what is perceived to be a prevailing premise: That writers don't write well enough themselves to "sell" a work; that the "real value" in a stage work comes from the director, without whom the writer would have only an unfinished, uninteresting piece. This overlooks the fact that directors, too, must learn to improve: Some writers are angry and exasperated that too often their conversations with directors proceed on the assumption that the director's work is wonderful, maybe even flawless, and the writer should be thankful for the director's attention and input.

Not all directors are right for every work, and sometimes a director's work isn't all that good. A writer might legitimately ask, "If the reason my director is not being offered the chance to direct the commercial production is that we were unhappy with his or her work—or we would just rather have someone else direct next—why should I be obligated to pay him or her not to work? And why should I be obligated to pay that person a share of my subsidiary income in perpetuity?"

Writers are also very nervous about becoming locked into one director's vision of a piece. Working on the same piece with different directors is a natural part of the creative process for stage writers that should not be stifled by any one director's career considerations. Indeed, writers hope that they will have the opportunity to work with many artists whose special talents can reveal a stage work's strengths and weaknesses. Even if the director was a good choice early in a work's life, the work can and will change over time, and some writers have found themselves obligated to one director despite the fact that he or she is no longer the best choice for the work. This shift is not surprising, given the number of years it takes for a work to get produced in the more visible arenas. And the author's concern that the hallmark production show off the work to the best of its ability should be afforded significant weight.

Consequently, writers are especially uncomfortable about signing directors' contracts for readings, staged readings, workshops, showcase and Equity-waiver productions, mid-range not-for-profit productions, even regional theatre mainstage productions. (This is not to suggest that directors are "entitled" to such contracts for commercial productions, only that writers generally find that the vast majority of contractual demands made fall outside the realm of realistic consideration.)

There is unfairness in every industry, and directors (among others, including writers) are sometimes passed over for any number of reasons, not all of them having to do with the quality of the work. Politics may reign; friends do betray friends for the sake of advancement; etc. Certainly, both writers and directors have war stories to tell. But are these concerns sufficient to drive writers into contractual agreements with directors? For a director, being passed over for subsequent productions of a work may be personally painful, but it rarely destroys a career.

Directors ask: In the case of multiple directors, a writer may be seeking different interpretations of the work, but what protects a first director from later directors copying his or her direction? Certainly not the stage writer. This is a wholly different issue that does not seem to have any connection to the terms of compensation and job security found in the contracts directors want writers to sign. And at some point it should be acknowledged that this is a problem created by other directors. The directors' union—the Society of Stage Directors and Choreographers—handles grievances between directors.

Some directors argue it is unfair for only the writers to earn money over the life of a work they have directed. This ignores the fact that directors' and writers' careers are simply structured differently, and that they follow different paths over a lifetime is not inherently unfair. Directors can and do direct back-to-back works throughout their careers; even multiple works within one theatre season. The stage writer, on the other hand, typically may have only a few financially successful works in his or her lifetime. The writer's investment in the work—representing years of writing and marketing without payment—far exceeds the director's investment during the production; and the income the writer may make over the life of the work is rightfully earned.

Writer's vulnerability

Future employment/buyout. The artistic approvals spelled out in an author's production contract provide for author and producer together to select the director. When an author has already signed a contract with a director, promising the right of first refusal on future productions, the author has in essence curtailed the next producer's right to be involved in that decision-making. Directors don't consider this a problem, since they include an escape clause: the buy-out provision, through which the director is paid a not insignificant amount of money—sometimes a full director's fee—if not chosen to direct. Directors—positing that experienced producers anticipate paying off previous financial interests in a work—tell writers, "It doesn't come out of your pocket," but writers *do* find these pre-existing obligations risky and sometimes problematic, because the writer who signs such a contract may find a potential producer disenchanted by the "package" presented, neither interested in hiring the particular director nor willing to pay both that director and the one who will actually do the work. Given a choice between producing two good works—one that comes with a director attached and one that doesn't—the producer could easily decide to take the unencumbered path. If not, often the producer will require something of value from the writer in return for paying the director's buyout fee: maybe dollars or royalty percentage points, or a concession on some other issue such as artistic or script approvals, subsequent option monies, etc.

Given the difficulties of the marketplace these days, writers necessarily consider attaching any potential hurdles to their works ill-advised. At a time when part of their job is to make producing a work as easy as possible (whether in terms of number of actors, set require-ments or other elements affecting the production budget), ultimately it is the writer who will "pay" for having signed a pre-existing contract.

Percentage of author's subsidiary rights income. In addition to all the problems discussed above, another reason writers should not agree to add directors to the list of those ordinarily sharing their sub-sidiary rights earnings is the possibility of opening the door to similar demands from others, such as actors and designers who ostensibly also could claim to have contributed to the "visual component" and the suc-cess of the hallmark production. Indeed, as of this writing it appears that a few dramaturgs have decided the best way to get paid—rather than to look solely to the producer—is to demand a percentage of the writer's subsidiary rights income. These concerns are not so farfetched.

It should also be noted that, at the "higher" levels of production, the directors' union has been successful in negotiating for the director to receive a percentage of the producer's share of the writer's subsidiary rights proceeds. Writers take the position that it is patently unfair for the director to receive *both* a direct share of what the writer earns *and* a share of the producer's portion of those very same monies. (By con-trast, many directors *don't* consider this double payment, but rather as separate compensation for two distinct contributions to the piece: once via the production itself, and once through the so-called "collabora-tion" with the author.)

Bilateral obligations

Many writers posit that if new relationships with directors are to be created, they should be based upon *bilateral* obligations and benefits. Writers complain that a contract with a director is wholly one-sided, in that the writer is bound by obligations to the director, but the reverse is not true, presumably because directors want to keep their career options open, never knowing when a better opportunity might come along. Perhaps directors who want contracts with writers should be obliged to direct that writer's work in the future, and if that director refuses any subsequent production—for whatever reason—the writer should be freed of all future obligations to that director. And since directing one writer's work may launch or significantly enhance the career of a director, writers ask why they shouldn't be compensated for their contributions to directors' careers. Few directors take on new works out of altruism. By working on new material, directors and other theatre artists exchange services for exposure, experience and, they hope, a growing reputation for the quality of their work (in addition to payment from the producer if there is payment to the artists, including the writer). Perhaps the writer should be able to negotiate a percentage of the director's future income.

These are probably not notions on which productive relationships are likely to be based. They are presented to highlight problems of logic in the position of some directors, and to better express the stage writer's concerns.

Organizational positions

The Dramatists Guild. The Dramatists Guild is adamantly opposed to authors signing contracts with directors for many of the same reasons addressed herein. Years ago, it created a stringent three-prong test which establishes and defines that only authorial contributions (not direction) should enable sharing in a writer's subsidiary rights monies. Admittedly, not many people qualify.

This test was most recently codified in the Guild's Approved Production Contract (for both plays and musicals) as follows: "The term 'Author' shall include any person who is 1) involved in the initial stages of a collaborative process, *and* 2) who is deserving of billing credit as an author, *and* 3) whose literary or musical contribution will be an integral part of the work as presented in subsequent productions by other producers."

"Initial stages" refers to the very beginning—the blank page—and the vast majority of directors cannot pass this test since they typically come to the work after it has been written. (To be fair, there are some writer/director teams that work together from the very first moment, hashing out virtually every part of the work, but these are the exceptions, not the rule.) "Collaborative process" does not refer to the fact that theatre is a collaborative art form—that is, it does not refer to the way in which directors and writers usually "collaborate" simply by working together—but rather to collaboration as the word is used in the body of copyright law. Deserving of authorial billing credit refers to input of an authorial nature, not just offering ideas about revision. And, finally, "an integral part of the work" means what it says: that the work *would not* be presented *without* the contribution in question— which would be *very* difficult to assert about any one director's ideas. (While an author may adopt a director's ideas for one production, he or she has the ultimate right to change the work again in the future.)

Society of Stage Directors and Choreographers. By contrast, the Society of Stage Directors and Choreographers (SSDC) is *not* opposed to directors entering into contracts with authors. SSDC lists factors for each director to take into consideration when evaluating individual situations (note that the parenthetical comments are this author's analysis of these factors, not necessarily those of the SSDC):

1) Who the director is and her or his level of achievement within the theatre. (The greater the prestige of the director, the stronger the demand for compensation.)

2) The relationship between the writer and director. Do they know each other well? Have they known each other for a long time? Have they worked together in the past? (The longer the working relationship, the greater the director's feeling that he or she is owed "something.")

3) The state of the script. (If, in the director's opinion, the script needs a lot of work, the director might want to negotiate compensation, but no guidelines exist for distinguishing a "normal" amount of revision from an amount waranting additional compensation.)

4) The stageworthiness of the script (which would seem to refer to somewhat unusual circumstances, since the primary focus of the director's job is to take a written script and transfer it to the stage).

5) The business acumen and professional contacts of the writer. (If the director has been working in the industry longer and therefore is better able to bring the script to the attention of

theatres or producers, the director may feel the writer should pay for this access; but, as addressed earlier, the analysis should include the reality of how the director exploits these contacts. Presumably, too, the opposite situation—the writer is the more experienced of the two—could be equally true.)

6) The extent of the director's interest in the work and her or his desire to be involved in future productions. (Which again raises the question: If the director demands the *right* to be offered future productions of the work at issue, should the director be *obligated* to continue?)

7) Where the work is in its life and development; that is, whether it has yet had a reading, a staged reading or a production. (One could argue that the more fully developed a work already is, the less credible the director's call for extraordinary compensation. But, as discussed earlier, it is exceedingly dangerous— and disadvantageous—for writers to be locked into contractual arrangements with directors in the early stages of a work's development.)

8) The likelihood that the director will contribute a "crucial component" to the work (although the definition of a "crucial component" has yet to be made).

SSDC suggests a process of negotation in which both parties talk honestly about their expectations and needs, both positive and negative. The parties would analyze who has what at stake, respective vulnerabilities, etc. However, the Dramatists Guild believes this discussion remains inappropriate in all but a select few situations.

Timing

The question inevitably arises: When is it appropriate for a director to approach these issues with a writer? Most writers believe the director should raise any contract issues at the beginning of the relationship, so that the writer can decide whether to work with that person or, if not, to move on before the relationship becomes difficult. Some directors agree, believing problems arise when such issues are not discussed up front; however, some directors disagree strongly, insisting that they cannot know how much or what kind of work will be involved until they have actually come to grips with the writer and the work over a period of time. (It should perhaps be noted that among those factors on the SSDC-recommended list concerning the script itself, they do *not* focus in hindsight on the work actually done, but rather seem to assume that a director can tell by looking at a script and talking with the writer how much "assistance" will actually be required.)

Thus, some directors wait to raise these issues until the work has been done—that is, often, well into rehearsals or performances, perhaps the worst possible time for such a discussion. Having proceeded that far with the expectations provided by the production contract, the writer may recoil in anger or horror, or at least react defensively. In response to the writer's reaction, the director may feel unfairly attacked.

Imagine a director making what amounts to an ultimatum—"Sign this contract or I walk"—during rehearsals or previews. This may not be the best way to approach a writer about a sensitive issue; but, since writers are, understandably, legitimately concerned about jeopardizing productions in midstream, sometimes they *will* sign such contracts, fearing they have no choice.

But writers are hereby placed on notice: If you do sign such a document—even if you believe that were "forced," or didn't have time to read the contract carefully or discuss it with your agent or lawyer—there is a good chance you will be held to its terms. Your signature *does* mean commitment, whatever the circumstances, so don't blithely proceed thinking you can later renege.

You may feel "squeezed" or threatened, but you do have a choice, albeit not a comfortable one: to refuse to sign the contract and to look for another director. You might think a director would hesitate to walk off of a production because of the legal ramifications of breaking the contract with the producer and because of the negative impact on the director's reputation; but, it does happen. The end result might be that the production is delayed or postponed while the producer looks for a new director.

It would be foolish to deny that there are writers who have consciously decided to enter into some types of contractual relationship with directors, but this is not mandated or even considered standard practice. Unfortunately, a resolution for this increasingly uncomfortable situation does not appear imminent, since there is no longer agreement within the industry on fundamental precepts. For the foreseeable future, writers and directors will have to struggle with these issues on a case-by-case basis.

AUTHORSHIP

The question of who is an author, or rather who qualifies to be called an author and thus an owner of the work, has become a point of contention in recent years. On its face, the issue seems simple, not worthy of as much discussion as it generates: The author of the play or musical is the person(s) who writes it. But lately some people who feel they deserve compensation for having "contributed" to a work are claiming joint authorship. All stage writers are hereby placed on notice that your position as sole author of a work may come under attack, and it is in your best interest to protect yourself as best you can from what could become an unpleasant situation.

Definition of an author

Interestingly, Section 101 of the copyright law—the definitions provision—does not define the word "author" despite repeated use of the word throughout the law. However, in 1989, in the case *Community for Creative Non-Violence v. Reid*, the Supreme Court stated that "the author is the party who actually creates the work, that is, the person who translates an idea into a fixed, tangible expression [that is] entitled to copyright protection" under Section 102 of the law. The copyright law *does* define the term "joint work," as follows:

> A joint work is a work prepared by two or more authors with the intention that their contributions be merged into inseparable or interdependent parts of a unitary whole.

All stage writers should know about two important cases involving playwrights, decided in recent years, establishing the appropriate test to apply to the definition of joint authorship and ultimately strengthening the author's position as the sole author of such works.

The first case was decided by the Second Circuit Court of Appeals, which includes New York City, in 1991. The actress Clarice Taylor wanted Alice Childress, the late playwright, to write a play about Moms Mabley in which Taylor would star. Taylor assembled material about Mabley by interviewing Mabley's friends and family, collecting her jokes and reviewing library resources. She turned all of these research materials over to Childress, including subsequent research she conducted. Taylor testified that she and Childress talked about which scenes and characters from Mabley's life should be used in the play, and she gave a number of examples of her ideas they had discussed, some of which Childress included in the play which she, alone, wrote. In order to determine who would qualify as a joint author according to the definition set forth in Section 102, above, the Court focused both on the sufficiency of the contribution and on the parties' intentions at the time they created the work.

As many courts both before and after this case have done, the Court acknowledged that this issue had never been resolved in the Second Circuit, and that it was faced with deciding which of two tests should be the sole test of joint authorship (which is generally known as an "issue of first impression"). The first test, and the one that has been adopted by the overwhelming majority of federal courts, is that *each* contribution must be copyrightable on its own. This is known as the "Goldstein test," named after its author, Professor Paul Goldstein.

The second test, devised by Professor Melville Nimmer, is often referred to as the "de minimus test," which posits that the primary focus should be on the end result—that is, whether the final product is copyrightable—so long as there was a *de minimus amount* (more than a word or a line) contributed by each person. This is a crucial distinction in situations where an author is the sole writer of a work but someone else proffered suggestions or ideas.

The crux of this distinction lies in the fact that under Section 102 of the copyright law, ideas are not copyrightable; only the *expression* of ideas is protected by copyright (hence the language stating that the work of authorship must be "fixed in a tangible medium of expression"). Nimmer believed that if one person contributed only uncopyrightable ideas and another person incorporated those ideas into the copyrightable expression, the two people should be considered joint authors. Goldstein strongly disagreed. He argued that any contribution that could not "stand on its own as the subject matter of copyright" should not be afforded copyright protection. If the courts only look at the combined result—a finished play or musical—the person who has made suggestions but *has not written* has a greater chance of being called a joint author than if each person's contribution could independently be afforded copyright protection.

In the *Childress* case, the Second Circuit Court carefully analyzed the pros and cons of both the Goldstein and Nimmer tests against the backdrop of existing case law (judicial decisions), statutory language, the goals of the Copyright Act and the risks to a "real" author of people bringing specious claims of joint authorship. The Court's final determination—which relied on previous cases that had required the copyrightability of each person's contribution—was to adopt the Goldstein test. However, the Court stated that any person making a *non*-copyrightable contribution to a work was not precluded by their decision from negotiating a contract with the author to protect that contribution, premised of course on the willingness of the author to negotiate sharing his or her copyright.

The second, equally important factor the Court addressed was the intention of the parties at the time the work was created; that is, did both (or all) participants regard themselves as joint authors? By way of example, the Court discussed editors who make revisions to a work and research assistants who may contribute copyrightable expression to a work, neither of whom would ever consider themselves to be joint authors with the primary writer. Again, the Court stated that people who "are not in a true joint authorship relationship with an author [are] free to bargain for an arrangement" via contract negotiation.

In the *Childress* case, Taylor's claims failed both tests: Her suggestions were not copyrightable, and Childress never shared Taylor's intention of joint authorship. The Court concluded by stating that "there was no evidence that these aspects (contributed ideas, suggestions and perhaps even minor bits of expression) ever evolved into more than the helpful advice that might come from the cast, the directors or the producers of the play. A playwright does not so easily acquire a co-author."

The second case, *Erickson v. Trinity Theatre, Inc.*, arose in the Seventh Circuit Court of Appeals, encompassing Chicago, in 1994. Karen Erickson was one of the founding members of Trinity Theatre and had worked there in a number of capacities. The lawsuit focused on her role as playwright of several works which were created, in part, by Erickson taking rehearsal notes while actors improvised. Erickson would then compile her notes, decide what ideas to use (and not) and she alone controlled and wrote the script.

In reaching its decision that Erickson was the sole author of the work, the Seventh Circuit Court also had to decide which of the two tests—Goldstein or Nimmer—was most appropriate to adopt, and it joined the majority of courts that have supported the Goldstein approach, stating:

> First, Professor Nimmer's test is not consistent with one of the Copyright Act's premises: Ideas and concepts standing alone should not receive protection. Because the creative process necessarily involves the development of existing concepts into new forms, any restriction on the free exchange of ideas stifles creativity to some extent. Restrictions on an author's use of existing ideas in a work, such as the threat that accepting suggestions from another party might jeopardize the author's sole entitlement to a copyright, would hinder creativity. Second, contribution of an idea is an exceedingly ambiguous concept . . .

The Goldstein test, by contrast, *did* advance creativity by "allowing for the unhindered exchange of ideas, and protects authorship rights in a consistent and predictable manner." It excludes ideas that are not copyrightable under the law and, as a practical matter, enables people to avoid what the Court calls "post-contribution disputes" over authorship.

These two cases (together with the relevant language defining an author from the Supreme Court case *CCNV v. Reid*) illuminate the over-riding issues confronting the author and resolves them in her or his favor. The conclusion is clear: Writers should not be forced to share copyright ownership with other artists whose contribution to a work is only ideas or suggestions. Unfortunately, the daunting threat of litigation may keep a writer from taking a firm position on his or her rights.

Notice that the courts are careful to mention that they are not taking away the parties' ability to negotiate documents addressing ownership rights. While this may have been important to judicial analysis, it is crucial that writers *not* jump to the wrong conclusion: Authors do *not* now need to sign contracts with every person on a production who might make a suggestion or offer an idea in order to make clear that that person has no rights in the author's work. But when a person involved in a production inquires about such a contract, be careful not to answer "yes" unless you have worked with that other person in such a way as to create a strong reason to negotiate.

Protect yourself

The conclusions reached in these cases comport with the fundamental language that should be found in the script approvals clause of *every* production contract, stating that no one has the right to make any changes in the work without the prior written consent of the author, *and* that any changes so made shall also remain the property of the author, free from any liens or encumbrances (i.e., claims) of any third parties, such as actors, directors, designers and any other person working on a production. It is also suggested that authors include language in their production contracts which states, in essence, that the producer will not allow employees (or any other persons over whom the producer has control even if there is no strict employer/employee relationship) to make joint authorship or collaboration claims on the author's work. This language places responsibility on the producer's shoulders as well as the author's, and serves to reinforce the fact that the writer alone will be the sole author of the work.

If the concerns expressed here seem irrelevant to you or farfetched, here's a reality check: One team of writers in this country is currently fighting such a battle resulting from ideas that were simply tossed around at production meetings. Consequently, it is imperative that authors: 1) be clear on where the lines are drawn and not waiver, equivocate, or somehow send mixed signals to those with whom you are working; 2) have a fully executed production contract containing the strongest possible script approvals protection language; and 3) if you feel an "ambiguous" or difficult situation arising, confront and resolve it as amicably as possible right away.

Be vigilant in demanding that any contrary or ambiguous language affecting sole authorship be eliminated from any proposed production contract, and do not enter into a contract with any other person which gives or acknowledges any copyrightable rights of authorship unless you feel confident that that person's contribution will be of an authorial nature.

As difficult as it may be to pull back from working with someone who might be able to help your play, you don't want to find yourself in a difficult situation. While the law is on the side of the actual authors, that may be cold comfort if you find yourself in the middle of a very unpleasant dispute. Remember that the law is fluid, never static: Do not assume that because the playwrights won in the two lawsuits described above that you would automatically or necessarily win yours. If in doubt about a particular situation, consult with a lawyer who can provide you with substantive legal advice.

ELECTRONIC RIGHTS

The term "electronic rights" is used to encompass a wide range of electronic technologies—such as online publishing, distribution and databases, CD-ROM, etc.—that continues to develop rapidly. No one knows what directions the technology will take in the future. The technology of today could be obsolete in five years or even sooner. No one knows how sophisticated the products will become, to what extent consumers will be attracted to the products, how long it will be before these products become an integral part of the consumer's everyday life, even how much money—if any—can be made. For writers, the electronic future is both exciting and scary, because every technological advance inevitably raises substantive intellectual property questions which are not at all easy to answer.

Consider this partial list of important issues: 1) Who will own these new creations? 2) Who will control these new creations; that is, who will have the authority to make deals? 3) What approval rights will be retained by the creators, both in products that are solely or primarily textual and in products that combine the creativity of a number of different contributors such as writers, sound designers and graphic artists? 4) Will the creators be compensated fairly and, if so, will the traditional system of advances and royalties be incorporated, either on a per-use or per-sale basis? 5) Since there is no established market yet, how does anyone know what could be considered "fair" compensation? 6) Should traditional print publishers become the licensors of electronic rights even if they are not set up to handle such rights and, if so, what is an appropriate division of the monies received? 7) How can the creator be protected from granting rights too broadly to the publisher and also provide for a reversion of rights if the publisher doesn't actively promote them? 8) How can you protect against unauthorized copying through the use of new technologies?

As is to be expected when standing on the threshold of something entirely new, everyone is trying to position themselves for the future, to protect their interests in the face of the unknown. For writers being asked to resolve such question-riddled matters, one hopes there is a natural tendency to negotiate conservatively; this means being vigilant about *not* granting too much too soon—that is, proceeding cautiously— seeing the new technology not for what it's worth today but for what it may be worth in the future. For publishers, this means grabbing the broadest rights possible now so that when the dust settles they already control all or most of the value without being forced into subsequent negotiations with writers. Unfortunately, writers are being asked to agree to concrete terms *now,* in the absence of reliable information, rather than to agree to negotiate those terms later, when much more will be known.

Add to this confusion the fact that Internet users have come to expect, and receive, free information and materials: The online world has been referred to as a "gift economy," and it's becoming increasingly obvious that in an environment in which free distribution has been established as the norm, successfully charging fees is a difficult proposition at best. Copyright is *already* a concept that some people fail to grasp, and in the current electronic marketplace, consumers do not fully appreciate that a creator's intellectual labor deserves payment, or that each time someone accesses someone else's creation a fee might be appropriate, just as there would be a royalty each time a book or a ticket is purchased. Although technological safeguards and payment accounting systems are in development, there is a great deal of resistance to fee-based information and entertainment online, and some commentators warn that it may *not* be technologically feasible. These concerns only increase the need for writers to remain vigilant about protecting their copyrights.

The Authors Guild, the National Writers Union and the American Society of Journalists and Authors have been leading the fight to protect writers' rights in these areas, promulgating position papers enumerating the range of issues confronting their members and urging specific approaches in negotiations between individuals and publishers. While most of the debate has thus far centered around book, magazine and newspaper publishing, electronic rights language has begun to seep into stage writers' publishing contracts, and thus stage writers should heed the information and warnings distributed by these organizations. It appears to be just a matter of time before dramatic and musical works are affected, if they aren't affected already.

It is strongly believed that authors should retain ownership of their work in this area. For stage writers, this encompasses electronic versions of their works (for example, publishing a play on CD-ROM or making it available for download from an online "bookstore"). The writers' organizations are particularly concerned about authors retaining control over the form and content of multimedia products incorporating their works, rather than simply turning them over to software companies or other electronic publishers in a work-for-hire situation.

Decisions in the multimedia arena may ultimately depend on the extent of an author's contribution to a finished product. The author's bargaining position might be different depending on whether a stage work is used as only one of a number of elements or whether the text is the central element. The writers' organizations have taken the position that in group-contribution situations, it is possible to divide the elements and allow each "contributor" to retain ownership of the element he or she created (so that authors would retain their claim on the text); the overall "developer" could have a copyright on the finished product (which is similar to existing situations with anthologies), and the author's royalty would depend on the magnitude of his or her contribution.

From the author's perspective, it is best to refuse to grant electronic rights to publishers at this time. This allows each individual to negotiate rights as markets and opportunities open up. However, this may not always be realistic. If an author agrees to grant *some* rights, based on reasonable expectations that the publisher will exploit them to the author's benefit, she or he should *not* relinquish control in a blanket manner. It is preferable to grant rights only in formats that already exist, avoiding language such as "in all electronic formats now existing or not yet invented." And if the publisher does not exploit the granted electronic rights within some agreed-upon period of time, the rights should revert automatically to the author. Once specific rights to be granted are enumerated, the author should double-check to be sure there is a strong reservation of rights clause; that is, a paragraph which states that all rights not *expressly* granted remain with the author.

Remember: These rights *do* have value, at least potentially. This doesn't mean authors will make bundles of money from the exploitation of these rights, not at first anyway. But publishing contracts typically can last for the life of a work's copyright, and no author should be expected to give away rights without fair compensation. This means electronic rights should *not* simply be lumped in with all existing rights already being granted. If the grant of rights broadens beyond the usual—whether in geographic scope, duration or breadth of types included—so should the level of compensation. Authors deserve to receive an advance for granting additional rights, and also a fair, ongoing royalty structure. (For example, negotiate percentage fees or specific dollar amounts for each time a work is accessed electronically or the CD-ROM version is purchased. Avoid one-time flat fees for unlimited distribution rights.)

It is not good enough for publishers to say they don't know how to structure access or use fees, or how to account for these new uses and products; the technology is already sophisticated enough to create some protections and payment structures, and publishers must work with data carriers and distributors to provide the necessary tracking systems. Online transaction systems, involving electronic debits, digital cash, etc., already exist on the World Wide Web; some sites allow consumers to read about authors and their works before using credit cards to make online purchases of fiction, nonfiction and drama titles.

Copyright protection

An author's concern with protecting the copyright in his or her work remains of paramount importance in electronic media. Until very recently, there was some question about whether the existing copyright law, dating from 1976, encompassed electronic media or instead required amendment to address issues that clearly did not exist when the law was drafted and passed.

The Clinton Administration has recently issued a report on copyright and the new electronic media, entitled "Intellectual Property and the National Information Infrastructure." This document takes the position that the 1976 Copyright Act is "fundamentally adequate and effective" in addressing questions of online distribution and new products such as CD-ROM, and it views online transmission as one of the exclusive rights under Section 102 of the copyright law. However, perhaps with appropriate caution it suggests that the Act should be amended in certain ways, and takes into account the fears of many concerning unauthorized copying. And more recently still, suggestions for amendments to copyright law both nationally and internationally have raised more questions and concerns than they have answered.

Authors are hereby warned *not* to place their copyrighted materials (scripts, lyrics, etc.) online, which will remain dangerous in terms of copyright protection until appropriate safeguards can be devised and implemented. Some stage writers post their works on the Internet hoping to use it as a new promotional tool; but, the risk of copyright infringement is great, since you typically have no way of knowing who has accessed and downloaded your work, nor could you easily—if ever—trace or prove it. There is nothing wrong with using the Internet to tell people *about* you and your work, and this may be a good way to connect with producers and others across the country and around the world; but, if someone wants to read your work, you should resort to the "old-fashioned" method of mailing a copy together with a clear cover letter, retaining a copy of the letter for your files "just in case." As tempting as it may be to send your work electronically (whether for ease, lower cost or whatever), you are strongly urged not to do so.

It is also suggested that authors discuss their copyright concerns with their publishers if they do grant electronic rights, to find out what steps the publisher will take to protect the work from unauthorized copying. While there isn't yet a foolproof way to prevent such copyright infringement, the publisher should at least be required in the case of any electronic publication to include strongly worded warnings addressing ownership and infringement, and to investigate and, if possible, implement the most effective means of thwarting copyright violation available today.

Royalties

When publishers decide to obtain electronic rights from authors, they should reasonably be expected to figure out or create ways to pay for them. Keep in mind that many of a publisher's normal costs (such as printing and binding, storage, spoilage, shipping, etc.) either don't exist or else are dramatically reduced in electronic formats such as CD-ROM, thus increasing the publisher's potential profit margin. (Although, to be fair, it should be noted that production costs may be dramatically higher before the first disk ships.) While the potential income in these areas remains unknown, writers' groups are pushing for higher royalties on such products so that income is more fairly allocated, with the writer receiving roughly fifty percent of the sales price.

Some publishers have proffered tautological arguments, positing that they cannot begin to estimate the value of their products because the markets are still in their infant stages, while at the same time they try to lock authors into certain terms, such as exceedingly high commissions on licenses they will negotiate. Writers' organizations argue that the normal (ten to twenty percent) commission for subsidiary rights should apply to the electronic markets, too, but some publishers are using a fifty percent figure instead.

Substantive, creative control is also a serious issue. When a stage work is published, the author retains final approval over the text. She or he should have the same rights as regard electronic formats. (In some ways, the writer is at greater risk with multimedia formats, since the use of other elements, such as sound and graphic images, may distort the meaning of the text.)

There is also concern about redefining the term "out of print" as regards reversion of rights. Since a work can easily remain available online at little cost to a publisher, it probably will never go out of print in the traditional sense. Consequently, writers' organizations take the position that if *usage* falls below a negotiated minimum point, the work will be deemed to be out of print, and the rights will revert.

Authors who have already signed publishing contracts should check the language carefully to see if it could be interpreted as encompassing electronic rights, and then discuss these issues with their publishers. For example, if the publishing contract states that the author grants to the publisher "the right to publish the Work throughout the world," the publisher may interpret this language as broadly as possible. There are a limited number of twentieth-century court cases that have addressed the question of how to handle new technologies (such as movies, television and videocassettes) that were invented after a contract was signed; the decisions are not wholly consistent as to whether broad, nonspecific granting language includes or excludes later-created new technology, but the majority have held that future rights *are* included. If you and your publisher have differing opinions about what is and is not included in existing contracts, *now* is the time to negotiate those issues, not later, when the publisher may have expended financial resources to exploit your work via new technologies.

Systems for payment of royalties

A problem for all authors is how to collect royalties owed for electronic uses. For example, if your play is available online and someone downloads it, how do you collect a user or access fee? Fortunately, authors' organizations, agents and individual authors have gotten together to create a system modeled after ASCAP, in the music industry, to monitor, collect and distribute payments for electronic uses of copyrighted works. The Authors Guild, the Dramatists Guild, the American Society of Journalists and Authors, the Association of Authors' Representatives and an impressive list of bestselling authors recently joined together to create the Authors Registry for this purpose. Publishers and others have apparently complained about the cost, impracticality and other problems associated with establishing such a use-payment system, in part because payments to each author will not likely be large enough to justify the effort and expense. The hope is that the Authors Registry will efficiently assume responsibility for all these matters. (The National Writers Union has founded the Publication Rights Clearinghouse, also modeled on the ASCAP system, as a collection/licensing agency focusing on the electronic reuse of freelance writers' materials, such as magazine and journal articles, essays and even book excerpts that have appeared in magazines.)

The Authors Registry will create a comprehensive directory which ultimately will be available on the Internet, too, so that anyone trying to obtain rights will be able to find the necessary contact information easily. Each author included in the Registry can list a personal address or the address of a representative, a phone number, a fax number and an e-mail address. They can even choose to post terms for the use of their work.

The information revolution

This discussion presents only the tip of the iceberg of the issues which need to be addressed regarding electronic media; many other issues exist or will come into being in the not-too-distant future. The National Writers Union, in its 1993 "Working Paper on Electronic Publishing Issues," has said we are on the "verge of an information revolution." The world of marketing entertainment and information is changing rapidly and will continue to metamorphose. The parameters, boundaries and standards of this developing industry are being created and established now, piece by piece. There is rampant confusion throughout the marketplace, and it seems that the "winners" will be those who jump in and vociferously stake claims. If authors don't speak up and protect their rights, the important decisions will be made by publishers and vendors. If that happens, one is almost assured that the electronic marketplace will be structured to benefit them, not authors.

Copyright in your creative output is the key to your professional success. It's imperative that these fundamental concepts—copyright protection and fair payment for commercial use—not be eroded by the new electronic media. Now is the time to place these important issues on the table.

RADIO DRAMA

One of the hottest, expanding areas for production is radio drama, sometimes also called audio drama. More and more people are interested in listening to theatre at home, in their cars and at work, and opportunities continue to be created in response to the growing demand. Radio drama is an enormous industry in England and the rest of Europe for a number of reasons—not least of which is that the arts are more a part of the European social structure, so there's more money available— and the United States is slowly awakening to its vast potential, both in the broadcast and audiocassette markets.

Production costs

Radio dramas with the highest quality production values are relatively inexpensive to produce (although set designers may not be happy about this new development). Current multi-track and computer technology allows engineers to create layered sounds and other audio effects that would have been unimaginable to earlier generations.

In 1994, Susan Loewenberg, producing director of L.A. Theatre Works (which produces plays for radio broadcast in collaboration with NPR and the BBC) was quoted as saying that the usual radio recording with "top-quality actors and superb production values" cost about

$20,000; an epic work with, say, fifty characters—and what was the last play you *saw* with fifty characters?—could cost $70,000, considered by some to be an uppermost limit. Sarah Montague, another prominent New York audio/radio producer, believes that even a full series of radio drama costs less than keeping a single play running or making one independent film.

Lower cost translates into lower risk, which often means audio producers may be willing to take chances on emerging writers, new works and even risky ideas. One such producer attending the 1995 National Black Theatre Network Conference was very well received in part because the attendees viewed radio as a means of workshopping new work, and of reaching a broader audience.

In addition, lower cost means that a single producer can produce many different works each year, in different cities. As of this writing, one radio producer produces fourteen full-length radio dramas per year in Los Angeles and ten per year in Chicago, and is looking to expand to Washington, D.C. and other markets. A New York producer recently talked of being able to produce ten shows at one radio station in the first nine months of 1995, which didn't include work he had done at other stations in the tri-state region. A third produced twenty pieces in 1995, while holding down a separate day job. This is a refreshing development for new plays, given today's economic climate.

Writing for radio

Writers who have worked in this area extol its virtues: The caliber of the people involved (engineers, directors, actors) is high and, from the writer's perspective, anything is possible. Writers are not forced into what one producer called an "economical model" which can be "stifling when the physical and economic realities" demand utmost attention. Conceptual works can be explored, free of encumbrances, burdens and boundaries such as sets, physical reality and so on. Plus, radio drama can create the illusion of intimacy with every listener, even if you are reaching out to 2,500 or 250,000 listeners on any given night.

To write radio drama, you must think aurally, not visually; it has been called "theatre of the ear." A repeated refrain by both writers and producers of radio drama is that playwrights have to learn to think differently when writing for radio; it isn't an effective use of the medium's idiosyncratic possibilities just to broadcast a stage play and have the stage directions read. New ways must be discovered to use words, music and sound effects to project the author's imagined world. Some producers even steer clear of narration, feeling that it is, essentially, the same as stage directions. (The BBC apparently has put out a funny and informative tape about how *not* to write a radio play called "The Gun in My Left Hand is Smoking.")

As a practical matter, it is a writer-driven medium generally imbued with a fundamental reverence for authors and language. For the most part, producers remain committed to respecting the writer's approval over the script and any changes that need to be made. (Interestingly, writers for this medium express less resistance to producer's suggestions, since many are related to the idiosyncrasies of radio and the need, in most circumstances—given strict time constraints—for extremely tight writing. Remember, too, that the FCC controls the airwaves, and that means producers must be particularly conscious about obscenity.)

Radio is a liberating medium for actors, too. Producers talk of eliciting extraordinary performances from actors who have been freed of typecasting or pigeonholing due to physical attributes. Working in radio allows actors to expand their range.

The topics are wide open: Mystery, horror, comedy, fantasy, science fiction—you name it—all have found an audio audience. And the lengths of radio dramas varies. Many productions are thirty to forty-five minutes long, with a half hour generally considered standard. Some works, such as children's bedtime stories, are as short as four to eleven minutes; some producers believe that eighty-five minutes is the maximum length a listener's attention can be held. Still other producers, however, believe full-length works can run as long as any stage production would. If you are interested in the audio market, contact an organization near you to find out how you can best learn to write for it. For instance, the Midwest Radio Theatre Workshop (KOPN Radio, 915 East Broadway, Columbia, MO), has materials that can be purchased or borrowed. Consult your local library for regional information.

Money

Commission opportunities are beginning to open up in radio drama. For example, Radio Stage in New York (a co-production of New York Public Radio and the Radio Consortium, a group of theatre organizations in the tri-state region including New Dramatists, the Playwrights Theatre of New Jersey, the Atlantic Theater Company, and Company One in Hartford Connecticut), recently gave writers $2,000 commissions to create half-hour radio dramas, and last year the BBC commissioned at least six American writers.

Writers do receive royalties from initial broadcasts, plus the possibility of a percentage of the proceeds if audiocassettes are sold or if the broadcast is licensed to National Public Radio or any other radio networks, as discussed below. But don't expect to be able to make a living in this venue for a while to come, if ever. Because funding for public radio—the primary home of radio drama—is increasingly tight, the amounts paid to writers is limited, although the producers interviewed for this book say they strive to be fair and reasonable. (As an aside, one typically doesn't find much agent or even union involvement in radio drama, ostensibly because there just isn't enough money to be earned in this medium yet to command their attention.)

National movement

Another wonderful facet of radio drama is that it can be produced anywhere, not just in large urban centers. Local radio stations, including those at colleges and universities may have good production services and people interested in radio drama. One way to get started is to get involved with a group or a station already creating radio drama. If none is being done in your area, consider starting a group and talking to the local radio station about it. Some of the people most interested in radio drama live in remote areas of the country.

Radio drama really is a grassroots movement, created and supported by a tremendous corps of volunteers. Writers and actors often work in this medium in exchange for the phenomenal exposure it provides, not just a paycheck. (Depending on the size of the radio station and its geographic reach, a writer's work might be heard by thousands if not tens or hundreds of thousands of listeners.) It certainly isn't this writer's intention to excuse anyone from paying artists, but those involved have said again and again that radio drama is a community effort that takes no more advantage of writers than anyone else.

As with any new area, there are skeptics. Some are concerned that radio exposure can hurt a dramatic work that might have had a life elsewhere. Others simply doubt this is an area worth pursuing. But the majority of those writing, acting and producing in this field believe that radio drama is a valuable vehicle for cross-marketing and promotion, enhancing the demand for work by whetting the public's appetite, with potential spillover onto stage and into the film and television industries. As of this writing, it appears to be a wide-open field.

Potential hurdles

Convincing local stations to create and broadcast radio drama might be an uphill battle. Some writers have found that program directors of local radio stations need to be educated about the value of drama and the existence of an audience. But an equal number of people polled have had quite a different experience, discovering that local stations are clamoring for new ideas and new product. You may have to campaign for what you want, so prepare yourself to be a strong salesperson, not a hostile one.

Marketing remains an important consideration. There are three primary public radio networks: National Public Radio, Public Radio International and Pacifica. (There used to be a fourth—American Public Radio—but it was recently absorbed by PRI.) By way of example, NPR has roughly 300 to 400 noncommercial member radio stations, and although it is involved with radio drama, it does not produce; rather, it broadcasts previously produced packages. Roughly half of the NPR stations broadcast some amount of spoken-word programming on a consistent basis. (By contrast, the BBC provides spoken-word programming twenty-four hours a day, albeit not all of it drama.)

There is no single marketing mechanism in place to reach these markets. In its absence each producer (and sometimes writer) attacks the market individually.

One writer purchased a list of member stations from NPR. (You can too, by *writing* to Angelina Lee, NPR, 635 Massachusetts Avenue N.W., Washington, D.C. 20001; NPR charges one dollar for each member on the list, and you must purchase the entire list, so this would cost hundreds of dollars. The Federal Trade Commission may also be able to provide an extensive list of public radio stations.) The same writer supplemented the broadcast of his work with a print ad campaign, direct mail marketing, press releases, and efforts to get interviews and articles into local newspapers and magazines. He focused zone by zone, depending on where his work received airplay or he received encouraging responses. He also has very creatively generated interest, articles and publicity with tie-in marketing: Since his work touches upon environmental conservation efforts, he donates one dollar from the sale of each audio CD to a prominent river conservation organization.

Your initial response to this might be, "That costs money, and it take *a lot* of time and energy." Yes, it does. But no one can create a career as a professional stage writer without an investment of money, time, energy or all three.

Funding

It is no secret that public broadcasting and public radio are not favored children these days. Consequently, producers are constantly trying to solve the great funding quagmire.

When trying to make inroads at local radio stations, it may help to think creatively about enticements for advertisers or sponsors to present along with your work. Of course, since these are *public* stations, they may be very cautious about certain sponsors, so use discretion as well as creativity. Do not count on money from the government to support these programs; current indications are strong that that will not be a significant source of funding in future years.

Audiocassettes

The audiocassette market for books may still be in its infancy, but the market is enormous and growing by leaps and bounds. As this market continues to grow explosively, many of those actively involved in radio drama believe that drama audiocassettes are not far behind. The long-term prospects seem excellent for this virtually untapped market.

Research

Unfortunately, there doesn't seem to be a comprehensive list of resources for the field of radio drama. Writers interested in learning more about it should contact the organizations mentioned here as well as local sources of information.

VIDEOTAPING

As discussed in the chapter on copyright, copyright ownership includes the right to control videotaping of the work. Thus, the stage writer who has created a play or musical possesses the sole right to decide whether to allow the videotaping of a production, and under what conditions. The right to control the videotaping of the work is not a developing area. This topic is included here because the past five years have seen a dramatic increase in people wanting to videotape productions.

The author's rights

This right is frequently misunderstood by theatre companies across the country. It is unfortunately not unusual to read an advertisement for a new play contest which states that the winning work will receive a full production and a copy of the videotape that the theatre company will make of the production. While this may seem like a nice offer to some writers, the theatre companies involved obviously do not understand that they do not have the right to videotape unless the writer expressly grants it to them. Typically, the theatre company does not include in any of its contest materials, guidelines or entry forms any language that would grant such permission. Even when the theatre company has enough business savvy to understand that there should be a production contract, there often isn't any mention of the videotaping in that document, either.

In other words, many theatres assume *they* have the right to decide whether or not to videotape a production, and consequently they don't request permission. So it is of utmost importance that writers assert their lawful right to control videotaping of their work from the beginning of the relationship. Perhaps the writer ultimately *will* want to allow the videotaping to take place, but this should happen only after permission has been granted and, one hopes, only after narrowly drafted restrictions have been agreed to, as discussed below.

The author's concerns

There are three concerns for writers on the issue of videotaped productions. First, a version of the work will exist over which the writer will have no control, assuming the absence of specific, restrictive language in the production contract. On its most basic level, this means that the videographer, together with the theatre, will decide how the production is filmed and edited, ultimately deciding what the finished product will be and what it will be used for. It is possible that a writer would later decide that the tape made does not represent his or her vision of the work, and she or he would therefore prefer that it not be shown, since it might interfere with efforts to market the work to future producers; but, in the absence of specific restrictions, the theatre could distribute copies of the videotape as it wished.

The second concern involves future marketing of the potentially valuable audiovisual rights in the work, of which videotaping is but one. For example, if there is subsequent interest in obtaining the film rights to a stage work, the film producer presumably will also, reasonably, be thinking of distributing the movie on videocassette. While the earlier videotape would not have preempted the videocassette market, the existence of such a video, if the theatre company is able to make copies of and market it as the work increases in value, could affect the film producer. (While some writers dismiss this concern as "implausible" or a "longshot," writers should not assume that videos of a premiere production will never create a problem.)

Last, even though it happens far less often than archival videotaping, one must anticipate that a theatre may try to sell a videotape, perhaps to audience members who enjoyed the show but potentially to others, and thus the writer's third concern should be fair compensation. If there is no agreement in writing, the writer may not participate in this stream of income. This is not to say that if the writer receives a royalty, all copyright issues should be overlooked. As stated above, all writers are strongly encouraged to reclaim their videotaping rights from producers who don't understand them. But if a writer *does* decide to allow a videotape to be made for sale, at the very least the writer should receive a fair royalty from those sales. The theatre should not be allowed to profit from sales to the exclusion of the writer.

A more sensible approach is to address the problem when you first submit your work to a theatre or producer that offers a videotape as part of a prize. State that you would like the theatre to consider your work for production, but include a friendly yet firm "reminder" that the right to videotape the work is part of the creator's copyright ownership. If you are not averse to videotaping, you can indicate your willingness to discuss the parameters of the videotaping while making it clear that you are not willing to simply turn all videotaping rights over to the theatre company.

The theatre's needs

Many theatres want to videotape a production for their "archives." If this is the theatre's response, inquire as to the logistics of these archives. Larger, ongoing institutional theatres typically maintain some type of library or archive on the premises of the theatre. Smaller theatre companies might operate on a less formal basis, perhaps lacking the resources to limit access and carefully monitor the use of such videotapes.

Theatres use videotapes to promote themselves in a variety of ways. Often video may be used in the theatre's fundraising efforts (for example, to show a potential donor the quality of the work being done). An increasing number of grantors require theatre companies to submit a videotape of work produced with their funding applications, and this may include excerpts from your work. It is also possible that an artist coming to work at a theatre for the first time might be interested in seeing what past productions looked like.

Theatres which do maintain on-premises archives are generally careful about restricting and monitoring those who view videotapes to ensure that no copies are made and that the original does not leave the premises. For smaller or less well-established theatre companies, controls might not be in place, whether for reasons of staffing, funding, space considerations or whatever, leaving the writer's work at greater risk, but this is not insurmountable; some writers are not uncomfortable with these situations, viewing them as no more risky than others having access to their scripts.

Off-premises libraries or archives

Theatres may also try to establish that a copy of the videotape they make of their own production can be deposited in more formal off-premises archives, such as the New York Public Library for the Performing Arts at Lincoln Center in Manhattan, the Music Center of Los Angeles, or the Huntington Library in Pasadena, California. While these institutions presumably have strict controls and restrictions in place to prevent any incidents of copyright infringement, the reality is that they may not impose the same rules on previously made videotapes received from third parties as they do on those videotapes they initiate and produce themselves. Thus, the writer who blindly relies on the protections of such institutions might discover the sad truth belatedly.

It is wise to include in any permission clause regarding videotaping a statement that the writer will receive written notice of any third party who asks to view the videotape. It is unusual for a writer to retain the authority to refuse to let anyone see the tape; but, at minimum, you can be notified each time someone asks to view it, and you would not be precluded from contacting that individual privately if you were concerned about the request.

Of greater concern is the fact that some theatres seek expansive language about placement of such tapes, such as in "other similar historical, library or educational collections." While on its face this seems harmless enough ("Why shouldn't a graduate playwriting student at the University of Wherever view a videotape of my play filmed five years ago at the XYZ Theatre Company?"), it is possible that you won't end up wanting that particular production on display, nor do you need a reason to decide you simply don't want to relinquish those rights.

No writer should be put on the defensive on these issues. The more proper questions might be, "Why *should* this theatre company have the right to place a videotape of my work's production in all of these locations? To what end am I granting these permissions and whose best interests do they serve?" Just because the technology exists, and just because others may want the videotape to be broadly accessible to the public, does not mean that that is the best path for the writer to take.

Other artists' work

There are other valid concerns that cannot be overlooked: those of the other artists involved in a production, and the rules of their unions and guilds. While the writer might believe that the XYZ Theatre production is the highest quality production for marketing purposes, it is possible that not every actor believes her or his best work was done in that production, so she or he might not want that particular videotape to be shown around. And the same could be true of the director and the designers.

While the writer owns the right to control the videotaping of his or her work, that copyright does not extend to the work of others. Consequently, if the production involves professional artists, the theatre may be required to obtain proper permission from their respective guilds or unions before proceeding. As a matter of course, if an institution such as the New York Public Library for the Performing Arts at Lincoln Center initiates the videotaping of a production, they require the signatures of all artists whose work will appear on the videotape to sign a special form granting permission (and even then, restrictions on the use of these tapes are *very* stringent). This practice should always be followed by any theatre or institution that videotapes such productions.

Protective clauses

For those writers who decide to grant limited archival videotaping rights to a theatre or producer, be sure to include a provision in your contract addressing the terms and parameters of those recordings such as the following:

> The Theatre shall have the right to make a single videotape recording of the Play in its entirety subject to the following restrictions: (a) that the Theatre shall receive no compensation or profit from said recording, either directly or indirectly, other than reimbursement for out-of-pocket expenses; (b) that said recording may be used only for library or archival purposes on the premises of the theatre; (c) that copies of said recording shall reside only in the archives of the New York Public Library for the Performing Arts at Lincoln Center; (d) that the Author will be provided with written notice of a request by any outside party to view the Theatre's copy of the tape; and (e) that the Theatre indemnifies the Author from any liability from applicable unions and guilds in connection with this videotaping.

If negotiating with a regional or resident theatre that is a member of the League of Resident Theatres, the following provision may also be included in the document:

> The Author agrees to permit the videotaping of a performance of the Work by the Theatre subject to the LORT Archive Rider of the collective bargaining agreement between the League of Resident Theatres and Actors Equity Association.

If the theatre plans to use excerpts of your work for grant or other funding applications, you might want to consider including language in your contract granting permission for this use. However, do not mistakenly think the theatre must contact you to use the video in this way. Addition of this language would be only for clarity. Last, no writer should expect additional payment for this use of excerpts.

The producer's right to promote or advertise

Do not confuse the creation of this videotape of a production for future use with the normal and necessary creation of marketing and promotional pieces to be used both before and during the production's run (for example, having promotional excerpts run on television or radio). All production contracts typically contain a clause that allows for the creation of short radio and/or television excerpts, usually no more than ten to twelve minutes in length, for the specific purposes of exploiting and publicizing that production of the work, and for use on awards programs. These excerpts might be subject to the writer's approval, but they are often not since producers strongly believe, and not unreasonably so, that the marketing of the work is within the province and expertise of the producer's business office. In addition, it should be expressly stated in this clause that the author is not paid for these excerpts, provided that the producer receives no compensation or profit from them other than reimbursement of out-of-pocket expenses.

Index